the unharried hostess

The Orion Press

New York

The Unharried Hostess

BY REBECCA REIS

Contents

TO HELP YOU MEASURE

tsp.   *means teaspoon*
Tbsp. means tablespoon
pt.   *means pint*
qt.   *means quart*

3 tsp.	*equal*	*1 Tbsp.*
2 Tbsp.	*equal*	*⅛ cup*
4 Tbsp.	*equal*	*¼ cup*
5 Tbsp. and 1 tsp.	*equal*	*⅓ cup*
8 Tbsp.	*equal*	*½ cup*
16 Tbsp.	*equal*	*1 cup*

½ pt.	*equals*	*1 cup*
1 pt.	*equals*	*2 cups*
1 qt.	*equals*	*4 cups*

1 medium lemon yields 3 Tbsp. lemon juice
¼-lb. bar of butter yields ½ cup or 8 Tbsp.

Introduction

A great French chef once said to me: "Cooking is not hard; it's simply a matter of knowing how." And he added: "But the ingredients must be impeccable."

This is precisely the principle behind this book. Cooking is not hard, but the "know how" is essential. In addition, there must be a standard of perfection, which comes largely as a result of experience in fine eating.

My husband and I have always looked upon great cooking — accompanied by good wines — as one of the fine arts. Consequently, for nearly forty years on our frequent trips to Europe and to the Far East we have sought it out as one of our two major interests, the other being beautiful works of art and their acquisition. These two loves seem of a piece to us, as they evidently do to many others. In fact, it always amuses and delights us when in France to observe that somewhere in the vicinity of great art sites there is invariably a fine restaurant, often of a grand order, many times simple, but always superb.

This is, I admit, a most enviable background for the cultivation of a good palate, and I strongly recommend it. However, one must eat and drink with attentive perception, or the experience is useless. (You might just as well spend your husband's money on horrendous souvenirs!) These memories and high standards come back with you. How many cooks I have trained by virtue of them! And how many French cookbooks I have devoured to help me attain the desired results!

It has been twenty years since I have dispensed with all cooks so that I might have the pleasure of cooking by myself. Our guests, many distinguished and knowledgeable, find it great. For me, I find good eating with good wines the surest way to lively, stimulating conversation. This book, encouraged by friends I've entertained, has been a natural outcome of this experience, as have the various magazine articles I've written.

Thirty dinners in thirty minutes each is, of course, not the sum of my cooking experience, but it is, in a sense, a summation of certain specific areas of cooking. It limits itself to just those dishes which demand short, precise cooking to be correct. By continued use of this book, the reasons for everything you do will be clarified, the cooking methods you are employing, and the precise timing and heat intensity you are using.

I have given detailed shopping instructions for each dinner and have repeated correct timing specifications for each menu. Wines and liquors in cooking as well as herbs in flavoring are precisely indicated. Tasting is urged to achieve the proper flavor — there can be no good cooking without it and, when possible, I have said what taste the end result must have.

Use this book trustingly and sensibly. After you've chosen a dinner, read through the whole menu. Then, read the specific recipes in the second section of the book, those which correspond to the major dishes involved in the dinner you undertake. Finally, take a good look at specific charts on all categories of foods and wines which are grouped in the third section, in the event you need substitutions for lack of suggested items in your markets.

Each dinner is presented as a complete entity, saving you the annoyance of referring to other pages in the book.

Do not worry if you cannot find time to do all the extras suggested. True, breads are delicious when buttered and heated but this and others are details you can skip if necessary.

With practice, I assure you, you will find time for everything. You will be doing in-between things unconsciously. You will develop an internal clock as I have. You will use ingredients correctly without measuring. That is cooking in the real sense.

Constant use of this book will lure you on to attempt other fascinating culinary delights. That is its ultimate intention.

I wish you "Bon Appetit."

Thirty Dinners in Thirty Minutes

Sautéed Oysters

Filet of Beef Limousin
Artichoke Hearts and Button Mushrooms

Cucumber Salad

Melon Crescents with Cointreau

Coffee

WINES:

For the first course:
Pouilly-Fuissé

For the main course:
Vosne-Romanée
or
Château Haut-Brion

This is a most distinguished company dinner. Yet, little advance preparation is required, since each dish is prepared while another is cooking. The main course is named for the French province of Limousin.

TO SUBSTITUTE:

If sweet ripe melon is not available, substitute bananas flambée. Should you wish to substitute another salad for the cucumbers, see page 114 for alternate suggestions.

what to buy

Everything except the fresh oysters and fresh bread may be purchased the previous day, if more convenient. For a dinner of this importance, wines should be bought the day before, allowing white to chill well and red to be opened hours ahead so it may breathe.

24 fresh oysters in their own liquor: Refrigerate. Or 2 (8 oz.) cans small oysters.

1 fresh loaf French or Italian bread: Or 1 package of partially baked French bread.

4 puff-pastry patty shells: For oysters. Buy frozen, or from a good bakery. Or substitute 4 slices white bread, for toast.

2 lbs. filet of beef: Same cut as filet mignon, but usually less expensive when bought in one piece for roasting. Do not have butcher wrap in fat.

¼ lb. salt pork: For filet. Very inexpensive. Should be pure white. Have butcher cut into strips ¼ in. thick, 2¼ in. long.

1 small (2 or 3 oz.) can paté de foie gras: For filet. Get least expensive variety.
If not available, buy any liver paté.

2 (9 oz.) cans or 2 packages frozen artichoke hearts.

1 (6 oz.) can of button mushrooms.

1 large bunch fresh parsley: You will need 3 cups, cut fine.

2 firm green cucumbers: Avoid extremely plump ones; they are seedy. Refrigerate.

1 medium-sized ripe melon: Buy best variety currently available — honeydew, Persian, Cranshaw, Casaba, Spanish. If cantaloupes are best, buy 2. Refrigerate.

If substituting bananas flambée, buy 4 medium-sized all-yellow bananas. You will also need brown sugar and ⅓ cup bourbon or rum.

½ pt. heavy sweet cream: You will need about ½ cup for oysters and ¼ cup for meat.

Extras: 3 lemons (½ for oysters, ½ for vegetables, 1 for cucumbers, 1 for melon); salt; pepper; 1 lb. butter; sugar and cream for coffee; drip grind coffee (breakfast blend and Italian after-dinner roast); 1 cup dry Madeira wine (½ cup for oysters, ½ cup for filet). *For Oysters* — flour; cayenne pepper; Worcestershire sauce; paprika. *For Melon* — ⅓ cup Cointreau. Suggest buying sweet butter.

Wines: If serving only one wine, omit white wine.

For first course:
1 bottle Pouilly-Fuissé (a white Burgundy)

For main course:
1 bottle Vosne-Romanée (a red Burgundy)
or
1 bottle Château Haut-Brion (a red Bordeaux)

See page 111 for correct wine service and less costly wine selections.

what to do

1. Early in the day (or the night before), attend to wines. Chill white wine well. De-cork red wine and lay in wine basket. Leave open, at room temperature, to breathe.

2. As early as possible (if not done before storing), wash parsley: Rinse quickly in running cold water. Remove discolored leaves. Shake well; wrap in paper towels to absorb extra moisture. Seal wrapped in plastic bag, and refrigerate until needed.
3. One or two hours before dinner, if possible, remove filet from refrigerator. Unwrap, so it can breathe and acquire room temperature.

30 minutes before serving first course

1. Remove butter and needed frozen foods from refrigerator.
2. Start first course:

   Open oysters; drain well. Remove any bits of shell.

   In skillet slowly melt 2-in. lump of butter. Do not brown.

   Add oysters. Salt lightly; shake on just a dash of cayenne pepper. Sprinkle on 1 Tbsp. flour. Cook gently 4 minutes, or until edges curl.
3. Place frozen patty shells in 400° oven. Will take about 25 minutes to bake and brown.
4. Open canned vegetables; drain well. Combine mushrooms and canned or frozen artichokes in saucepan. If using frozen artichokes, cover and cook very gently 4 or 5 minutes, or until tender. Drain; turn off heat.
5. To oysters add 1 Tbsp. Worcestershire sauce and 1 Tbsp. lemon juice. Add more butter if needed. Stir in ½ cup heavy sweet cream and ⅓ cup dry Madeira. Cook gently 4 or 5 minutes so mixture thickens slightly into a nice creamy sauce. Turn off heat.
6. Cut washed parsley quite fine with kitchen scissors. You need 3 cupfuls— 1 apiece for oysters, vegetables and cucumbers.
7. Peel cucumbers. (I find a potato peeler fastest.) Slice thin; lay tastefully on flat platter. Salt lightly. Sprinkle juice of 1 lemon over slices. Refrigerate until serving.
8. Lard filet on top in 10 or 12 places. Very easy; just make a 2 in. deep gash with slim knife and slip in strip of salt pork along knife blade. Lightly brown 2-in. lump of butter in roasting pan on top of stove. Place filet in pan. Do not roast yet.
9. Slice bread; if a long loaf, cut into 2 in. chunks. If a round loaf, cut into ½ in. slices, then cut loaf in half. Butter slices well on one side. Then put all slices in form of loaf on bakepan, ready to heat.

5 minutes before serving first course

10. Remove small circles of pastry from centers of baked patty shells.

    Or: Place bakery patty shells in 400° oven for 5 minutes to warm.

    Or: Cut crusts off 4 slices white bread; toast.

11. Taste oyster sauce for flavor. Adjust seasoning if needed. Reheat over gentle flame. If sauce thickens too much, stir in a little more cream or Madeira. Just before serving, stir in ¾ cup cut parsley.
12. Place warm patty shells (or buttered toast) on individual plates; heap hot oyster mixture over and around. Sprinkle with cut parsley and paprika.
13. If using partially baked bread, place on bottom rack of oven now. Takes about 15 minutes to bake and brown.
14. Turn oven to highest heat. After serving first course, salt filet and place on middle or top rack of oven, to roast while you eat. Roast 6 minutes; then return to kitchen to finish preparing main course.

If you feel uneasy watching the clock when eating first course, start roasting the filet *after* the first course has been eaten. It must be served rare. (There is no greater culinary calamity than an overcooked filet—and it can happen in just a minute.) Because this meat is so tender and so small, it takes only 10 to 12 minutes to roast. In this case, preheat oven during first course. If using partially baked bread, place it in oven when you put filet in; it can finish baking while you carve the filet.

serve first course

Open chilled white wine. Do not serve over ice. Fill glasses a little over halfway.

assemble main course

1. Stir ½ cup dry Madeira into juices in roaster. Baste filet with juices. Roast 4 minutes more.

2. To artichokes and mushrooms, add a 2-in. lump of butter, a squeeze of lemon juice and a dash of salt. Cover; heat over gentle flame.
3. Look at partially baked bread. If browning too fast, remove.
Or: Place fresh bread on bottom rack of oven for 5 to 8 minutes to warm.
4. Examine filet for rareness: Cut gash in center with small knife. If too raw, cook only another minute; look again. (Remember, ends always cook more than center, so can be served to those desiring less rare meat.)

IMPORTANT:
Remove roaster from oven the moment filet is ready, or it will continue to cook even if oven is turned off. Let stand at room temperature 1 or 2 minutes before carving.
5. Turn off oven. Place serving platter, bowl, and dinner plates in oven to warm. Put partially baked bread back in oven if necessary.
6. Blend ¼ cup heavy sweet cream into paté. Stir in some juices from roaster, to thin paté to the consistency of very heavy cream.
7. Carve filet in roaster: Cut slices ¼ in. thick. Overlap neatly down center of warm platter. Pour a little paté sauce around meat—not over it. Pour remaining sauce into sauceboat.
8. Taste vegetables; adjust seasoning if necessary. Turn off heat. Add a generous cup of parsley; mix well. Spoon carefully into warm bowl.

serve main course

Place warmed bread in basket, covered with napkin.
Pour red wine. Fill glasses a little over halfway.

assemble salad course

1. Fill coffeemaker: Suggest combining half breakfast blend and half Italian after-dinner roast for hearty flavor.
2. Decorate cucumber salad with cut parsley.

serve salad course

assemble dessert course

1. Cut chilled melon into quarters; remove seeds. Then, working over dessert platter to catch all juice, slice each quarter into crescents ½ in. thick at base. Peel crescents, removing all of white portion, which is not sweet. Arrange attractively on platter. Squeeze lemon juice over all, and pour on ⅓ cup of Cointreau.
Or: Prepare bananas flambée: Melt 2-in. lump of butter in skillet while you peel 4 bananas and slice in half lengthwise. Add bananas to skillet; sprinkle with brown sugar. Cook gently 3 or 4 minutes, spooning butter over. Do not try to turn them; they break easily.
Meanwhile: In a small attractive saucepan, heat ⅓ cup bourbon or rum.
When bananas are cooked and liquor is hot but not boiling, slide bananas onto warm platter and top with sauce in skillet. Serve immediately.
2. Turn on coffeemaker.

serve dessert course

All of the guests should have spoons as well as forks, so they can take up juice.
Or: Serve bananas flambée: Bring platter of bananas, pan of steaming liquor and dessert plates to table. Pour liquor over bananas; light at once with a match. Let flame until it dies down.

serve after-dinner coffee

If coffee was not started earlier, make last-minute coffee in a saucepan. (See page 118)

3

Green Turtle Soup with Sherry

Tournedos of Beef
Tiny Peas with Shallots

Belgian Endive with Blue Cheese Dressing

Strawberries Romanoff

Coffee

WINES:

For the first course:
Pouilly-Fuissé

For the main course:
Chambertin
or
Château Haut Brion

This dinner is worthy of your most discriminating guests. Yet, curiously enough, it's one of the easiest to do, since it requires very little advance preparation.

As a special treat after dessert, why not surprise your guests with Coffee Brulot, or one of the other special variations on page118.

TO SUBSTITUTE:

Unfortunately, shallots are not always available. They are most delicate in flavor, and very different from scallions or onions. However, if necessary, use scallions with good green stems, or canned pearl onions.

If good Belgian endive is not available, substitute hearts of iceberg lettuce with blue cheese dressing. Or see page114 for other salad suggestions.

Another equally festive dessert is chocolate mousse.

what to buy

Everything except the fresh bread may be purchased the previous day, if more convenient. For a dinner of this importance, wines should be bought the day before, allowing white to chill well and red to be opened hours ahead to breathe.

1 fresh loaf French or Italian bread: Or 1 package of partially baked French bread.

3 (10½ oz.) cans of green turtle soup: Be sure it contains turtle meat.

4 filets of beef (filet mignon): Each should be at least 1½ in. thick. Do not have fat wrapped around them. And, it may be less expensive to buy the filet in 1 piece and cut it yourself. (A 2¼ lb. piece will cut into 4 nice filets.)

4 large fresh mushrooms: Should be pure white with an unbroken membrane connecting stem and cap. Refrigerate in original bag. *If not available,* buy 2 small (2 or 3 oz.) cans of button mushrooms.

¼ lb. shallots: You will need 14. *If not available,* buy 1 bunch scallions with good green stems, or 3 small white onions and 1 small jar of pearl onions.

1 large bunch fresh parsley: You will need 1½ cups, cut fine.

4 or 5 large fresh Belgian endive: Stalks should be tightly closed; white with

light green tips. Refrigerate. *If not available,* buy 1 large firm head of iceberg lettuce.

¼ lb. Danish blue cheese: Or Roquefort, or Gorgonzola. Buy only if serving endive or hearts of iceberg lettuce salad.

2 or 3 packages frozen tiny peas: Sometimes these are labeled "Baby Peas" or "Petite Peas." (Unless labeled thus, peas will probably be large and not too sweet.) Canned baby peas are good eating but lack fresh green color.

2 (1 lb.) cartons frozen whole strawberries: For Strawberries Romanoff. Do not keep in freezer.

1 pt. vanilla ice cream: For Strawberries Romanoff.

½ pt. heavy sweet cream: For Strawberries Romanoff.

Extras: Salt; pepper; ¾ lb. butter; sugar and cream for coffee; drip grind coffee (breakfast blend and Italian after-dinner roast). *For Soup —* ¼ cup dry sherry wine. *For Tournedos —* Worcestershire sauce; dry tarragon; ¼ cup dry Madeira wine. *For French Dressing —* paprika; dry mustard; 1 clove of garlic; olive oil; vinegar. *For Strawberries —* ¼ cup Cointreau. Suggest buying sweet butter.

Wines: If serving only one wine, omit white wine.

For first course:
1 bottle Pouilly-Fuissé (a white Burgundy).

For main course:

1 bottle Chambertin (a red Burgundy).
or
1 bottle Château Haut Brion (a red Bordeaux).

See page 111 for correct wine service and less costly wine selections.

what to do

1. Early in the day (or the night before), attend to wines. Chill white wine well. De-cork red wine and lay in wine basket. Leave open, at room temperature, to breathe and expand.
2. As early as possible (if not done before storing), wash parsley and endive (or lettuce): Do not separate endive (or lettuce) leaves. Rinse quickly in running cold water. Remove discolored leaves and edges. Shake well; wrap in paper towels to absorb extra moisture. Seal in plastic bag, and refrigerate until needed.

30 minutes before serving first course

1. Remove filets, butter, mushrooms, parsley and frozen peas and strawberries from refrigerator. Unwrap filets. Open strawberry cartons to hasten thawing.
2. Whip ½ pt. heavy sweet cream until it stands in soft peaks when beater is lifted. Refrigerate for dessert course.
3. Cut washed parsley quite fine with kitchen scissors. You need 1½ cupfuls—½ cup for meat, 1 cup for peas.
4. Slice bread: If a long loaf, cut into

2-in. chunks. If a round loaf, cut into ½-in. slices, then cut loaf in half. Butter slices well on one side. Then put all slices in form of original loaf on bakepan, ready to heat.
5. For the filets, melt 2-in. lump of butter in large skillet. For the peas, melt 2-in. lump of butter in saucepan.
6. Peel 14 shallots; sliver 6 into skillet you will use for the filets. Keep remaining 8 whole; place in saucepan to cook with peas.
Or: Cut 1 cup of scallions (white and green parts combined). Place half in skillet, half in saucepan.
Or: Peel 3 small onions; sliver into skillet. Open pearl onions; drain well, and place in saucepan.

15 minutes before serving first course

7. If using partially baked bread, place in 450° oven now. Takes about 15 minutes to bake and brown.
8. Cook slivered shallots (or scallions or onions) in skillet gently 4 minutes. Stir occasionally; add more butter if needed. When golden, remove from heat. Do not brown.
9. Wipe fresh mushrooms with damp paper towel. Do not wash or peel. Cut stems even with caps. Refrigerate stems for another meal. Place caps in small saucepan with 2-in. lump of butter. Cover; cook gently until serving first course.
10. Look at partially baked bread. If browning too fast, turn oven down.

Or: Place fresh bread in 450° oven for 5 to 8 minutes to warm.
11. Heat soup slowly about 4 minutes.
12. Mix French dressing while soup heats: Peel and split 1 clove garlic; place in small deep bowl with ½ tsp. paprika, ½ tsp. dry mustard, ½ tsp. salt and 3 Tbsp. vinegar. Mix well. Slowly stir in 6 Tbsp. olive oil. Taste; add more oil or vinegar for perfect balance. Set aside for salad course; do not refrigerate.
13. Add ¼ cup dry sherry to soup just before serving.
14. Turn off oven; turn off mushrooms.

serve first course

Place warmed bread in basket, covered with napkin.

Open chilled white wine. Do not serve over ice. Fill glasses a little over halfway.

assemble main course

1. For the peas, simmer whole shallots (or scallions or pearl onions) in saucepan about 5 minutes.
2. Reheat skillet. Salt filets lightly on both sides; place in skillet. Add 1 Tbsp. Worcestershire sauce, and more butter if needed. Cook 3 minutes on first side.
3. Place serving platter and dinner plates in oven to warm.
4. To mushrooms, add 1 Tbsp. dry Madeira, and more butter if needed. Cover; heat gently.
5. Turn filets; add 3 Tbsp. dry Madeira

and 1 heaping tsp. dry tarragon. Baste filets with this sauce. Cook 2 minutes more.

6. When shallots (or substitute) have softened and are golden, add to frozen peas (or well-drained canned peas) with another lump of butter. Salt lightly. Cover and cook gently 1 to 2 minutes.
7. Examine filets for rareness. Make small cut in center of 1 filet. If too raw, cook only another minute; look again.

   IMPORTANT:
   Place filets in center of warm platter the second they are ready, or the heated skillet will continue to cook them.
9. Turn off peas. Stir in 1 cup cut parsley.
10. Taste sauce in skillet. Adjust if needed. Turn off heat; stir in remaining cut parsley. Top filets with mushroom caps and pour sauce over.
11. Spoon peas onto platter around filets.
12. Taste strawberries. If defrosted, place cartons in refrigerator.

serve main course

Pour red wine. Fill glasses a little over halfway.

assemble salad course

1. Quarter endive stalks (or head of lettuce) lengthwise. Do not separate leaves. Salt lightly. Arrange on individual plates.
2. Mash blue cheese with enough French

dressing to make a thick creamy sauce. Do not include split garlic. Spoon over salad. Toss.

serve salad course

assemble dessert course

1. Place ice cream in large bowl; break apart with spoon. Let soften 1 or 2 minutes.
2. Fill coffeemaker while ice cream softens: Suggest combining half breakfast blend and half Italian after-dinner roast for hearty flavor.
3. Work ice cream with a spoon so it is smooth and firm but not soupy. (It will soften more as you add other ingredients.) Fold in whipped cream. Add strawberries with all juice, and ¼ cup Cointreau. Mix gently but thoroughly. Taste; add more Cointreau if desired. Transfer to dessert bowl.
4. Turn on coffeemaker.

serve dessert course

serve after-dinner coffee

If coffee was not started earlier, make last-minute coffee in a saucepan. (See page 118.)

Oysters or Clams on the Half Shell

Porterhouse Steak
Mushrooms Madeira
French Fried Potatoes

Baked Alaska

Coffee

WINES:

For the first course:
Pouilly-Fuissé

For the main course:
Châteauneuf du Pape
or
Beaune

A steak dinner is always great eating, provided the meat is tender and not overcooked. Steak is at its best when rare. For dessert, Baked Alaska makes a very impressive showing — yet it's astonishingly easy! Should you also want a salad course, choose a simple one. (See page 114.)

TO SUBSTITUTE:

If fresh oysters or clams are not available, serve frozen cream of shrimp soup or oyster stew. If Baked Alaska does not intrigue you for dessert, serve a soft-type French cheese with some French bread. (See page 117 for suggestions on buying and serving cheese.)

what to buy

Everything except the fresh oysters or clams and fresh bread may be purchased the previous day, if more convenient. For a dinner of this importance, wines should be bought the day before, allowing white to chill well and red to be opened hours ahead to breathe.

24 fresh oysters or cherry-stone clams: Have dealer open these as near dinner time as possible and pack on half shells over crushed ice. Refrigerate until serving.

If substituting frozen cream of shrimp soup or oyster stew, buy 3 (10 oz.) cans. You will also need a little heavy sweet cream and ¼ cup dry Madeira wine.

1 fresh loaf French or Italian bread: Or 1 package of partially baked French bread.

1 porterhouse steak: Tell butcher it is to serve 4. Should be nearly 2 in. thick, with a small tail. Buy well-aged beef, of "prime" or "choice" quality. Have butcher remove tail, cut off fat and grind twice. (This chopped tail can be served as hamburger the next day.)

2 or 3 packages frozen French fried potatoes: Do not keep in freezer.

16 large fresh mushrooms: Should be pure white with an unbroken membrane connecting stem and cap. Refrigerate in original bag. *If not available,* buy 3 or 4 small (3 or 4 oz.) cans of button mushrooms.

1 large bunch fresh parsley: You will need 2 cups, cut fine.

1 layer of spongecake: For Baked Alaska. Should be as large as a quart brick of ice cream — 7 in. long, 5 in. wide, 1 in. thick. Refrigerate.

1 qt. brick of ice cream, any flavor: For Baked Alaska. Keep solidly frozen.

1 small package of slivered almonds: For Baked Alaska.

Extras: 3 lemons (2 for oysters or clams, 1 for mushrooms); salt; pepper; ¾ lb. butter; sugar and cream for coffee; drip grind coffee (breakfast blend and Italian after-dinner roast). *For Oysters (or Clams)* — cocktail sauce; 1 package dark pumpernickel. *For Steak*—Bahamian or Dijon mustard; ⅓ cup Worcestershire sauce; olive oil or French dressing. *For Mushrooms*—dry tarragon; ⅓ cup dry Madeira wine. *For Baked Alaska* — 4 eggs; ¾ cup sugar. Suggest buying sweet butter.

Wines: If serving only one wine, omit white wine.

For first course:
1 bottle Pouilly-Fuissé (a white Burgundy).

For main course:
1 bottle Châteauneuf du Pape (a red Rhone).
or
1 bottle Beaune (a red Burgundy).

See page 111 for correct wine service and alternate selections.

what to do

1. Early in the day (or the night before), attend to wines. Chill white wine well. De-cork red wine and lay in wine basket. Leave open, at room temperature, to breathe.

2. As early as possible (if not done before storing), wash parsley. Rinse quickly in running cold water. Remove discolored leaves. Shake well; wrap in paper towels to absorb extra moisture. Place wrapped in plastic bag, and refrigerate until needed.

3. One or two hours before dinner, if possible, remove steak from refrigerator. Unwrap, so it can breathe and acquire room temperature.

30 minutes before serving first course

1. Remove butter, 4 eggs, parsley, mushrooms and frozen soups (if using them) from refrigerator.

2. Make meringue for Baked Alaska: Separate 4 eggs. Be sure not to get any yolk in the whites, or they will not beat stiff. (If some yolk does get in, pick it out with a broken egg shell.) Refrigerate yolks, covered with cold water for tomorrow's omelette.

   Beat whites until very dry and glossy, slowly adding ¾ cup sugar. (Meringue should not slide when bowl is partially inverted.) Refrigerate for dessert course.

3. Lay steak on shallow pan. Do not salt. Spread thin layer of Bahamian or Dijon mustard on both sides. Pour over ¼ cup Worcestershire sauce and 2 Tbsp. olive oil or French dressing (page 116). Dot with small lumps of butter in 4 or 5 places. Do not

broil yet.

4. Cut washed parsley quite fine with kitchen scissors. You need 2 cupfuls — 1 for mushrooms, 1 for steak.
5. Wipe fresh mushrooms with damp paper towel; do not wash or peel. Cut stems even with caps; refrigerate stems for another meal.

   Or: Open canned mushrooms. Drain liquid into measuring cup; add enough water to make ¾ cup liquid.

15 minutes before serving first course

6. For the mushrooms, bring ¾ cup water (or the liquid from canned mushrooms) to a boil. Add 3 Tbsp. butter, 1 Tbsp. lemon juice, dash of salt and mushrooms. Cover; cook quite actively about 15 minutes so most of liquid boils away, leaving mushrooms slightly glazed. Look occasionally so mushrooms do not scorch.
7. Spread potatoes on shallow pan; place on top rack of 400° oven for 25 minutes, or until crisp.
8. Slice bread: If a long loaf, cut into 2-in. chunks. If a round loaf, cut into ½-in. slices, then cut loaf in half. Butter slices well on one side. Then put all slices in form of the loaf on bakepan, ready to heat.
9. Prepare first course:
   Butter 6 slices pumpernickel thickly; cut in half and place on plate. Pack ice from oysters (or clams) on 4 individual plates. On each plate center ½ lemon. Surround lemon with

oysters (or clams), narrow ends of shells at center.

Or: Open soup. Taste before diluting as can label directs. Usually these soups are not too thick; you may want to serve "as is." If thinning is needed, add a little heavy sweet cream. Heat well. Just before serving, add ¼ cup dry Madeira for fine flavor.

10. Look at mushrooms. Liquid should be almost gone. Turn off heat.
11. Shake or stir potatoes. If browning too fast, remove from oven while you eat first course.
12. If using partially baked bread, place on bottom rack of oven now. Takes about 15 minutes to bake and brown.
13. Turn oven control to "broil." After serving first course place steak pan 3½ in. below high flame, to broil while eating first course. In 6 minutes top of steak will be brown; return to kitchen to turn it. If you feel uneasy watching the clock while with your guests, start broiling the steak *after* the first course has been eaten. It takes only 10 minutes at most, and is the best way to avoid overcooking. (Nothing is more detrimental to a cook's reputation than dry, overdone steak.) Remove potatoes and partially baked bread from oven if done. Put them back in if necessary when broiling steak.

serve first course

Buttered pumpernickel is served with oysters or clams.

Or: If serving soup, heat well and add Madeira just before serving.

Open chilled white wine. Do not serve over ice. Fill glasses a little over halfway.

assemble main course

1. Look at steak. If nicely browned, turn over. Baste with pan juices. Watch carefully from now on. Broil 3 minutes.
2. Move partially baked bread to top rack of oven to finish browning.

   Or: Place fresh bread on bottom rack of oven for 5 to 8 minutes to warm.
3. Look at potatoes. Remove, if necessary, until you carve steak.
4. To mushrooms, add ⅓ cup dry Madeira, a little lemon juice and 1 tsp. dry tarragon. Heat slowly.
5. Examine steak for rareness: Make small cut in center. If still raw, cook only another minute; look again. (Even 1 minute of extra cooking can make steak gray and tough.)

   IMPORTANT:
   Remove pan from broiler the second steak is ready or it will continue to cook even if broiler is turned off.
6. Turn off oven. Place serving platter and dinner plates inside to warm. Put potatoes back in oven if necessary.
7. Carve steak in pan: With a sharp knife, cut closely around bone to release both areas of meat — the small, which is the filet, and the large, called the contre filet. Then, holding knife slightly slanted away from you,

cut each area crosswise (across the grain), into slices 1 in. thick.

8. Slide whole steak (including the bone) onto warm platter so shape is retained. Lay a thick ribbon of cut parsley down center; pour pan juices over.
9. Turn off mushrooms. Toss in remaining cut parsley; cover pan and shake to mix well.
10. Place mushrooms at one end of steak; salt potatoes; place at other end.

serve main course

Place warmed bread in basket, covered with napkin.

Pour red wine. Fill glasses a little over halfway.

assemble dessert course

1. Prepare Baked Alaska:
Turn oven to 450°. Put serving platter in refrigerator. Lay spongecake on small bread board; center *solidly* frozen ice cream on top. Cake should be just slightly larger than ice cream. Quickly cover all with meringue. Swirl surface of meringue into attractive peaks with spatula. Sprinkle with slivered almonds. Place bread board on middle rack of oven; bake only 3 or 4 minutes, until meringue is lightly browned. Watch closely. (If you prefer to brown it under high broiler flame, it takes less time. But you must watch even more closely. Meringue scorches quickly.

2. Fill coffeemaker: Suggest combining half breakfast blend and half Italian after-dinner roast for hearty flavor.
3. Turn on coffeemaker.
4. Remove Baked Alaska from oven the moment it is ready. With two wide spatulas, slide it onto chilled platter. Serve immediately.
5. Turn off oven.

serve dessert course

Cut Baked Alaska into fairly thick slices when serving.

serve after-dinner coffee

If coffee was not started earlier, make last-minute coffee in a saucepan. (See page 118.)

Nova Scotia Salmon

Steak au Poivre
Parslied Potatoes
Frenched String Beans with Foie Gras

Boston Lettuce Salad

Vanilla Ice Cream
with
Mandarin Oranges and Cointreau

Coffee

WINES:

St. Emilion
or
Beaujolais

This is an impressive dinner because of its specialties. Nova Scotia salmon is a great delicacy if bought choice — absolutely saltless and slightly oily. Steak au Poivre is a tender peppered steak with cognac sauce.

TO SUBSTITUTE:

If fine Nova Scotia salmon is not available, use frozen lobster Newburg spiked with cognac. If good Boston lettuce is not in the market, use romaine lettuce if choice. Or see page 114 for other salad suggestions.

what to buy

Everything except the fresh bread may be purchased the previous day, if more convenient.

1 fresh loaf French or Italian bread: Or 1 package of partially baked French bread.

12 slices Nova Scotia salmon: This is expensive, no matter where bought, so it is worth the extra trouble to track down the best available. Have cut to order so slices are of uniform size, ⅛ in. thick. Ask for a taste: must be unsalted, slightly oily. Refrigerate.
If substituting lobster Newburg, buy 2 packages of frozen lobster Newburg. You will also need 1 lemon, cognac, and 4 patty shells, fresh or frozen. If patty shells are not available, substitute 4 slices white bread.

4 large shell steaks: Should be only ½ in. thick. Substitute small T-bone steaks, if you wish.

1 jar cracked black pepper: For steak. Or 1 box black peppercorns.

16 tiny new potatoes: Or 2 (1 lb.) cans small whole potatoes.

1 large bunch fresh parsley: You will need 1 generous cup, cut fine.

2 heads of crisp young Boston lettuce: Or 1 head of romaine lettuce.

2 packages frozen Frenched string beans.

1 small (2 or 3 oz.) can paté de foie gras: Get a nice but inexpensive variety.

1½ pts. vanilla ice cream.

2 (10 or 11 oz.) cans of Mandarin oranges: Refrigerate.

Extras: Salt; pepper; olive oil; ¾ lb. butter; sugar and cream for coffee; drip

grind coffee (breakfast blend and Italian after-dinner roast). *For Salmon —* 1 lemon; 1 package dark pumpernickel; peppercorns. *For Steak —* ¼ cup dry vermouth and cognac. *For French Dressing —* paprika; dry mustard; 1 clove of garlic; vinegar. *For Dessert —* ⅓ cup Cointreau. Suggest buying sweet butter.

Wine:
1 bottle St. Emilion (a red Bordeaux).
or
1 bottle Beaujolais (a red Burgundy).
See page 111 for correct wine service and alternate selections.

what to do

1. Several hours before dining, if possible, de-cork wine and lay in wine basket. Leave open, at room temperature, to breathe.
2. As early as possible (if not done before storing), wash parsley and salad greens: Separate leaves; rinse quickly in running cold water. Remove discolored leaves and edges. Shake well; wrap in paper towels to absorb extra moisture. Seal wrapped in plastic bag, and refrigerate until needed.

30 minutes before serving
first course

1. Remove steak, butter and needed frozen foods from refrigerator. Unwrap steak.
2. If serving frozen lobster Newburg,

empty packages into top of double boiler; heat uncovered over actively boiling water 25 to 30 minutes, stirring occasionally.
3. If using frozen patty shells, heat oven to 450°.
4. Scrub fresh potatoes in cold water. Do not peel. Place in deep saucepan; cover with cold water and 1 to 2 tsp. salt. Do not cook yet.
   Or: Open canned potatoes; empty into deep saucepan, liquid and all. Add water to cover. Do not cook yet.
5. Place frozen patty shells in oven. Turn oven to 400°. Bake 20 to 25 minutes.
6. Cut washed parsley quite fine with kitchen scissors. You will need 1 generous cupful for potatoes.
7. Mix French dressing: Peel and split 1 clove garlic; place in small deep bowl with ½ tsp. paprika, ½ tsp. dry mustard, ½ tsp. salt and 3 Tbsp. vinegar. Mix well. Slowly stir in 6 Tbsp. olive oil. Taste; add more oil or vinegar for perfect balance. Set aside for salad course; do not refrigerate.
8. Slice white bread: If a long loaf, cut into 2-in. chunks. If a round loaf, cut into ½-in. slices, then cut loaf in half. Butter slices well on one side. Then put all slices in form of loaf on bakepan, ready to heat.
9. Cut 1 lemon in quarters. Butter 6 slices pumpernickel; cut in half.
   Or: Taste lobster Newburg sauce. Add salt, lemon juice or a little cream if needed.

10. If using whole peppercorns instead of cracked pepper, place entire box in small plastic bag or between two dry paper towels, and crush with a rolling pin. Pieces should be larger than coarsest grinding of a pepper mill. Save for steaks.
11. Fill coffeemaker: Suggest combining half breakfast blend and half Italian after-dinner roast for hearty flavor.

5 minutes before serving first course

12. If using fresh potatoes, bring to an active boil. Then lower heat slightly. Cover; cook about 20 minutes.
13. Remove small circles of pastry from centers of baking patty shells.
    Or: Place bakery patty shells in 400° oven for 5 minutes to warm.
    Or: Cut crusts off 4 slices white bread; toast.
14. Prepare first course:
    Lay 3 slices of salmon, 1 lemon quarter and 3 pieces of buttered pumpernickel on each of 4 individual plates.
    Or: Stir lobster Newburg. Add dash of cognac. Taste sauce; add more lemon juice or cream if needed. Place warm patty shells (or buttered toast) on individual plates; heap hot lobster Newburg over and around. Top with paprika.
15. If using canned potatoes, bring to an active boil. Then lower heat slightly. Cover; cook about 15 minutes.

16. If using partially baked bread, place in 450° oven now. Takes about 15 minutes to bake and brown.

serve first course

Bring plates of salmon to table with a pepper mill, and possibly a cruet of olive oil.
Or: Bring plates of lobster Newburg to table.

assemble main course

1. Look at partially baked bread. If browning too fast, remove from oven for a few minutes, or turn oven down.
   Or: Place fresh bread in 450° oven for 5 to 8 minutes to warm.
2. Place string beans in saucepan with 2-in. lump of butter and ¼ tsp. salt. Cover; cook gently about 6 minutes.
3. Place serving platter and dinner plates in oven to warm.
4. Start steaks: You will probably need two skillets. In each, melt small lump of butter; add 2 Tbsp. olive oil.
   Salt steaks lightly. Press cracked pepper into both sides with heel of your hand.
   Lay steaks into skillets. Cook over medium flame, about 2 minutes on first side.
5. Test potatoes for doneness: Prick with thin-pronged fork. If cooked through, drain by sliding cover back just enough to let out the water. Quickly add ¼ lb. butter cut into

several pieces, and cut parsley. Cover. Do not cook more. Shake to mix; retained steam will melt butter and render potatoes to perfection.
6. Turn steaks over. Add more butter if needed; skillets should not be dry. Add 2 Tbsp. dry French vermouth and 1 Tbsp. cognac to each skillet. Swish around; cook another 2 minutes.
7. Open can of paté de foie gras.
8. Examine steaks for rareness: Cut small gash in center of one. If too raw, cook 1 minute or less; look again. (Steak this thin cooks in very little time.)

   IMPORTANT:
   Place steaks in center of warm platter the second they are ready, or the heated skillets will continue to cook them.
9. Test string beans with fork. If done, turn off heat; cut small pieces of foie gras into pan. Do not cook more or foie gras will dissolve.
10. Taste sauce in skillets for flavor; adjust if necessary. Pour over steaks.
11. Place string beans at one end of steaks. Salt potatoes; place at other end.
12. Turn off oven.

serve main course

Place warmed bread in basket, covered with napkin.
Pour wine. Fill glasses a little over halfway.

assemble salad course

1. Place Boston lettuce in salad bowl; keep leaves whole if possible.
   Or: Break romaine leaves into 2½ in. lengths.
2. Salt salad lightly. Toss with 4 or 5 Tbsp. French dressing (See page 116), or just enough to moisten all leaves. Do not include split garlic.

serve salad course

assemble dessert course

1. Spoon ice cream attractively into dessert bowl. Add Mandarin oranges with all juice, and ⅓ cup Cointreau.
2. Turn on coffeemaker.

serve dessert course

serve after-dinner coffee

If coffee was not started earlier, make last-minute coffee in a saucepan. (See page 118.)

Avocados Stuffed with Tiny Shrimp

Broiled Butterfly Lamb
Parslied Potatoes
Frenched String Beans with Bacon

Belgian Endive with Blue Cheese Dressing

Fresh Pineapple
filled with
Orange Ice

Coffee

WINES:

Beaujolais
or
Châteauneuf du Pape
or
Médoc

This unusual dinner has won many compliments — even from people who thought they didn't like lamb. The important thing is to serve the lamb while still pink inside. It takes close watching, but, I assure you, the taste and texture of rare lamb is far superior to the overdone gray lamb generally served in this country. The French never serve lamb, be it roasted or broiled, other than rare. They call it "à pointe" which means cooked to the point of perfection.

TO SUBSTITUTE:

If prime avocados are not available, use fresh water cress. If you cannot find choice Belgian endive, serve hearts of iceberg lettuce with blue cheese dressing. If fresh ripe pineapple is not in the market, you may substitute baked fresh rhubarb with sour cream.

what to buy

Everything except the fresh bread may be purchased the previous day, if more convenient.

1 fresh loaf French or Italian bread: Or 1 package of partially baked French bread.

2 large ripe avocados: Should be soft enough to yield readily to gentle pressure from palms of hands. Refrigerate. *If not available,* substitute 2 large bunches of crisp water cress, and buy twice as much shrimp or crabmeat.

2 (3 oz.) jars of tiny shrimp: If not available, substitute 1 (6 oz.) package of frozen Alaska king crabmeat. Refrigerate.

1 fresh leg of spring lamb: Top chops must be cut off by butcher; do not buy unless you want them. Have butcher cut remainder of leg open its full length and remove center bone, then lay meat out in butterfly shape. Very easy for him.

16 tiny new potatoes: Or 2 (1 lb.) cans small whole potatoes.

1 large bunch fresh parsley: You will need 2 generous cups, cut fine.

4 or 5 large fresh Belgian endive: Stalks should be tightly closed; white with light green tips. Refrigerate. *If not available,* buy 1 large firm head of iceberg lettuce.

1 large fresh ripe pineapple: A ripe pineapple smells sweet. Choose a fat one, with a handsome leafy crown. Fat pineapples are easier to scoop out. Refrigerate.

If substituting baked rhubarb, buy 2 bunches fresh crisp rhubarb. You will also need sugar and some sour cream.

1 qt. orange ice: For pineapple. Keep solidly frozen.

2 packages frozen Frenched string beans.

¼ lb. Danish blue cheese: For salad. Or buy Roquefort, or Gorgonzola.

½ pt. sour cream: You will need only 1 Tbsp. for first course. Remainder will keep for days in refrigerator. Serve over baked rhubarb, apple strudel, frozen whole strawberries, or borscht. Or make beef stroganoff, or veal smetana.

Extras: Salt; pepper; ½ lb. butter; sugar and cream for coffee; drip grind coffee (breakfast blend and Italian after-dinner roast). *For Avocados with Shrimp*—1 lemon; mayonnaise; Worcestershire sauce. *For Lamb* — dry thyme. *For French Dressing*—paprika; dry mustard; 1 clove of garlic; olive oil; vinegar. *For String Beans* — 2 slices bacon. Suggest buying sweet butter.

Wine: 1 bottle Beaujolais (a red Burgundy).
or
1 bottle Châteauneuf du Pape (a red Rhone).
or
1 bottle Médoc (a red Bordeaux).
See page 111 for correct wine service and alternate suggestions.

what to do

1. Several hours before dining, if possible, de-cork wine and lay in wine basket. Leave open, at room temperature, to breathe.
2. As early as possible (if not done before storing), wash parsley, endive (or lettuce), and water cress if using it: Do not separate endive (or lettuce) leaves. Rinse quickly in running cold water. Remove any discolored leaves and edges. Shake well; wrap in paper towels to absorb extra moisture. Seal in plastic bag, and refrigerate until needed.

30 minutes before serving first course

1. Remove lamb, butter, pineapple (or rhubarb), parsley and frozen string beans from refrigerator. Unwrap lamb and spread out flat so it can gain room temperature more quickly.
2. If using frozen crabmeat, take out of carton. Leave in wrapper; immerse in cool water for about 25 minutes to thaw. If defrosted in less time, place in a bowl and refrigerate until needed.
3. Start dessert; should take no more than 10 minutes:
   Cut off leafy crown far enough down on pineapple to give you a good opening for scooping out interior. Save crown so you can present a "whole pineapple" after filling. If edges of leaves are frayed, cut off all tips straight across with sharp knife to make a squared-off, bushy top.
   Using a sharp, long-bladed knife, cut deep into pineapple flesh, crisscross fashion, to free small pieces. Keep knife 1 in. away from outside skin so as not to puncture it. Use a curved grapefruit knife to scoop out more flesh if you wish. Don't try to scoop out all flesh; it's nearly impossible.
   Put crown back in place; refrigerate both pineapple shell and flesh.
   Or: Prepare rhubarb for baking. Cut green tops and dried ends off stalks. Do not peel. Rinse quickly in running cold water; do not dry. Cut pieces to fit across an oblong baking dish; or cut them half the diameter of a large pyrex pie plate and arrange like spokes of a wheel. Cover with 1 generous cup sugar. Do not bake yet.
4. Mix French dressing for lamb and salad: Peel and split 1 clove garlic; place in small deep bowl with ¾ tsp. paprika, ¾ tsp. dry mustard, ¾ tsp. salt and 5 Tbsp. vinegar. Mix well. Slowly stir in 10 Tbsp. olive oil. Taste; add more oil or vinegar for perfect balance.
5. Lay butterfly lamb out flat in shallow pan, cut side up. Do not salt. Pour 6 Tbsp. French dressing over. Sprinkle a scant ½ tsp. dry thyme over all. (Too much thyme creates a bitter taste.) Dot in 4 or 5 places with small pieces of butter. Do not broil yet.

6. Scrub fresh potatoes in cold water. Do not peel. Place in deep saucepan; cover with cold water and 1 to 2 tsp. salt. Do not cook yet.

   Or: Open canned potatoes; empty into deep saucepan, liquid and all. Add water to cover. Do not cook yet.
7. Cut washed parsley quite fine with kitchen scissors. You will need 2 generous cupfuls — 1 for meat, 1 for potatoes.
8. Slice bread: If a long loaf, cut into 2-in. chunks. If a round loaf, cut into ½-in. slices, then cut loaf in half. Butter slices well on one side. Then put all slices in form of loaf on bakepan, ready to heat.

5 minutes before serving first course

9. If using fresh potatoes, bring to an active boil. Cover; cook about 20 minutes.
10. Mix seafood sauce for shrimp (or crabmeat). Double these amounts if using water cress instead of avocados: Combine 2 Tbsp. mayonnaise with half as much sour cream, a dash of salt, ½ Tbsp. lemon juice and ½ Tbsp. Worcestershire sauce. Taste. Should be slightly pungent, but not too lemony. If so, add more mayonnaise or sour cream.
11. Open jars of shrimp; drain well. Mix into seafood sauce gently.

    Or: Separate crabmeat with fingers; keep lumps large. Eliminate any bits

of bone you feel. Mix into seafood sauce gently.
12. Wash avocados; cut in half lengthwise. Twist halves in opposite directions to separate. Remove pit and thin skin surrounding it. Salt flesh lightly; sprinkle with lemon juice to retain color.
13. Place each avocado half on an individual plate. Fill cavities generously with shrimp (or crabmeat) mixture.

    Or: Place shrimp (or crabmeat) mixture in center of round platter and surround with a thick garland of water cress.
14. If using canned potatoes, bring to an active boil. Then lower heat slightly. Cover; cook about 15 minutes.
15. If using partially baked bread, place in 450° oven now. Takes about 15 minutes to bake and brown.

serve first course

assemble main course

1. Look at partially baked bread. If browning too fast, remove from oven until turning lamb over.
2. Turn oven control to "broil"; place lamb pan 3 in. below high flame. Broil first side 5 or 6 minutes to brown. Watch closely; do not scorch.
3. Put 2 slices of bacon in skillet; fry over low heat until crisp but not brittle. Drain off grease as it collects; dry on paper towel.
4. Test potatoes for doneness while

bacon fries: Prick with thin-pronged fork. If cooked through, drain by sliding cover back just enough to let out the water. Quickly add ¼ lb. butter cut into several pieces, and 1 cup cut parsley. Do not cook more. Shake to mix; retained steam will melt butter and finish potatoes to perfection.
5. Place string beans in saucepan with 2-in. lump of butter and ¼ tsp. salt. Cover; cook gently about 6 minutes.
6. Turn lamb over; baste with pan juices. Broil only 3 minutes more.
7. Put partially baked bread back in oven if necessary.

   Or: Place fresh bread in oven for 5 to 8 minutes to warm.
8. Fill coffeemaker: Suggest combining half breakfast blend and half Italian after-dinner roast for hearty flavor.
9. Examine lamb for rareness: Make a small cut in thickest part. It should be pink; remember that ends and thinner areas will be cooked more. If too raw, cook only 1 minute more; look again. (This boned leg of lamb takes less time to broil than a thick steak. And like steak, it must be rare for really superb eating.)

IMPORTANT:
Remove pan from broiler the second lamb is ready or it will continue to cook even if broiler is turned off.
10. Turn off oven. Place serving platter and dinner plates inside to warm.
11. Carve lamb in pan: Cut in half, down the center. Then cut each area cross-

wise (against the grain) into slices ½ in. thick.

12. Test string beans with fork. If done, turn off heat; crumble in crisp bacon.
13. Slide lamb onto warm platter so slices overlap. Lay a strip of cut parsley down the center. Pour pan juices over.
14. Place string beans along one side of lamb, parslied potatoes along the other.

serve main course

Place warmed bread in basket, covered with napkin.

Pour wine. Fill glasses a little over halfway.

assemble salad course

1. If baking rhubarb, place in 400° oven now. Will take 15 to 20 minutes to bake. Should be soft but not mushy.
2. Quarter endive stalks (or head of lettuce) lengthwise. Do not separate leaves. Salt lightly. Arrange on individual plates.
3. Mash blue cheese with enough French dressing to make a thick creamy sauce. Do not include split garlic. Spoon over salad.

serve salad course

assemble dessert course

1. Quickly spoon orange ice into pineapple shell. If you like, layer in some scooped-out fresh pineapple as you go. Replace leafy crown; center pineapple on platter. Serve immediately.
Or: Taste rhubarb. Add more sugar if needed.
2. Turn on coffeemaker.

serve dessert course

serve after-dinner coffee

If coffee was not started earlier, make last-minute coffee in a saucepan. (See page 118.)

6 menu for 4

Jellied Madrilene with Caviar

Chicken Breasts à la Vallée D'Auge
Carrots Vichy

Avocado, Belgian Endive and Mushroom Salad

Peaches Melba

Coffee

WINES:

Hermitage
or
Pouilly-Fuissé

This is a deluxe dinner, suitable for any occasion. The main dish originated in Normandy, a French province famous for the quality of its cream and its apples. Here, cream and apple brandy (Calvados) are used to create a magnificent chicken specialty.

TO SUBSTITUTE:

If salad ingredients are not available, see page 114 for other delicious combinations. If you prefer a hot soup, you may serve Consommé Bellevue, a combination of clam juice and clear chicken consommé, spiked with dry sherry. Or make Boula, a combination of green turtle soup and purée of green pea soup. It, too, is spiked with dry sherry.

what to buy

Everything except the fresh bread may be purchased the previous day, if more convenient. The madrilene should be purchased the previous day to be chilled solid.

1 fresh loaf French or Italian bread: Or 1 package of partially baked French bread.

2 or 3 (13 oz.) cans madrilene: Plan to refrigerate at least 8 hours before serving, or buy already chilled.

1 (4 oz.) jar black caviar: Lumpfish (Danish) caviar is the least expensive, and not salty. If you wish, substitute red caviar mixed with sour cream to counteract its extreme saltiness.

4 large chicken breasts: Have butcher split in half to make 8 pieces. If you wish, substitute 2 young broilers, each 2¼ to 2½ lbs., cut up. Thighs and drumsticks may also be used; but, being less tender, they require 20 minutes of extra cooking.

1 large bunch fresh parsley: You will need about 2 cups, cut fine.

1 large ripe avocado: Should be soft enough to yield readily to gentle pressure from palms of hands. Refrigerate.

6 medium-sized fresh mushrooms: You need 3 for chicken, 3 for salad. Should be pure white with an unbroken membrane connecting stem and cap. Refrigerate in original bag. *If not available,* buy 1 small (3 or 4 oz.) can of sliced or button mushrooms for chicken, and omit mushrooms from salad.

3 fresh Belgian endive: Stalks should be tightly closed; white with light green tips. Refrigerate.

¼ lb. shallots: You will need 6 for the chicken. *If not available,* buy 1 bunch scallions with good green stems, or 3 small white onions.

2 (14 oz.) cans or 2 packages frozen whole baby carrots: If you have extra time to clean and cut fresh carrots, by all means substitute 1 bunch of young carrots.

1 pt. heavy sweet cream: You will need about half for the chicken, half for Peaches Melba.

1½ pts. vanilla ice cream: For Peaches Melba.

1 (1 lb. 13 oz.) can or 2 packages frozen sliced peaches: For Peaches Melba.

1 (8 oz.) jar red currant jelly: For Peaches Melba.

1 small package of slivered almonds: For Peaches Melba.

Extras: Salt; pepper; ¾ lb. butter; sugar and cream for coffee; drip grind coffee (breakfast blend and Italian after-dinner roast). *For Madrilene*—1 lemon. *For Chicken* — flour; dry tarragon. *For French Dressing* — paprika; dry mustard; 1 clove of garlic; olive oil; vinegar. Suggest buying sweet butter.

½ cup Calvados or American applejack: If necessary, substitute cognac or armagnac; the chicken will lack the traditional apple flavor, but will taste delicious.

Wine: 1 or 2 bottles Hermitage (a white Rhone).
or
1 or 2 bottles Pouilly-Fuissé (a white Burgundy).

NOTE: You will need ½ cup of this white wine for cooking, unless you wish to substitute dry French vermouth.

See page 111 for correct wine service and alternate selections.

what to do

1. At least 8 hours before dining, chill madrilene.
2. Three or four hours before dining, chill wine.
3. As early as possible (if not done before storing), wash parsley and endive (or other salad greens): Do not separate endive leaves. Rinse quickly in running cold water. Remove any discolored leaves or edges. Shake well; wrap in paper towels to absorb extra moisture. Seal in plastic bag, and refrigerate until needed.
4. If using fresh carrots, clean just before starting chicken. Slice into thin rounds directly into saucepan. Add 2-3-in. lump of butter; salt lightly. Cover; cook gently about 5 minutes. Reheat just before serving.

30 minutes before serving first course

1. Remove chicken, butter, mushrooms,

parsley and frozen carrots from refrigerator.

2. Start chicken dish:

In attractive casserole large enough for 8 chicken breasts, melt 3-in. lump of butter over gentle flame on top of stove. (If casserole is earthenware, prevent cracking by using asbestos pad over flame.)

Peel 6 shallots. (Or clean white parts of 5 or 6 scallions or peel 3 small white onions.) Sliver directly into casserole. Cook gently about 4 minutes, until soft and golden. Stir occasionally. Do not brown.

Salt and flour chicken lightly on both sides; lay into casserole, skin side down. Cook gently until skin side is golden brown. Add extra butter as needed; flour absorbs butter.

3. Slice bread: If a long loaf, cut into 2-in. chunks. If a round loaf, cut into ½-in. slices, then cut loaf in half. Butter slices well on one side. Then put all slices in form of loaf on bakepan, ready to heat.

4. When chicken is light golden brown on skin side, turn pieces over; brown other side. Add extra butter as needed.

5. Wipe 6 fresh mushrooms with damp paper towel. Do not wash or peel. Discard dry ends of stems. Set 3 mushrooms aside for salad.

Or: Open canned mushrooms; drain well.

6. Cut washed parsley quite fine with kitchen scissors. You need 2 cupfuls

— 1 for chicken, 1 for carrots.

7. Complete preparation of chicken dish:

Scatter 1 tsp. dry tarragon over chicken.

Pour in ½ cup Calvados or applejack (or cognac). Heat about 2 minutes.

When liquor is hot, put a lighted match to its surface to flame sauce. When flame dies, add ½ cup white wine from the bottle you are serving. (Or substitute dry French vermouth.)

Slice 3 mushrooms evenly down through stems directly into casserole. *Or: Add all of drained mushrooms.*

Cover casserole; use heavy aluminum foil if you have no cover that fits. Cook gently, stirring occasionally, until serving.

8. Whip ¾ cup heavy sweet cream with 2 Tbsp. sugar until it stands in soft peaks when beater is lifted. Refrigerate for dessert.

9. If using canned or frozen baby carrots, place in saucepan with 1½ cups salted water. Cover; cook actively about 15 minutes.

just before serving
first course

10. Spoon chilled, jellied madrilene into cups or bowls. Top each serving with 1 tsp. black caviar (or 1 tsp. red caviar mixed with sour cream). Lay a large

lemon wedge beside each serving.

11. If using partially baked bread, place in 450° oven now. Takes about 15 minutes to bake and brown.

12. Stir ½ cup heavy sweet cream into casserole. Test chicken with fork. If tender, turn off heat and reheat before serving.

serve first course

Pour chilled wine. Do not serve over ice. Fill glasses a little over halfway. Keep bottle cool.

assemble main course

1. Look at partially baked bread. If browning too fast, remove from oven for a few minutes, or turn oven down.

Or: Place fresh bread in 450° for 5 to 8 minutes to warm.

2. Test carrots with fork. If tender, drain and add 2-3-in. lump of butter. Salt lightly. Cover; cook gently until serving.

Or: Reheat cooked fresh carrots.

3. Stir casserole. Add more cream if necessary; this dish must have plenty of nice creamy sauce. Taste; adjust flavor if needed.

4. Place serving bowl and dinner plates in oven to warm.

5. Mix French dressing: Peel and split 1 clove garlic; place in small deep bowl with ½ tsp. paprika, ½ tsp. dry mustard, ½ tsp. salt and 3 Tbsp. vinegar. Mix well. Slowly stir in 6 Tbsp. olive

oil. Taste, add more oil or vinegar for perfect balance. Set aside for salad course; do not refrigerate.

6. Turn off carrots. Add 1 cup cut parsley; shake to mix well. Spoon into warm bowl.
7. Cover top of casserole with remaining cut parsley.
8. Turn off oven.

serve main course

Place warmed bread in basket, covered with napkin.
Pour more wine.

assemble salad course

1. Starting at base, cut several 1-in. sections from each endive stalk directly into salad bowl. Separate upper leaves.
2. Slice 3 remaining mushrooms evenly down through stems directly into bowl.
3. Slit skin of avocado in 4 places; strip it off. Cutting towards center pit, slice flesh into thin crescents directly into bowl.
4. Salt salad lightly. Toss carefully with 4 or 5 Tbsp. French dressing, or just enough to moisten all leaves. Do not include split garlic.

serve salad course

assemble dessert course

1. Fill coffeemaker: Suggest combining half breakfast blend and half Italian

after-dinner roast for hearty flavor.
2. Turn on coffeemaker.
3. Spoon ice cream attractively into dessert bowl. Pour on sliced peaches and juice. Here and there place tablespoons of currant jelly and dabs of whipped cream. Scatter slivered almonds over top.

serve dessert course

serve after-dinner coffee

If coffee was not started earlier, make last-minute coffee in a saucepan. (See page 118.)

Lobster Bisque

Filets of Sole Normandy
Parslied Potatoes

Escarole and Chicory Salad

Watermelon Half
with Inserts of
Ice Cream and Fresh Fruit

Coffee

WINES:

Meursault
or
Muscadet
or
Graves

An easy, yet spectacular, dinner in respect to both taste and appearance. Filets of Sole Normandy combines sole with shrimp and oysters for a truly superb dish. On page 105 you will find two other famous sole recipes, each cooked the same way as this, but using different accompanying ingredients for completely different results. The dessert is one of my favorites: light, refreshing and beautiful.

TO SUBSTITUTE:

You may have to alter the salad ingredients, depending on what is best in the market. See page 114 for other delicious salad combinations. If fresh sweet watermelon is not available, serve any choice ripe melon cut into crescents and dressed with Cointreau.

what to buy

Everything except the fresh sole, shrimp, oysters, bread and the watermelon may be purchased the previous day, if more convenient.

4 filets of fresh lemon or grey sole: Better to buy this domestic sole fresh than imported English sole which is invariably frozen. Refrigerate.

¾ lb. large fresh shrimp: Have dealer shell and clean, ready for you to cook. Refrigerate. *If not available, substitute ¾ lb. shelled and cleaned frozen uncooked shrimp. Do not keep in freezer.*

12 fresh oysters in their own liquor: Refrigerate. *If absolutely necessary, substitute 1 (7 oz.) can frozen oysters. Do not keep in freezer.*

1 fresh loaf French or Italian bread: Or 1 package of partially baked French bread.

½ of a large fresh watermelon: Choose a long slim melon. Insist that it be fully ripe. Have dealer cut in half lengthwise; buy nicer half. Protect cut surface with waxed paper. Refrigerate. *If substituting melon dressed with Cointreau,* buy 1 medium-sized ripe melon — the best variety currently available: honeydew, Persian, Cranshaw, Casaba, Spanish. If cantaloupes are best, buy 2. Refrigerate. You will also need ⅓ cup Cointreau.

1 small ripe cantaloupe or honeydew melon: For decorating watermelon. Refrigerate. *If not available, buy 1* package frozen melon balls. Do not keep in freezer.

½ lb. fresh white seedless grapes: For decorating watermelon. Refrigerate.

1 package frozen strawberry halves: For decorating watermelon. Do not keep in freezer.

1 pt. ice cream: For decorating watermelon. Choose mocha, pistachio or peach for a pleasing color and flavor balance.

20 tiny new potatoes: Or 2 (1 lb.) cans small whole potatoes.

1 large bunch fresh parsley: You will need 2 generous cups, cut fine.

½ lb. medium-sized fresh mushrooms: For sole. Should be pure white with an unbroken membrane connecting stem and cap. Refrigerate in original bag. *If not available,* buy 2 (3 or 4 oz.) cans of sliced mushrooms.

1 head of crisp escarole: Or any other choice salad green in the market.

1 small head of crisp chicory.

2 (13 oz.) cans concentrated lobster bisque.

1 (8 oz.) bottle or can of clear clam broth.

1 pt. heavy sweet cream: You will need a little for the bisque and about 1 cup for the sole. Serve the rest with coffee.

Extras: 2 lemons (½ for bisque, 1 for sole, ½ for dessert); salt; pepper; ¾ lb. butter; sugar for coffee; drip grind coffee (breakfast blend and Italian after-dinner roast). *For Bisque —* Worcestershire sauce; ⅓ cup dry sherry wine. *For Sole —* flour; dry tarragon; 2 eggs. *For French Dressing —* paprika; dry mustard; 1 clove of garlic; olive oil; vinegar. Suggest buying sweet butter.

Wine: 1 or 2 bottles Meursault (a white Burgundy).
or
1 or 2 bottles Muscadet (a white Loire).
or
1 or 2 bottles Graves (a white Bordeaux).

NOTE: You will need ½ cup of this white wine for cooking, unless you wish to substitute dry French vermouth.

See page 111 for correct wine service and alternate selections.

what to do

1. Several hours before dining, chill wine. Also chill melons early.
2. As early as possible (if not done before storing), wash parsley and salad greens: Separate leaves; rinse quickly in running cold water. Remove discolored leaves and edges. Shake well; wrap in paper towels to absorb extra moisture. Seal wrapped in plastic bag, and refrigerate until needed.
3. If using frozen shrimp or oysters, or frozen fruit, remove from refrigerator in plenty of time to defrost before using.

30 minutes before serving first course

1. Remove butter, parsley, lemons and melons from refrigerator.
2. Start dessert; should take about 7 minutes:

   With a melon-ball scoop (available in dime stores), scoop 12 or 16 small watermelon balls out of 3 different well-spaced places in watermelon. Place in a bowl.

   Scoop 12 small melon balls out of cantaloupe or honeydew; place in another bowl.

   Or: Empty frozen melon balls into separate bowl.

   Squeeze lemon juice over melon balls. Refrigerate them and melons.

   Or: Cut substitute melon into crescents: First cut into quarters; remove seeds. Then, working over a bowl to catch all juice, slice each quarter into crescents ½ in. thick. Peel crescents, removing all of white portion at base, which is not sweet. Place in bowl. Squeeze lemon juice over all, and pour on ⅓ cup Cointreau. Refrigerate.

3. Scrub fresh potatoes in cold water. Do not peel. Place in deep saucepan; cover with cold water and 1 to 2 tsp. salt. Do not cook yet.

   Or: Open canned potatoes; empty into deep saucepan, liquid and all. Add water to cover. Do not cook yet.

4. Slice bread: If a long loaf, cut into 2-in. chunks. If a round loaf, cut into ½-in. slices, then cut loaf in half. Butter slices well on one side. Then put all slices in form of loaf on bakepan, ready to heat.

15 minutes before serving first course

5. If using partially baked bread, place in 450° oven now. Takes about 15 minutes to bake and brown.
6. Start filets of sole Normandy:

   Use a good-looking cook-and-serve utensil; I like a shallow oval roasting pan. Place over two stove burners; keep both flames very gentle. Melt a 2-in. lump of butter at each end; swish around to cover bottom.

   While butter melts, wash filets and shrimp quickly in running cold water. Remove any visible black cords from shrimp. Pat all dry with paper towels. Salt and flour filets lightly on both sides; lay into center of pan.

   Continue to cook gently as you add other ingredients to pan. Add more butter as needed; it should always bubble around ingredients.

   Lay shrimp in uniform arrangement along one side of filets.

   Open oysters; drain well. Remove any bits of shell. Lay tastefully along other side of filets.

   Wipe fresh mushrooms with damp paper towel. Do not wash or peel. Discard dry ends of stems. Slice caps evenly down through stems. Lay in even arrangement between filets.

   Or: Open canned mushrooms. Drain well; lay in even arrangement between filets.

   Crumble 1 tsp. dry tarragon over all. Squeeze on juice of ½ lemon. Pour on ½ cup white wine from the bottle you are serving. (Or substitute dry French vermouth.)

   Baste pan juices over all. Do not turn or move anything; do not stir. Cook gently on lowered flame.

7. Look at partially baked bread. If browning too fast, remove from oven for a few minutes, or turn oven down.

   Or: Place fresh bread in 450° oven for 5 to 8 minutes to warm.

8. Blend lobster bisque and clam juice together in saucepan; heat gently.
9. If using fresh potatoes, bring to an active boil. Then lower heat slightly. Cover; cook about 20 minutes. Canned potatoes take only 15 minutes.
10. In a large cup, beat up 2 egg yolks with a fork. Add a generous ½ cup heavy sweet cream; blend well. Pour over ingredients in roasting pan. Continue cooking very gently so mixture will thicken slightly into a nice creamy sauce. Baste over ingredients frequently. No need to cover.
11. Taste bisque. Add what it needs for special flavor: salt, a dash of lemon juice or Worcestershire sauce, or some heavy sweet cream. When flavor pleases you, add ⅓ cup dry sherry. Ladle into soup plates.

serve first course

Place warmed bread in basket, covered with napkin.

Open chilled wine. Do not serve over ice. Fill glasses a little over halfway. Keep bottle cool.

assemble main course

1. Place serving bowl and dinner plates in oven to warm.
2. Baste sauce over ingredients in roasting pan. If sauce has thickened too much, add in a little more cream. Be careful not to disturb arrangement of ingredients.
3. Cut washed parsley quite fine with kitchen scissors. You will need 2 generous cupfuls — 1 for sole, 1 for potatoes.
4. Mix French dressing: Peel and split 1 clove garlic; place in small deep bowl with ½ tsp. paprika, ½ tsp. dry mustard, ½ tsp. salt and 3 Tbsp. vinegar. Mix well. Slowly stir in 6 Tbsp. olive oil. Taste; add more oil or vinegar for perfect balance. Set aside for salad course; do not refrigerate.
5. Test potatoes for doneness: Prick with thin-pronged fork. If cooked through, drain by sliding cover back just enough to let out the water. Quickly add ¼ lb. butter cut into several pieces, and 1 cup cut parsley. Do not cook more. Shake to mix; retained steam will melt butter and finish potatoes to perfection.
6. Taste sauce for the fish dish. Add more salt, or a dash of lemon juice or some cream or wine if needed. When serving a sauced dish like this, you should not serve extra lemon at the table. Sauce should be seasoned perfectly. Turn off heat. Decorate top with cut parsley.
7. Spoon potatoes into warm bowl.

serve main course

Pour more wine.

assemble salad course

1. Fill coffeemaker: Suggest combining half breakfast blend and half Italian after-dinner roast for hearty flavor.
2. Break salad greens into salad bowl in 3-in. pieces.
3. Salt salad lightly. Toss with 4 or 5 Tbsp. French dressing, or just enough to moisten all leaves. Do not include split garlic.

serve salad course

assemble dessert course

1. Enlarge hollows in watermelon if necessary. Heap one hollow high with defrosted strawberry halves. Pile mixed melon balls into another. Mound ice cream into the third. Add a few seedless grapes where they look best. Center watermelon on long platter.

   Or: Arrange melon crescents attractively on platter. Pour juice in bowl over all.
2. Turn on coffeemaker.

serve dessert course

Serve each guest a portion of each ingredient. What melon remains can be covered with heavy aluminum foil and served the next day.

Or: Serve melon crescents: Guests should have spoons as well as forks, so they can take up juices.

serve after-dinner coffee

If coffee was not started earlier, make last-minute coffee in a saucepan. (See page 118.)

Clams Casino

Broiled Lobsters

Corn on the Cob

Combination of Fruit Ices:
Pineapple, Raspberry and Lime

Coffee

WINES:

Pouilly-Fuissé
or
Montrachet

A great dinner to serve if feasible in your kitchen. Lobsters prepared this way are so much juicier than those ordinarily served. However, you must have two broiling compartments because each split lobster must be close to broiler flame at all times. One oven broiler, unless it is much wider than average, will just not accommodate two lobsters spread out flat. Of course, if you have a supplementary electric broiler you have no problem.

TO SUBSTITUTE:

If fine fresh clams are not available, substitute frozen cream of shrimp soup or canned lobster bisque. Should you prefer a salad instead of corn on the cob, avocado crescents with mixed greens is a happy choice.

what to buy

Everything except the fresh clams, lobsters, corn and bread may be purchased the previous day, if more convenient. For a dinner of this importance, wines should be bought the day before so they have plenty of time to chill before serving.

24 fresh cherry-stone clams: Have dealer open these as near dinner time as possible and pack on half shells over crushed ice. Refrigerate until needed. *If substituting frozen cream of shrimp soup,* buy 3 (10 oz.) cans. You will also need a little heavy sweet cream and ¼ cup dry Madeira wine.

If substituting lobster bisque, buy 2 (13 oz.) cans concentrated lobster bisque and 1 (8 oz.) bottle or can of clear clam broth. You will also need 1 lemon, Worcestershire sauce, a little heavy sweet cream and ⅓ cup dry sherry wine.

2 large, live lobsters: Each should weigh 2½ lbs. Ask for females; besides the delicious green liver (tomalley) present in all lobsters, females have red roe, or "coral," a great delicacy. Have dealer split in half, clean, and crack large claws. Refrigerate until needed.

4 fresh ears of sweet corn: Husks and tassels should be fresh, not dry-looking. Corn that squirts milk when kernels are punctured is most tender. Do not buy if already husked. Refrigerate. *If not available,* buy 4 packages of frozen corn on the cob.

1 fresh loaf French or Italian bread. Or 1 package of partially baked French bread.

¼ lb. shallots: You will need 5 or 6 for clams. *If not available,* buy 1 bunch scallions with good green stems, or 3 small white onions.

2 large green peppers: For clams. Should be firm and crisp. Refrigerate.

1 small (2 oz.) can or jar of pimientos: For clams.

3 or 4 (½-pt.) packages of fruit ice: Choose flavors and colors that complement one another. Pineapple, raspberry and lime are nice together. Or orange, raspberry, lemon and lime.

1 small box of coarse salt: For clams.

Extras: 7 lemons (3 for clams, 4 for lobsters); salt; pepper; ¾ lb. butter; cream and sugar for coffee; drip grind coffee (breakfast blend and Italian after-dinner roast). *For Clams*—Worcestershire sauce; 3 slices bacon. *For Lobsters* — paprika; dry mustard; 1 clove of garlic; olive oil; vinegar. *For Fruit Ices* — ⅓ cup Cointreau or Crème de Menthe (optional). Suggest buying sweet butter.

Wine: 1 or 2 bottles Pouilly-Fuissé (a white Burgundy).
or
1 or 2 bottles Montrachet (a great white Burgundy).

See page 111 for correct wine service and alternate selections.

what to do

Early in the day (or the night before) chill wine.

22

30 minutes before serving
first course

1. Remove lobsters, clams, butter, bacon, green peppers, 3 lemons and frozen corn on cob from refrigerator. Do not remove fresh corn on cob.
2. Start first course:
   Wash and dry 2 green peppers; remove stems and seeds.
   Peel 5 or 6 shallots (or 3 small onions).
   Or: Clean white and green parts of all scallions.
   Open pimientos; drain well.
   Chop all together rather fine. Salt lightly; add 1 Tbsp. Worcestershire sauce. Taste for pleasant flavor; should not be very salty. (Bacon topping will provide extra salt.) Set aside until ready to dress clams.
3. Mix French dressing for lobsters: Peel and split 1 clove garlic; place in small deep bowl with ½ tsp. paprika, ½ tsp. dry mustard, ½ tsp. salt and 3 Tbsp. vinegar. Mix well. Slowly stir in 6 Tbsp. olive oil. Taste; add more oil or vinegar for perfect balance.
4. Spread lobster halves flat, flesh side up, in two shallow pans. Break ends of tails open completely to prevent their curling up when broiling. Over each half pour the juice of ½ lemon and 1 Tbsp. French dressing. Dot generously with butter. Do not broil yet.
5. In large attractive shallow baking dish, make a bed of salt ½ in. deep. Place clams on the half shell on top in a tasteful pattern. Flavor each clam with less than ½ tsp. lemon juice. (Two juicy lemons are enough for 24 clams.) Mound some of previously chopped mixture on each clam. Lay a small square of bacon atop each.

10 minutes before serving
first course

6. Place baking dish in 500° oven. Takes about 9 minutes for clams to bake and bacon to crisp.
7. Slice bread: If a long loaf, cut into 2-in. chunks. If a round loaf, cut into ½-in. slices, then cut loaf in half. Butter slices well on one side. Then put all slices in form of loaf on bakepan, ready to heat.
8. Look at clams. Turn baking dish around, if necessary, so all bacon cooks evenly.
   Or: Prepare cream of shrimp soup: Taste before diluting as can label directs. Usually these soups are not too thick; you may want to serve "as is." If thinning is needed, use heavy sweet cream. Heat gently.
   Or: Prepare lobster bisque: Blend with clam juice in saucepan. Taste; add what it needs for special flavor: salt, a dash of lemon juice or Worcestershire sauce, or some heavy sweet cream. Heat gently.
9. Turn oven control to "broil" on both units you will use for lobsters; place each pan 2½ to 3 in. below high flame. Lobster must be broiled as close to high flame as possible without scorching; otherwise it will exude moisture, and be ruined. Total time for broiling is approximately 18 minutes.
10. Husk fresh corn. Cut off stem at base and husks come off easily. Place ears in cold water until ready to cook.
    Or: Open packages of frozen corn.
11. Look at clams. If bacon is still raw, bake another minute; look again. (Bacon scorches quickly.) When nice and crisp, but not charred, remove baking dish immediately. Place 8 quarters of lemon on bed of salt.
    Or: Taste cream of shrimp soup. Add more heavy sweet cream if needed. Stir in ¼ cup dry Madeira. Ladle into soup plates.
    Or: Taste lobster bisque. When flavor pleases you, add ⅓ cup dry sherry. Ladle into soup plates.
12. Baste lobsters with pan juices. Add more butter if needed. If tops are beginning to brown, lower pans slightly.
13. If using partially baked bread, place in oven now. Takes about 15 minutes to bake and brown.

serve first course

Bring baking dish of Clams Casino to table. Each guest lifts 6 clams and 2 lemon wedges to his plate. He does not take any salt.

Open chilled wine. Do not serve over ice. Fill glasses a little over halfway. Keep bottle cool.

assemble main course

1. Look at partially baked bread. If browning too fast, remove from oven until you remove lobsters from broilers.

   Or: Place fresh bread in oven for 5 or 6 minutes to warm.

2. Baste lobsters with pan juices. Add more butter if needed. Do not turn lobsters over; they would lose juices. Frequent basting will cook them properly.

3. Place 1 or 2 serving platters and dinner plates in oven to warm.

4. Fill large saucepan or kettle with water for cooking corn. (Must be enough water to cover corn.) Salt well. Do not add corn. Do not heat yet.

5. Baste lobsters again. Should be about done; you can tell by looking. If not, broil another minute or two; look again.

   IMPORTANT:
   Remove pans from broilers as soon as lobsters are done, to prevent drying out.

6. Turn oven and additional broiling unit off. Put partially baked bread back in oven if necessary.

7. Place lobsters on warm platter; pour pan juices over. Add ½ lemon for each diner.

8. Begin heating water for corn. Do not add corn.

serve main course

Be sure to have a nutcracker or lobster cracker at table if claws are not thoroughly cracked.

Place warmed bread in basket, covered with napkin.

Pour more wine.

assemble vegetable course

1. Drop corn into actively boiling water. Cover; bring to a boil again. Cook defrosted frozen corn 2 or 3 minutes, fresh corn 6-8 minutes.

2. Place oblong serving platter in oven to warm.

3. Fill coffeemaker: Suggest combining half breakfast blend and half Italian after-dinner roast for hearty flavor.

4. Remove cooked corn from boiling water with tongs. Place on warm platter.

serve vegetable course

assemble dessert course

1. Spoon fruit ices attractively into dessert bowl. Pour on ⅓ cup Cointreau or Crème de Menthe if you wish.

2. Turn on coffeemaker.

serve dessert course

Serve each guest a portion of each fruit ice.

serve after-dinner coffee

If coffee was not started earlier, make last-minute coffee in a saucepan. (See page118.)

9 *menu for 4*

Salad Niçoise
Beef Stroganoff
Whole String Beans
Crepes Suzettes
Coffee

WINES:

Pouilly-Fuissé
or
Sancerre

A very attractive, out-of-the-ordinary dinner combining French and Russian specialties. Salad Niçoise originated in the south of France. Combinations can vary, but this one is very good, and makes a pretty platter. Beef Stroganoff is perhaps the most famous of all Russian dishes, and one of the easiest! For greatest enjoyment, serve it with black bread or the darkest pumpernickel you can find.

TO SUBSTITUTE:

If canned Crepes Suzettes are not available, substitute frozen apple strudel or frozen whole strawberries dressed with sour cream.

what to buy

Everything except the fresh bread may be purchased the previous day, if more convenient.

1 fresh loaf black bread: Or 1 loaf or large package of the darkest pumpernickel you can find.

1 (7 oz.) can solid pack white meat tuna: For salad. Refrigerate.

½ lb. black Greek olives: For salad. Are sold by weight at delicatessen counters. Also available dried in jars; these need to be soaked in warm water about ½ hour to expand. *If not available,* substitute 1 (8 oz.) jar domestic black olives — the largest possible. Refrigerate.

2 large firm tomatoes, ripe for slicing: For salad. Beefsteak tomatoes are best. Refrigerate.

2 medium-sized green peppers: For salad. Should be firm and crisp. Refrigerate.

1 bunch fresh scallions: For salad. Stems should be firm and green. Refrigerate. *If not available,* buy 1 large Spanish or Bermuda onion.

1 large yellow onion: For beef.

1 bunch fresh dill: For beef. Do not wash. Refrigerate in sealed plastic bag. *If not available,* substitute fresh parsley.

1½ lbs. beef tenderloin: This is not the expensive filet mignon. Should be cut in strips about ½ in. thick, 4½ in. long.

2 or 3 packages frozen whole string beans.

½ pt. sour cream: You will use most of this for the meat.

3 small (5½ oz.) cans of French crepes: A variety flavored with purée of chestnuts is extremely good. But get what you can. Suggest buying a fourth can

because your guests will love them.

If substituting apple strudel, buy 1 frozen package. Do not keep in freezer. Sour cream is a delicious topping. *If substituting frozen strawberries,* buy 2 (1 lb.) cartons of frozen whole strawberries. Do not keep in freezer. You will need to buy extra sour cream for these substituted desserts.

Extras: 1 lemon; salt; pepper; flour; ¾ lb. butter; sugar and cream for coffee; drip grind coffee (breakfast blend and Italian after-dinner roast). *For Salad —* 4 eggs; paprika; dry mustard; 1 clove of garlic; olive oil; vinegar. *For Crepes —* 1 orange; ½ cup Cointreau or Grand Marnier. Suggest buying sweet butter.

Wine: 1 or 2 bottles Pouilly-Fuissé (a white Burgundy).
or
1 or 2 bottles Sancerre (a white Loire).
See page 111 for correct wine service and alternate selections.

what to do

Several hours before dining, chill wine.

30 minutes before serving first course

1. Remove beef, butter, 4 eggs, vegetables and needed frozen foods from refrigerator. Unwrap beef. If using frozen whole strawberries, open cartons to hasten thawing.

2. Place 4 eggs in small saucepan; cover

with cool water. (Warm water may make chilled eggs crack.) Cover; bring to boil. Boil gently just 12 minutes (14 minutes if eggs are very large). Then plunge into cold water to facilitate peeling.

3. Prepare rest of salad while eggs cook: Open can of tuna. Drain off oil; turn out whole in center of round platter. (If you open both ends of can and remove one end, you can push down on the other and press tuna out unbroken.) As you prepare other ingredients, arrange each tastefully in its own area around tuna.

Slice tomatoes in thin rounds directly onto platter.

Starting at the bottom, slice green peppers in thin rounds directly onto platter. Discard seeds and stem.

Clean scallions; cut white tips 3½ in. long. Arrange on platter.

Or: Peel Spanish or Bermuda onion; slice in thin rounds directly onto platter.

Scatter black olives wherever they look best.

4. Refrigerate dressed platter until serving.

5. Mix French dressing: Peel and split 1 clove garlic; place in small deep bowl with ½ tsp. paprika, ½ tsp. dry mustard, ½ tsp. salt and 3 Tbsp. vinegar. Mix well. Slowly stir in 6 Tbsp. olive oil. Taste; add more oil or vinegar for perfect balance. Set aside for Salad Niçoise; do not refrigerate.

6. Fill coffeemaker: Suggest combining

half breakfast blend and half Italian after-dinner roast for hearty flavor.

7. Shell eggs; cut in half lengthwise and add to Salad Niçoise.

8. Cut bread into ½-in. slices; butter generously. Arrange on platter.

9. Salt and pepper beef strips; flour lightly all over.

10. If baking apple strudel, place in 400° oven now. Will take about 30 minutes to bake and brown.

just before serving
first course

11. Salt tomatoes lightly. Pour several Tbsp. French dressing over all parts of salad except scallions. Do not include split garlic.

serve first course

Open chilled wine. Do not serve over ice. Fill glasses a little over halfway. Keep bottle cool.

assemble main course

1. Place serving platter and dinner plates in oven to warm. (If not baking strudel, turn oven to 350°.)

2. Place string beans in saucepan with 3-in. lump of butter and ¼ tsp. salt. Cover; cook gently about 6 minutes.

3. Start beef stroganoff:
In large skillet melt 3-in lump of butter. Do not brown.

Add beef strips to skillet.

Peel 1 yellow onion; grate (do not sliver) directly into skillet. Cook all gently about 4 minutes, turning strips with spoon. Add more butter as needed; skillet should not be dry.

Stir 4 heaping Tbsp. sour cream into skillet.

With scissors snip a little fresh dill (or parsley) into skillet; stir to mix in. Cook all 2 minutes more to blend well. Do not let cream boil.

Taste sauce; you may wish to add salt or a squeeze of lemon juice.

4. Place beef stroganoff in center of warm platter; snip more fresh dill (or parsley) over top. Surround with string beans.

5. Turn off oven.

6. If baking strudel, prick center with a fork to see if apples and pastry are baked. If so, remove from oven. If not, leave inside to finish baking with oven turned off.

Or: If frozen strawberries are defrosted, place cartons in refrigerator.

serve main course

Pour more wine.

assemble dessert course

1. If serving crepes or strudel, place serving platter in oven to warm.

2. Turn on coffeemaker.

3. Empty canned crepes into large skillet; be sure to utilize all sauce. Add 1 Tbsp. Cointreau, a little lemon and

orange juice. Warm gently 3 or 4 minutes; move around carefully with spoon.

Meanwhile: In a small attractive saucepan, heat ½ cup Cointreau or Grand Marnier, but do not boil.

When both crepes and liqueur are hot, slide crepes onto warm platter and top with sauce in skillet. Serve immediately.

Or: Prepare apple strudel: Slide onto warm platter. Cut into 3-in. portions. Empty sour cream into bowl.

Or: Prepare strawberries: Empty into dessert bowl with all juice. Mix in 3 or 4 heaping Tbsp. sour cream.

serve dessert course

Bring platter of crepes, pan of steaming liqueur, and dessert plates to table. Pour liqueur over crepes; light at once with a match. Let burn until flame dies.

Or: Bring apple strudel and dessert plates to table with bowl of chilled sour cream.

Or: Bring strawberries and dessert dishes to table. Pass extra sour cream if you wish.

serve after-dinner coffee

If coffee was not started earlier, make last-minute coffee in a saucepan. (See page 118.)

Tomatoes à la Provençale

Steak Diane
Baby Lima Beans and Frenched String Beans
with
Fresh Dill

Mixed Salad

French Dessert Cheese
Ripe Anjou Pears

Coffee

WINE:

Beaujolais

This dinner features two French specialties worth knowing. The savory first course comes to us from Provence and, like most cooking of this area, uses both garlic and olive oil. Steak Diane embellishes thin slices of beef with bourbon or Madeira, and is cooked in only 5 or 6 minutes. The mixed salad is an important part of the dinner too; this one combines 3 different greens with fresh chives, radishes, mushrooms, avocado and hard-boiled eggs.

TO SUBSTITUTE:

Major substitutions should be unnecessary. However, you may have to alter the salad ingredients or the fresh fruit, depending on what is best in the market. See page 114 for other appetizing salad combinations.

what to buy

Everything except the fresh bread may be purchased the previous day, if more convenient.

1 or 2 fresh loaves French or Italian bread: Or 2 packages of partially baked French bread. Remember, you will need some for dessert course.

4 fairly large, firm, ripe tomatoes: Refrigerate.

1 bunch fresh dill: Do not wash. Refrigerate in sealed plastic bag. *If not available*, substitute fresh parsley.

1 large bunch fresh parsley: You will need ¾ cup, cut fine. (Cut 1¾ cups if you have no dill.)

1 large bunch fresh chives: You will need about ⅓ cup, cut fine, for tomatoes and salad. Refrigerate in sealed plastic bag. *If not available*, buy 1 bunch scallions with good green stems, or 1 large Spanish or Bermuda onion. Refrigerate scallions.

1 small head of crisp escarole: Or any other choice salad green in the market.

1 small head of crisp chicory.

1 bunch of crisp water cress: Not essential, but a tasty addition to salad if prime in market.

3 or 4 medium-sized fresh mushrooms: For salad. Should be pure white with an unbroken membrane connecting stem and cap. Refrigerate in original bag.

1 bunch red radishes: For salad. Should be firm and unblemished. Clean, then refrigerate in a sealed plastic bag.

1 small ripe avocado: For salad. Should be soft enough to yield readily to gentle pressure from palms of hands. Refrigerate.

4 large ripe Anjou pears: Check ripeness by pressing gently near stem. *If not available,* buy 4 Golden Delicious apples, or seedless white grapes, or any other good eating pears or apples. Refrigerate.

20 slices beef tenderloin: This is not the expensive filet mignon. Should be cut ¼ in. thick.

2 packages frozen baby lima beans.

1 package frozen Frenched string beans.

French dessert cheese: Choose any ripe soft-type French cheese, imported or domestic. (See page 117 for specific suggestions and cheese-buying and serving tips.) Buy a whole or a half cheese if practical; it makes a more handsome appearance than individual portions. Do not refrigerate. Must be served at room temperature.

Extras: Salt; pepper; 3 cloves of garlic (2 for tomatoes, 1 for salad); olive oil; ¾ lb. butter; sugar and cream for coffee; drip grind coffee (breakfast blend and Italian after-dinner roast). *For Tomatoes* — dry basil; dry thyme; ½ cup seasoned bread crumbs. *For Steak* — Worcestershire sauce; ½ cup bourbon or dry Madeira wine. *For Salad* — 2 eggs; paprika; dry mustard;

vinegar. Suggest buying sweet butter.

Wine: 2 bottles Beaujolais (a red Burgundy).

Remember you will need wine for the dessert course. See page 111 for correct wine service and alternate selections.

what to do

1. Several hours before dining, if possible, de-cork wine. You need not lay in wine basket because Beaujolais, being a young wine, has no sediment. Leave open, at room temperature, to breathe.
2. As early as possible (if not done before storing), wash parsley and salad greens. (But do not wash dill.) Separate leaves; rinse quickly in running cold water. Remove discolored leaves and edges. If using water cress, cut off most of stems. Shake well; wrap in paper towels to absorb extra moisture. Seal wrapped in plastic bag, and refrigerate until needed.

30 minutes before serving first course

1. Remove beef, butter, 2 eggs, parsley, chives or scallions and tomatoes from refrigerator. Unwrap beef.
2. Place 2 eggs in small saucepan; cover with cool water. (Warm water may make chilled eggs crack.) Cover; bring to boil. Boil gently just 12 minutes (14 minutes if eggs are very large). Then plunge into cold water to facilitate peeling.

3. Prepare first course while eggs cook: Cut washed parsley quite fine with kitchen scissors. You need ¾ cupful — ¼ cup for tomatoes, ½ cup for meat. If you have no dill, cut 1 extra cup for vegetables.

   Pre-heat oven to 400°. Put 2 Tbsp. olive oil in attractive shallow baking dish.

   Wash and dry 4 tomatoes; do not peel. Cut in half horizontally. Lay into baking dish, cut side up. With a small knife, gash each surface to make a recess in center. Salt and pepper lightly.

   Peel 2 cloves of garlic; sliver very fine directly into tomatoes. Noticeable garlic flavor is good.

   Wash chives; dry in paper towel. With kitchen scissors, cut about 3 Tbsp. directly into a bowl.

   Or: Clean scallions; cut a scant ⅓ cup of green stems very fine directly into a bowl.

   Or: Peel 1 large Spanish or Bermuda onion; sliver half of it directly into bowl.

   Add ½ cup seasoned bread crumbs, ¼ cup cut parsley, 1 tsp. dry basil and ¼ tsp. dry thyme to cut chives (or scallion stems or onion). Mix well; stir in 3 Tbsp. olive oil.

   Stuff tomatoes with bread crumb mixture evenly over top. Dot each tomato half with ½ tsp. butter.
4. Slice bread: If a long loaf, cut into 2-in. chunks. If a round loaf, cut into ½-in. slices, then cut loaf in half.

Butter slices well on one side. Then put slices in form of loaf on bakepan, ready to heat.

15 minutes before serving first course

5. Place tomatoes on middle rack of oven. Bake 15 minutes, or until crumbs are golden and tomatoes are soft, but not mushy. Baste every 5 minutes with sauce in baking dish.
6. If using partially baked bread, place on bottom rack of oven now. Takes about 15 minutes to bake and brown.
7. Place baby lima beans in saucepan with 2-in. lump of butter; salt lightly. Cover; cook over gentle flame until serving first course. Look occasionally; add more butter if needed so beans do not scorch.
8. Baste tomatoes.
9. Shell hard-boiled eggs.
10. Mix French dressing: Peel and split 1 clove garlic; place in small deep bowl with ½ tsp. paprika, ½ tsp. dry mustard, ½ tsp. salt and 3 Tbsp. vinegar. Mix well. Slowly stir in 6 Tbsp. olive oil. Taste; add more oil or vinegar for perfect balance. Set aside for salad course; do not refrigerate.
11. Baste tomatoes.
12. Move partially baked bread to top rack of oven to finish browning.
    Or: Place fresh bread on bottom rack of oven for 5 to 8 minutes to warm.
13. Break lettuce leaves into salad bowl; pieces should be no more than 2½

in. long. Clean 4 or 5 radishes; place in bowl whole. Add quartered eggs.
14. Turn off lima beans. Add Frenched string beans and a 2-3-in. lump of butter. Cover.
15. Turn off oven; leave oven door closed.

serve first course

Baste sauce in baking dish over tomatoes when you serve. Sauce is worth dipping up with bread.

Place warmed bread in basket, covered with napkin.

Pour wine. Fill glasses a little over half-way.

assemble main course

1. Place serving platter and dinner plates in oven to warm.
2. Heat vegetables over gentle flame until serving.
3. Start steak Diane:
   In large skillet gently melt 2-3-in. lump of butter. Do not brown.
   Salt and pepper beef lightly on both sides; lay into melted butter. Cook gently only 3 or 4 minutes to keep tender. Turn slices over carefully. Add more butter as needed; skillet should not be dry.
4. Fill coffeemaker: Suggest combining half breakfast blend and half Italian after-dinner roast for hearty flavor.
5. Add 2 Tbsp. Worcestershire sauce and ½ cup bourbon or dry Madeira to skillet. Swish all around to blend. Taste

sauce for flavor; adjust if necessary. Turn off heat.
6. Turn off vegetables. With kitchen scissors, cut some fresh dill directly over them.
   Or: Stir 1 cup cut parsley into vegetables.
7. Mound vegetables in center of warm platter; arrange beef around edge. Sprinkle beef with remaining cut parsley; pour sauce over.

serve main course

Pour more wine.

assemble salad course

1. Prepare salad:
   Remove salad bowl from refrigerator. Cut radishes into thin slices. With scissors, cut about 2 Tbsp. washed chives directly into bowl.
   Or: Sliver white parts of several scallions directly into bowl.
   Or: Sliver remaining half of onion directly into bowl.
   Wipe fresh mushrooms with damp paper towel; discard dry ends of stems. Slice caps evenly down through stems directly into bowl.
   Slit skin of avocado in 4 places; strip it off. Cutting towards center pit, slice flesh into thin crescents directly into bowl.
   Salt salad lightly. Toss with 4 or 5 Tbsp. French dressing, or just enough

to moisten all leaves. Do not include split garlic.

2. Remove fruit from refrigerator. May be served slightly chilled, but not ice cold.

serve salad course

assemble dessert course

1. Wash and dry fruit. Arrange in basket or bowl.
2. Place cheese and cheese knife on cheese tray or large plate. Have bread on table.
3. Turn on coffeemaker.

serve salad course

Pour more wine.

serve after-dinner coffee

If coffee was not started earlier, make last-minute coffee in a saucepan. (See page 118.)

Onion Soup in Casserole au Gratin

Ham in Cream Sauce
Tiny Peas in Lettuce Cups

Iceberg Lettuce Salad

Oranges Arabian

Coffee

WINE:

Muscadet
or
Beaujolais

This dinner is noteworthy because it combines several familiar dishes in an exciting new way. Although not intended for special occasions, it's very good eating. It is also very easy.

Creamed dishes generally call for a white wine. But ham is a highly flavored meat, so a light red wine like Beaujolais is appropriate too.

TO SUBSTITUTE:

Everything needed should be readily available except perhaps California navel oranges. If these are not in season, substitute fresh figs with orange juice, or canned figs heated with rum and served with heavy sweet cream.

what to buy

Everything except the fresh bread may be purchased the previous day, if more convenient.

1 or 2 fresh loaves French or Italian bread: Or 2 packages of partially baked French bread. You will need 6 slices for onion soup, so allow extra.

1 box (2 packets) of dehydrated (dry) onion soup.

2 center slices ready-to-eat ham: Each should be cut ⅜ in. thick.

2 cans beef consommé.

2 or 3 packages frozen tiny peas: Sometimes these are labeled "Baby Peas" or "Petite Peas." (Unless labeled thus, peas will probably be large and not too sweet.) Canned baby peas are good eating but lack fresh green color.

1 large head of crisp iceberg lettuce: Or 2 heads of young Boston lettuce.

¼ lb. shallots: For peas. You will need 4. If not available, buy 2 small white onions.

1 large bunch fresh parsley: You will need 1½ cups, cut fine.

3 large California navel oranges: For Oranges Arabian. Refrigerate.

If substituting fresh figs, buy 8 large ripe figs and 1 large juicy orange. Refrigerate.

If substituting canned figs, buy 2 (8 oz.) cans whole figs. You will also need ½ cup rum and ½ pt. heavy sweet cream.

1 (8 oz.) package pitted dates: For Oranges Arabian.

1 small package slivered almonds or shredded coconut. For Oranges Arabian.

1 small (8 oz.) can tomato sauce.

½ lb. Swiss Gruyère cheese: For soup. Should be in one piece for grating. Or buy 1 (8 oz.) jar of grated Parmesan cheese. (Swiss cheese is more traditional for onion soup, but Parmesan tastes excellent too.)

½ pt. light sweet cream: For ham. If you prefer, use 1 cup milk.

½ pt. heavy sweet cream: You will need a little for ham.

Extras: Salt; pepper; flour; ¾ lb. butter; sugar for coffee; drip grïnd coffee (breakfast blend and Italian after-dinner roast); ½ cup dry Madeira wine (¼ cup for soup, ¼ cup for ham). For Ham — dry tarragon. For French Dressing — paprika; dry mustard; 1 clove of garlic; olive oil; vinegar. For Oranges Arabian — sugar; ⅓ cup Cointreau or Grand Marnier. Suggest buying sweet butter.

Wine: 1 bottle Muscadet (a white Loire). or
1 bottle Beaujolais (a red Burgundy).
See page 111 for correct wine service and alternate selections.

what to do

1. Several hours before serving, chill Muscadet. If serving Beaujolais instead, remove cork. You need not lay in wine basket because Beaujolais, being a young wine, has no sediment. Leave open, at room temperature, to breathe.

2. As early as possible (if not done before storing), wash parsley and salad greens: Separate leaves; rinse quickly in running cold water. Remove discolored leaves and edges. Shake well; wrap in paper towels to absorb extra moisture. Seal in plastic bag, and refrigerate until needed.

30 minutes before serving first course

1. Remove ham, butter, cheese, parsley and frozen peas from refrigerator. Unwrap ham.

2. Start first course:
   In large saucepan, heat 2 cans beef consommé. Stir in 2 packets of dry onion soup; cover and boil gently for about 10 minutes.

   Cut 6 slices of French bread ½-in. thick; toast. (Or use the equivalent of Italian bread.)

   If using Swiss Gruyère cheese for top of soup, grate now.

   To give soup more "body," mix 1 level Tbsp. flour into ½ cup cool water; pour into soup slowly as you stir.

   Add 1 or 2 Tbsp. tomato sauce and ¼ cup dry Madeira for good flavor. Taste; correct seasoning if needed.

   Pour soup into 2-qt. casserole; lay toasted bread slices on top.

   Cover top generously with grated cheese. Put rest of cheese in a bowl to serve separately.

Place casserole on middle rack of 375° oven to brown before serving.

3. Cut washed parsley quite fine with kitchen scissors. You need 1½ cupfuls — ½ cup for ham, 1 cup for peas.

4. Make a tasty cream sauce for ham: Melt 4 Tbsp. butter in large skillet over gentle flame. Do not brown.

   Turn flame very low; stir in 3 level Tbsp. flour and dash of salt to make a smooth paste.

   Slowly pour in 1 cup light sweet cream or milk as you continue to stir to keep everything smooth. If mixture starts to lump, remove skillet from heat and work out lumps with spoon. Add more cream or milk.

   When sauce has thickened slightly, crumble in 1 tsp. dry tarragon. Stir in ¼ cup dry Madeira. Taste for flavor; adjust if necessary.

5. Cut each ham slice in half; lay into sauce. Simmer gently while you slice and butter bread.

6. Slice bread: If a long loaf, cut into 2-in. chunks. If a round loaf, cut into ½-in. slices, then cut loaf in half. Butter slices well on one side. Then put all slices in form of loaf on bakepan, ready to heat.

7. Turn off ham.

8. For peas, peel 4 shallots (or 2 small white onions); sliver into saucepan. Add 2-in. lump of butter; cook gently about 3 minutes, until soft and golden. Stir occasionally; add more butter if needed. Do not brown.

9. Mix French dressing: Peel and split

1 clove garlic; place in small deep bowl with ½ tsp. paprika, ½ tsp. dry mustard, ½ tsp. salt and 3 Tbsp. vinegar. Mix well. Slowly stir in 6 Tbsp. olive oil. Taste; add more oil or vinegar for perfect balance. Set aside for salad course; do not refrigerate.

10. Stir peas into shallots; add 4 outside leaves of lettuce. Salt all lightly. Add more butter if needed. Cover; cook gently 1 or 2 minutes.

just before serving
first course

11. If using partially baked bread, turn oven to 450°; place bread inside. Takes about 15 minutes to bake and brown.

    Or: If using fresh bread, turn off oven. Do not put bread inside yet.

serve first course

Bring casserole to table with bowl of grated cheese.
Pour wine. Fill glasses a little over halfway. Keep white wine cool.

assemble main course

1. Look at partially baked bread. If browning too fast, remove from oven for a few minutes, or turn oven off.

   Or: Place fresh bread in oven for 5 to 8 minutes to warm.

2. Gently reheat ham in cream sauce. If sauce thickens too much, stir in a little heavy sweet cream or more Madeira.

3. Place deep serving platter and dinner plates in oven to warm.

4. Heat peas gently. Add more butter if needed.

5. Fill coffeemaker: Suggest combining half breakfast blend and half Italian after-dinner roast for hearty flavor.

6. Slide ham onto platter; pour all sauce over. Scatter on about ½ cup cut parsley.

7. Turn off peas. Remove lettuce leaves and add remaining cut parsley. Shake or stir to mix well. If ham platter is large enough, place lettuce leaves around edge; fill with peas. Otherwise, serve in same fashion on small platter.

serve main course

Place warmed bread in basket, covered with napkin.
Pour more wine.

assemble salad course

1. Break iceberg lettuce leaves into salad bowl in 3-in. pieces.

   Or: Place Boston lettuce in salad bowl; keep leaves whole if possible.

2. Salt salad lightly. Toss with 4 or 5 Tbsp. French dressing, or just enough to moisten all leaves. Do not include split garlic.

serve salad course

assemble dessert course

1. Wash 3 large navel oranges. Don't peel: cut into ¼-in. slices. Dip both sides of each slice in sugar. Overlap slices on flat platter. Place ½ lb. pitted dates in clumps here and there. Pour ⅓ cup Cointreau or Grand Marnier over all; sprinkle liberally with slivered almonds or shredded coconut.

   Or: Prepare fresh figs: Cut 8 figs in half; place 4 halves on each of 4 individual plates. Squeeze fresh orange juice over all.

   Or: Prepare canned figs: Empty 2 (8 oz.) cans whole figs into saucepan. Add ½ cup rum; heat gently. Spoon into 4 dessert dishes.

2. Turn on coffeemaker.

serve dessert course

serve after-dinner coffee

If coffee was not started earlier, make last-minute coffee in a saucepan. (See page 118.)

32

Prosciutto with Melon

Veal Scaloppine al Marsala
Spinach, Italian Style

Large Ripe Strawberries
with
Powdered Sugar

Coffee

WINE:

Valpolicella
or
Neuchâtel

Enthusiasts of Italian cooking will recognize this superlative all-Italian dinner. Prosciutto, thinly sliced Italian ham, is now successfully made in this country, and should be readily available. The main course, thin slices of veal cooked with mushrooms and Marsala wine, is perhaps the best loved of all Italian veal dishes.

Following dinner, it might be fun to serve an Italian coffee specialty called Caffè Poncino. See page 118 for directions and ingredients.

TO SUBSTITUTE:

If either prosciutto or good ripe melon is not available, substitute Zuppa alla Pavese, an unusual Italian soup that floats an egg on top of each serving. If large ripe strawberries are not available, you may serve small ripe strawberries mixed with sour cream, sugar and Marsala wine. Or substitute frozen whole strawberries dressed with crushed frozen raspberries and slivered almonds.

what to buy

Everything except the fresh bread may be purchased the previous day, if more convenient.

1 fresh loaf Italian or French bread: Or 1 package of partially baked French bread.

12 slices very thin prosciutto: Should be cut to order on an electric slicer; butchers and dealers who carry it know how. Refrigerate.

1 medium-sized ripe melon: Buy best variety currently available—honeydew, Persian, Cranshaw, Casaba, Spanish. If cantaloupes are best, buy 2. Refrigerate.

If substituting Zuppa alla Pavese, buy 3 (10½ oz.) cans of clear chicken or beef consommé. You will also need 2 chicken or beef bouillon cubes, 4 fresh eggs, 1 (6 oz. jar) grated Parmesan cheese and 1 box Italian bread sticks.

20 slices milk-fed veal: Should be cut paper thin, each about 2¼ in. square. This meat is expensive, so do not accept leftover driblets; insist that it be freshly cut. (Generally slices are cut from the leg, like veal cutlet, or from the loin, like veal chops. Much less expensive to buy a small rump of good quality and have butcher slice it for you.)

½ lb. medium-sized fresh mushrooms: Should be pure white with an unbroken membrane connecting stem and cap. Refrigerate in original bag. *If not available,* buy 2 (3 or 4 oz.) cans of sliced mushrooms.

1 large bunch fresh parsley. You will need 1 cup, cut fine.

2 qt. boxes of fresh ripe strawberries: Must be unblemished. To serve whole with powdered sugar, berries must be very large with fresh green hulls.

If only small berries are available, you will need ½ pt. sour cream, granulated sugar and ½ cup dry Marsala wine.

If substituting frozen strawberries, buy 2 (1 lb.) cartons of frozen whole strawberries, 1 package frozen raspberries and 1 small package slivered almonds. Do not keep strawberries and raspberries in freezer.

3 packages frozen whole leaf spinach.

Extras: Salt; pepper; ½ lb. butter; sugar and cream for coffee; drip grind Italian after-dinner roast coffee. *For Melon —* 1 lemon. *For Veal —* flour; ½ cup dry Marsala wine. *For Spinach —* olive oil; vinegar. *For Large Fresh Strawberries —* powdered sugar. Suggest buying sweet butter.

Wine: 1 or 2 bottles Valpolicella (an Italian red).
or
1 or 2 bottles Neuchâtel (a Swiss white).
See page 111 for correct wine service and alternate selections.

what to do

1. Several hours before serving, chill Neuchâtel. If serving Valpolicella, remove cork. (Or you may wait until later.) You need not lay in wine basket; Valpolicella has no sediment.
2. As early as possible (if not done before storing), wash parsley: Rinse quickly in running cold water. Remove discolored leaves. Shake well; wrap in paper towels to absorb extra moisture. Seal wrapped in plastic bag, and refrigerate until needed.

30 minutes before serving first course

1. Remove veal, butter, parsley, spinach and strawberries from refrigerator. Unwrap veal. If using frozen raspberries, empty into small bowl; leave out to thaw.
2. Wash fresh strawberries under running cold water. If very large and perfect, do not hull; just pat dry with paper towels. Refrigerate unsugared. If strawberries are small, remove hulls. Rinse again quickly; pat dry. Place in dessert bowl. Stir in 4 heaping Tbsp. sour cream, sugar to taste, and ½ cup dry Marsala. Refrigerate.

   Or: Open cartons of frozen whole strawberries to hasten thawing.
3. Cut melon into quarters; remove seeds. Then, working over bowl to catch all juice, slice each quarter into crescents 1-in. wide at base. Peel crescents, removing all of white portion, which is near peel. Lay into bowl, squeeze lemon juice over all, and refrigerate.
4. Cut washed parsley quite fine with kitchen scissors. You need 1 cupful for veal.
5. Wipe fresh mushrooms with damp paper towel. Do not wash or peel. Discard dry ends of stems. Slice caps evenly down through stems.

   Or: Open canned mushrooms; drain well.
6. Place spinach (defrosted or not) in saucepan. Cover; heat gently so all water exudes. Drain. Turn off heat.
7. Slice bread: If a round loaf, cut into ½-in. slices, then cut loaf in half. If a long loaf, cut into 2-in. chunks. Butter slices well on one side. Then put all slices in form of loaf on bakepan, ready to heat.
8. Salt and flour veal lightly on both sides.

just before serving first course

9. Lay 3 crescents of chilled melon and 3 slices of prosciutto on each of 4 individual plates.

   Or: Make Zuppa alla Pavese: Heat consommé without diluting. Taste; may need salt, or enriching with bouillon cubes. Meanwhile, break 1 egg into center of each of 4 soup plates. Gently pour steaming hot consommé over; it will poach eggs at once. Top each egg with 2 Tbsp. grated Parmesan cheese. Put rest of grated Parmesan in a small serving bowl.
10. If using partially baked bread, place in 450° oven now. Takes about 15 minutes to bake and brown.

serve first course

Bring plates of melon and prosciutto to table.

Or: Bring soup plates to table with bowl of grated Parmesan and basket of Italian bread sticks.

Pour wine. Fill glasses a little over halfway. Keep white wine cool.

assemble main course

1. Look at partially baked bread. If browning too fast, remove from oven for a few minutes, or turn oven down.

   Or: Place fresh bread in 450° oven for 5 to 8 minutes to warm.
2. Place large serving platter (or serving platter and bowl) and dinner plates in oven to warm.
3. In large skillet melt 3-in. lump of butter over gentle flame; do not brown. Add veal; cook gently about 2 minutes.
4. Turn veal over; it should not be browned, but kept white for tenderness. Add more butter if necessary; skillet should not be dry. Stir in mushrooms and ½ cup dry Marsala. Cover; cook gently about 2 minutes.
5. Salt spinach lightly. Add 3 Tbsp. olive oil and a generous ½ Tbsp. vinegar

or lemon juice. Mix lightly with fork to separate leaves. Cook 2 to 3 minutes, or until hot and soft. Too much cooking will destroy lovely green color.

6. Fill coffeemaker while veal cooks: Suggest you use all Italian after-dinner roast for this dinner, especially if you plan to serve Caffé Poncino.
7. Taste sauce in skillet; adjust flavor if necessary.
8. Place veal on warm platter; pour sauce and mushrooms over. Top with cut parsley.
9. Taste spinach; adjust flavor if necessary. Arrange around veal if platter is large enough. Otherwise, transfer to a warm bowl.
10. If frozen strawberries and raspberries are defrosted, place back in refrigerator.

serve main course

Place warmed bread in basket, covered with napkin.

Pour more wine.

assemble dessert course

1. Arrange large unhulled strawberries attractively on platter; do not heap in a bowl. Fill a small bowl or shaker with powdered sugar.
   Or: Taste small hulled strawberries. Add more sugar, sour cream or Marsala if needed.
   Or: Prepare frozen strawberries: Empty cartons into dessert bowl with all

juice. Squash raspberries with a fork; stir in. Scatter slivered almonds over top.
2. Turn on coffeemaker.

serve dessert course

Bring platter of unhulled strawberries, powdered sugar and dessert plates to table. Each guest puts a mound of powdered sugar on his plate, then lifts several berries from platter with his fingers. Holding each by the stem, he dips it into sugar. No spoon needed.

Or: Bring bowl of hulled or frozen strawberries and dessert dishes to table.

serve after-dinner coffee

If coffee was not started earlier, make last-minute coffee in a saucepan. (See page 118.) If making Caffé Poncino, see page 118.

13 *menu for 4*

Eggplant Parmigiana

Veal Smetana
Frenched String Beans with Almonds

Purée of Chestnuts
with
Heavy Sweet Cream

Coffee

WINE:

Soave
or
Vouvray
or
Graves

1237642

An interesting dinner because of Eggplant Parmigiana, an Italian specialty, and Veal Smetana, a delicious concoction of veal, sliced mushrooms and sour cream. "Parmigiana" always indicates that a food is prepared with Parmesan cheese.

TO SUBSTITUTE:

If fresh eggplant is not available, substitute broiled shrimp. If sweetened purée of chestnuts is not available, serve canned figs heated with rum and served with heavy sweet cream. Or the best fresh fruit in the market.

what to buy

Everything except the fresh bread may be purchased the previous day, if more convenient.

1 fresh loaf Italian or French bread.

1 large eggplant, or 2 small ones: Choose firm ones with shiny purple skins and no rust spots. Refrigerate.

If substituting broiled shrimp, buy 2 lbs. of large fresh shrimp, shelled and cleaned but not cooked. Or 2 lbs. shelled and cleaned frozen shrimp. Refrigerate. You will also need 1 large Spanish or Bermuda onion, 2 cloves of garlic, 3 lemons, olive oil and capers.

1 (1 lb.) can peeled Italian plum tomatoes: For eggplant Parmigiana. Get those seasoned with basil, if possible. If not available, buy 1 (1 lb.) can of peeled whole tomatoes.

¼ lb. medium-sized fresh mushrooms: For veal. Should be pure white with an unbroken membrane connecting stem and cap. Refrigerate in original bag. If not available, substitute 1 (3 or 4 oz.) can of sliced mushrooms.

1 large bunch fresh parsley: You will need 2 cups, cut fine.

20 slices milk-fed veal: Should be cut paper thin, each about 2¼ in. square. This meat is expensive, so do not accept leftover driblets; insist that it be freshly cut. (Generally slices are cut from the leg, like veal cutlet, or from the loin, like veal chops. Much less expensive to buy small rump of good quality and have butcher slice it for you.)

2 or 3 packages frozen Frenched string beans.

1 small package of slivered almonds. For string beans.

1 large Mozzarella cheese: For eggplant Parmigiana. Should weigh about 1 lb.

1 (3 oz. jar) grated Parmesan cheese: For eggplant Parmigiana.

½ pt. sour cream: You will use most of this for the meat.

1 (1 lb.) can sweetened purée of chestnuts: Sometimes these are labeled "crème de marrons."

If substituting canned figs, buy 2 (8 oz.) cans whole figs. You will also need ½ cup rum.

½ pt. heavy sweet cream: For sweetened purée of chestnuts or canned figs.

Extras: Salt; pepper; ½ lb. butter; sugar and cream for coffee; drip grind coffee (breakfast blend and Italian after-dinner roast). For Eggplant — olive oil; 2 cloves of garlic; 1 cup seasoned bread crumbs; dry basil (or oregano). For Veal — flour; 1 lemon; ⅓ cup cognac or bourbon; paprika. For Purée of Chestnuts — rum (optional). Suggest buying sweet butter.

Wine: 1 or 2 bottles Soave (an Italian white).
   or
1 or 2 bottles Vouvray (a white Loire).
   or
1 or 2 bottles Graves (a white Bordeaux).
See page 111 for correct wine service and alternate selections.

what to do

1. Several hours before dining, chill wine.

2. As early as possible (if not done before storing), wash parsley: Rinse quickly in running cold water. Remove discolored leaves. Shake well; wrap in paper towels to absorb extra moisture. Seal wrapped in plastic bag, and refrigerate until needed.

30 minutes before serving first course

1. Remove veal, butter, eggplant (or shrimp), parsley and frozen string beans from refrigerator. Unwrap veal.
2. Cut washed parsley quite fine with kitchen scissors. You need 2 cupfuls — 1 for eggplant (or shrimp), 1 for veal.
3. Start first course:
Pre-heat oven to 450°. In attractive casserole heat ¼ cup olive oil over gentle flame on top of stove. (If casserole is earthenware, prevent cracking by using an asbestos pad over flame.)

Peel 2 cloves of garlic; sliver directly into casserole.

Peel eggplant; cut into ⅛-in. slices. Salt and pepper; lay into casserole. Move slices around so all cook evenly until soft, about 3 minutes on each side.

While eggplant cooks, open canned tomatoes; drain well.

Move most of softened eggplant slices to one side. Leave only a single layer on bottom of casserole. Keep cooking as you layer on several tomatoes, a little dry basil (or oregano), cut parsley, grated Parmesan cheese and bread crumbs. Salt lightly; moisten all with 1 tsp. olive oil.

Add another identical layer, and another, each time starting with eggplant and ending with bread crumbs. Dot top layer here and there with butter and 1 or 2 Tbsp. olive oil.

Fifteen minutes before serving, place casserole on middle rack of oven.

Or: Prepare shrimp for broiling: Rinse quickly in running cold water.

Remove all visible black cords. Pat dry with paper towels; lay flat in shallow pan. Peel 1 large onion and 2 cloves of garlic; sliver very fine directly over shrimp. Add juice of 1 lemon, ¼ cup olive oil and 1 Tbsp. capers. Salt lightly. Mix well.

Ten minutes before serving, place pan 3 in. below high broiler flame. Broil only 9 or 10 minutes, stirring occasionally so all cooks evenly.

4. Slice bread: If a round loaf, cut into ½-in. slices, then cut loaf in half. If a long loaf, cut into 2-in. chunks. Butter slices well on one side. Then put all slices in form of loaf on bakepan, ready to heat.

6 minutes before serving first course

5. Place bread on middle or bottom rack of oven for 5 or 6 minutes to warm.
6. Cover entire top of casserole with ¼-in. slices of Mozzarella cheese. Continue baking to melt cheese into a creamy blanket. (Do not bake longer than 5 minutes or cheese will toughen.)

Or: Stir shrimp; place serving platter in oven to warm.

7. Salt and flour veal lightly on both sides.
8. Look at casserole; if cheese is nicely melted, remove from oven. Cheese does not brown.

Or: Taste shrimp sauce. Add more lemon juice if needed. Broil shrimp 1 or 2 minutes more if not quite cooked. But remember they toughen if cooked too long. When done, mix in 1 cup cut parsley and transfer to warm platter, juice and all. Garnish with 4 halves of lemon.

9. Turn off oven.

serve first course

Carry casserole or platter to table.

Place warmed bread in basket, covered with napkin.

Open chilled wine. Do not serve over ice. Fill glasses a little over halfway. Keep bottle cool.

assemble main course

1. Place serving platter and dinner plates in oven to warm.
2. Place string beans in saucepan with 3-in. lump of butter and ¼ tsp. salt. Cover; cook gently about 6 minutes.
3. Start Veal Smetana:
   In large skillet melt 3-in. lump of butter over gentle flame; do not brown.

Add veal; cook gently about 2 minutes. Wipe fresh mushrooms with damp paper towel. Do not wash or peel. Discard dry ends of stems. Slice caps evenly down through stems directly into skillet.

Or: Open canned mushrooms. Drain well; add to skillet.

Turn veal over; it should not be browned, but kept white for tenderness. Add more butter if necessary; skillet should not be dry. Cover; cook gently about 2 minutes.

4. Fill coffeemaker: Suggest combining half breakfast blend and half Italian after-dinner roast for hearty flavor. Or use all Italian after-dinner roast.
5. Stir 4 heaping Tbsp. sour cream into skillet. Cook 1 or 2 minutes more to blend well. Do not let cream boil.
6. Taste sauce; you may wish to add salt or a squeeze of lemon juice.
7. Turn off string beans. Add slivered almonds, and more butter if needed. Mix well.
8. Add ⅓ cup cognac or bourbon to veal; blend well.
9. Place veal on warm platter; pour sauce over. Top with remaining cut parsley, and sprinkle a little paprika here and there. Surround with string beans.

serve main course

Pour more wine.

assemble dessert course

1. Whip about ¾ cup heavy sweet cream

to soft peak stage; carefully blend into sweetened purée of chestnuts. Add 2 Tbsp. rum, if you like. Spoon into 4 dessert dishes.

Or: Spoon sweetened purée of chestnuts into 4 dessert dishes directly from can.

Or: Prepare figs: Empty 2 (8 oz.) cans whole figs into saucepan. Add ½ cup rum; heat gently. Spoon into 4 dessert dishes.

2. Turn on coffeemaker.

serve dessert course

Pass a pitcher of heavy sweet cream if you are serving sweetened purée of chestnuts or figs.

serve after-dinner coffee

If coffee was not started earlier, make last-minute coffee in a saucepan. (See page 118.)

Spaghetti Alfredo

Saltimbocca alla Romana
Spinach Soufflé

Zabaglione

Coffee

WINE:

Chianti Antinori

Some years ago Alfredo of Rome so delighted customers with his new Spaghetti Bianca, a creamy white spaghetti creation, that two of them presented him with a gold spoon and fork for tossing it at the table before serving. Saltimbocca alla Romana combines thin pieces of veal and ham in a delicious wine sauce. The dessert, zabaglione, is famous the world over. You can make it in minutes, for it is simply a frothy mixture of egg yolks, sugar and Marsala wine. Just follow my simple foolproof directions.

TO SUBSTITUTE:

If by chance frozen spinach soufflé is not available, substitute frozen Italian broad green string beans. If you do not wish to make zabaglione, serve vanilla ice cream topped with marrons glacé, whole or in pieces. (Marrons glacé are chestnuts bottled in heavy syrup.) Or, if you can buy a good Gateau St. Honoré at a patisserie, serve that. Although this is a French dessert, Italians love it. It has lots of whipped cream.

what to buy

Everything except the fresh bread may be purchased the previous day, if more convenient.

1 fresh loaf Italian or French bread: Or 1 package of partially baked French bread.

1 lb. spaghetti.

1 large (8 oz.) jar grated Parmesan cheese: For spaghetti. Keeps well in refrigerator.

8 slices pre-cooked ham: Should be cut ¼ in. thick, about 2¼ in. square.

8 slices milk-fed veal: Should be cut ¼ in. thick, and same size as ham.

2 packages frozen spinach soufflé: Do not keep in freezer. *If not available,* substitute 2 or 3 packages frozen Italian green beans.

½ pt. heavy sweet cream: You will need ½ cup for spaghetti. Buy extra for coffee.

Extras: Salt; pepper; 1 lb. butter; sugar and cream for coffee; drip grind Italian after-dinner roast coffee. *For Saltimbocca* — flour; dry sage; ½ cup dry French vermouth. *For Zabaglione* — 6 eggs; 6 Tbsp. sugar; 1 cup dry Marsala wine. Suggest buying sweet butter.

Wine: 1 or 2 bottles Chianti Antinori (an Italian red).

See page 111 for correct wine service and alternate selections.

what to do

30 minutes before serving first course

1. De-cork Chianti, if not previously done.
2. Remove meats, butter, 6 eggs and spinach soufflé (or Italian beans) from refrigerator. Unwrap meats.
3. Remove spinach soufflé from packages; place on pan. If still frozen, put on middle rack of 350° oven now; bake until serving main course.

   Or: Place Italian green beans in saucepan with 2-in. lump of butter and ¼ tsp. salt. Do not cook yet.
4. Separate 6 eggs. Place yolks in top of double boiler for zabaglione. Refrigerate whites in a covered jar; use another day for Baked Alaska or meringue.
5. Stir 6 Tbsp. sugar and dash of salt into egg yolks. Do not cook yet.
6. Salt and flour veal lightly on both sides.

20 minutes before serving first course

7. For spaghetti, put 6 qts. water and 2 Tbsp. salt in large kettle. Bring to an active boil; will take about 10 minutes over high flame.
8. If spinach soufflé is defrosted, place on middle rack of 350° oven now; bake until serving main course.
9. Slice bread: If a round loaf, cut into ½-in. slices, then cut loaf in half. If a long loaf, cut into 2-in. chunks. Butter slices well on one side. Then put all slices in form of loaf on bakepan, ready to heat.
10. When water is boiling hard, take whole sheaf of spaghetti in your hand and push down against bottom of kettle. Sheaf becomes limp in 1 or 2 minutes. Never break spaghetti. (Broken spaghetti looks like leftovers.)
11. Stir spaghetti. Cook actively until done, anywhere from 7 to 9 minutes, depending on thickness.
12. Fill coffeemaker while spaghetti cooks: Suggest you use all Italian after-dinner roast for this dinner. Or combine half breakfast blend and half Italian after-dinner roast.
13. In large skillet gently melt 3-in. lump of butter for saltimbocca. Do not brown. Turn off heat.
14. Place half of grated Parmesan cheese in a small serving bowl.
15. Place large serving bowl and 4 first-course plates in oven to warm.
16. When spaghetti has boiled 7 minutes, taste: To be right, it must be cooked "al dente," as the Italians say. (Firm to the bite, but not hard.) If too hard the first time, keep tasting every minute or two until it is ready. (Watch carefully; overcooking makes spaghetti pasty and slimy.)

IMPORTANT:
The moment spaghetti is ready, drain entire kettle into a colander standing in the sink. Never run cold water over spaghetti "to wash off starchiness," as some cookbooks suggest. (If properly cooked, there is no such starchiness.)

17. Let spaghetti drain about 1 minute; then return it to kettle, but do not cook.
18. To spaghetti, add several 1-in. lumps of butter and half of the remaining grated Parmesan cheese (about ½ cup). With large fork and spoon, gently lift spaghetti high, then let it fall, to blend all ingredients. Continue mixing in this way, gradually adding ½ cup heavy sweet cream and the rest of the grated Parmesan. Mix gently but quickly, so spaghetti does not cool too much; takes less than 2 minutes to blend all.
19. Quickly transfer Spaghetti Alfredo to warm bowl.
20. If using partially baked bread, place on bottom rack of oven now. Takes about 20 minutes to bake and brown at this temperature.

serve first course

Bring bowl of spaghetti to table with warm plates and bowl of grated Parmesan cheese. Give each guest a soup spoon which he can use to help roll up the spaghetti on his fork. One should never cut spaghetti into small pieces.

Pour wine. Fill glasses a little over halfway.

assemble main course

1. Reheat skillet. Lay in veal. Cook

gently 3 minutes.

2. Move partially baked bread to top rack of oven to finish browning.

   Or: Place fresh bread on bottom rack of oven for 5 to 8 minutes to warm.

3. Test spinach soufflé: Insert knife in center. If it comes out clean, soufflé is done; remove from oven and cover to keep warm. If not done, continue to bake; test again in a few minutes.

   Or: Cover Italian beans; cook gently about 6 minutes.

4. Turn veal over. Crumble a little sage over each slice; use no more than ½ tsp. altogether.

5. Place ham slices in same skillet; cook gently 2 minutes.

6. Turn ham slices over. Lay a veal slice on each ham slice. Baste with butter. Add more butter if needed; skillet should not be dry.

7. Pour in ½ cup dry French vermouth. Cover; cook gently 2 or 3 minutes more.

8. Place serving platter and dinner plates in oven to warm.

9. Test soufflé; remove from oven when ready.

   Or: Turn off Italian beans. Taste; add more butter if needed.

10. Look at bread. If nicely browned, remove. If pale, place bread under broiler for 1 or 2 minutes. Watch closely.

11. Taste sauce in meat skillet; adjust flavor if necessary.

12. Transfer veal and ham combination to warm platter; pour sauce over.

13. Cut spinach soufflé into portions;

place at ends of platter.

Or: Arrange Italian beans around edge of platter.

14. Begin heating water in lower part of double boiler. Do not put upper part with egg yolks on top.

serve main course

Place warmed bread in basket, covered with napkin.

Pour more wine.

assemble dessert course

1. Turn off actively boiling water in lower part of double boiler. Place top of double boiler over lower for 1 minute to warm egg yolks slightly. (The secret of making zabaglione successfully is not to let egg yolks get too hot.) Remove top, and immediately begin stirring eggs with wire whip.

2. Repeat this sequence of heating eggs, then stirring them, 2 or 3 times, or until water is no longer too hot.

3. Then leave top of double boiler over lower while you beat eggs with rotary beater, slowly adding 1 cup dry Marsala. Be sure to beat mixture on bottom and sides of pan. Continue until all Marsala is beaten in. Takes about 5 minutes. (Mixture should become creamy and fluffy, somewhat like the frozen custard you buy at highway stands in summer.)

IMPORTANT:

If mixture does not seem to be cooking, the water beneath is too cool.

Turn on heat for only 1 minute. Then turn heat off, or very, very low. Remember, egg yolks cannot stand sustained heat.

If mixture starts to thicken too fast, into a sort of spongecake consistency on bottom or sides of pan, there is too much heat below. Immediately lift off pan and stir mixture with spoon from bottom up so all is well blended. (Small solid parts on sides or bottom of pan may be safely mixed into the creamy center.

4. As soon as zabaglione is ready, spoon into stemmed glasses (or dessert dishes), removing every bit from pan with rubber spatula. Serve immediately; wine and eggs separate on standing.

5. Turn on coffeemaker.

serve dessert course

serve after-dinner coffee

If coffee was not started earlier, make last-minute coffee in a saucepan. (See page 118.)

Stracciatella

Veal Parmigiana
Zucchini with Walnuts

Mocha Mousse

Coffee

WINE:
Orvieto Est-Est-Est
or
Soave

This is an exceptional Italian dinner which I first had in the beautiful town of Orvieto. Stracciatella is a rich egg drop soup served with grated Parmesan cheese. The veal dish is one of the finest I have ever eaten. Do not be surprised that so thick a cut can be cooked in so short a time. Mocha mousse, a wonderful dessert, does not take long to do either.

TO SUBSTITUTE:

If zucchini are not available, substitute frozen broccoli spears with chunks of walnuts. Should you wish a fruit dessert instead of mocha mousse, white pears baked in wine is most appropriate.

what to buy

Everything except the fresh bread may be purchased the previous day, if more convenient. I suggest buying the heavy sweet cream 2 or 3 days ahead, if possible; it will thicken in your refrigerator, and make a richer dessert.

1 pt. heavy sweet cream:

1 fresh loaf Italian or French bread: Or 1 package of partially baked French bread.

3 (10½ oz.) cans of clear chicken or beef consommé: Be sure there is no rice in it. You will also need 2 chicken or beef bouillon cubes.

2 slices milk-fed veal cutlet: Should be cut between ½ and ¾ in. thick.

4 or 5 medium-sized fresh zucchini: Should be firm, with no dark spots. Refrigerate. Or buy 2 or 3 packages frozen zucchini. *If not available,* substitute 2 or 3 packages frozen broccoli spears.

1 small package walnut halves: For zucchini. If substituting broccoli spears, buy 1 small package broken walnut pieces.

1 small box fresh white marshmallows: You need 16 for the mousse. "Campfire" is a good brand.

1 large (8 oz.) jar grated Parmesan cheese: For stracciatella and veal. Keeps well in refrigerator.

1 large Mozzarella cheese: For veal. Should weigh less than 1 lb.

Extras: Salt; pepper; 4 eggs (2 for stracciatella, 2 for veal); ¾ lb. butter; sugar and cream for coffee; drip grind Italian after-dinner roast coffee. *For Veal —* 1 cup seasoned bread crumbs. Suggest buying sweet butter.

Wine: 1 bottle Orvieto Est-Est-Est (an Italian white).

or
1 bottle Soave (an Italian white).
See page 111 for correct wine service and alternate selections.

what to do

Several hours before dining, chill wine.

30 minutes before serving
first course

1. Remove veal, butter and zucchini (or broccoli) from refrigerator. Unwrap veal.
2. Start dessert:
   In small saucepan, bring 1¼ cups water to a near boil.

   Place 16 marshmallows in deep bowl; place fine sieve next to bowl.

   When water is near boiling, stir in 2 Tbsp. drip grind coffee (breakfast blend or after-dinner roast). Let boil up to top of pan; stir as it boils. Turn off heat.

   Quickly pour this double-strength coffee through sieve into bowl with marshmallows. Stir well; then beat into smooth cream with rotary beater. Put bowl in coldest part of refrigerator (but not the freezing compartment) for about 15 minutes to chill well.
3. Start veal Parmigiana:
   Cut each cutlet in half; lightly salt both sides of all pieces.

   Break 2 eggs into shallow bowl; with a fork, beat in 2 Tbsp. cold water until all is well mixed.

In small shallow pan, mix 1 cup seasoned bread crumbs with 3 Tbsp. grated Parmesan cheese.

Dip each slice of veal into beaten egg to moisten both sides; then coat well with bread crumb mixture. Place on waxed paper until ready to cook.

4. Slice bread: If a round loaf, cut into ½-in. slices, then cut loaf in half. If a long loaf, cut into 2-in. chunks. Butter slices well on one side. Then put all slices in form of loaf on bakepan, ready to heat.

15 minutes before serving first course

5. If using partially baked bread, place in 450° oven now. Takes about 15 minutes to bake and brown.
6. Finish making dessert:
In large deep bowl whip ¾ pt. (1½ cups) heavy sweet cream until firm but not dry. (Should stand in soft peaks when beater is lifted.) Do not add sugar.

Test refrigerated coffee-marshmallow mixture with finger; It *must* be well chilled. If so, pour very slowly into whipped cream, folding it in with a spoon as you pour. (Lift spoon from bottom to top. Do not stir around and around.)

You may not use all of coffee-marshmallow mixture; stop pouring when whipped cream is smooth-textured and the consistency of the frozen custard you buy at highway stands in summer. Blend should not be too thin. (I cannot be more exact than this about the amounts because marshmallows differ considerably in composition.)

Transfer blend to dessert bowl. Put back in coldest part of refrigerator. But do not freeze. Mousse should be creamy and light, not solid.

7. Look at partially baked bread. If browning too fast, remove from oven for a few minutes, or turn oven down.
Or: Place fresh bread in 450° oven for 5 to 8 minutes to warm.
8. Wash fresh zucchini. Remove stems; do not peel. Slice in thin rounds directly into saucepan.
Or: Place frozen zucchini or broccoli spears in saucepan.
9. Heat consommé without diluting. Taste; may need salt, or enriching with bouillon cubes. In small bowl, beat 2 eggs very well with a fork. When soup boils, slowly pour egg into it, stirring constantly. Heat of soup cooks egg into tiny shreds. Ladle into soup plates.

serve first course

Bring soup plates to table with bowl of grated Parmesan cheese.

Place warmed bread in basket, covered with napkin.

assemble main course

1. In large skillet melt 2-in. lump of butter. Do not brown. Lay in veal; cook 4 minutes over medium flame. Add butter as needed; bread crumbs absorb a great deal. Do not brown.
2. Fill coffeemaker: Suggest you use all Italian after-dinner roast for this dinner. Or combine half breakfast blend and half Italian after-dinner roast.
3. Add 2-in. lump of butter to zucchini (or broccoli). Do not add water. Salt lightly. Cover; cook gently about 5 minutes. Look occasionally; add more butter if needed.
4. Turn veal over. Add more butter if necessary. There should always be enough to bubble in skillet. Baste butter over veal often to keep it succulent. Cook 3 or 4 minutes more.
5. Place serving platter and dinner plates in oven to warm.
6. Lay ¼-in. slices of Mozzarella cheese over veal, covering completely. Cover skillet; cook gently about 3 minutes to melt cheese into a creamy blanket. (Do not cook longer or Mozzarella will toughen.)
7. Test zucchini (or broccoli) with fork. If cooked through, turn off heat; mix in walnuts.
8. Slide veal onto warm platter without separating pieces; melted Mozzarella is very stringy, and hard to cut apart.
9. Add zucchini (or broccoli) to platter.

serve main course

Open chilled wine. Do not serve over ice. Fill glasses a little over halfway.

assemble dessert course

1. Mocha mousse is ready to serve in

dessert bowl.
2. Turn on coffeemaker.

serve dessert course

serve after-dinner coffee

If coffee was not started earlier, make last-minute coffee in a saucepan. (See page 118.)

16 *menu for 4*

Creamed Mushrooms in Patty Shells

Sautéed Veal Cutlet
Braised Celery Hearts with Almonds

Apple Strudel

Coffee

WINE:

Sancerre
or
Riesling

This is one of my favorite dinners, since I'm very fond of veal cooked this way. American milk-fed veal is tender and delicate in flavor, and should be cooked gently in plenty of butter to keep it succulent. All too often people fry veal, which ruins it in my opinion. Braised celery hearts are a pleasant complement to the veal, and very easy to do.

TO SUBSTITUTE:

There should be no need for substitutions. However, if you wish a lighter dessert, serve a combination of fruit ices. Pineapple, raspberry and lime are nice together. Or orange, raspberry, lemon and lime.

what to buy

Everything may be purchased the previous day, if more convenient.

1 or 2 packages fresh "gem" rolls: Sometimes also labeled "butterflake" rolls, these are made of several segments of rich dough layered together.

4 puff-pastry patty shells: Buy frozen, or from a good bakery. Or substitute 4 slices white bread.

1 package frozen apple strudel: Do not keep in freezer. Or 1 bakery strudel.

2 slices milk-fed veal cutlet: Should be cut ½ in. thick.

1 slice pre-cooked ham: For mushrooms. Should be only ⅛ in. thick, about 4 in. square.

½ lb. medium-sized fresh mushrooms: Should be pure white with an unbroken membrane connecting stem and cap. Refrigerate in original bag. *If not available,* buy 2 (3 or 4 oz.) cans of sliced mushrooms.

4 large (or 8 small) fresh hearts of celery: Or 2 large bunches of crisp clean Pascal celery. Refrigerate in sealed plastic bag.

1 small package of slivered almonds.

½ pt. heavy sweet cream.

½ pt. sour cream: A delicious topping for hot apple strudel.

Extras: Salt; pepper; flour; 1 lb. butter; sugar and cream for coffee; drip grind coffee (breakfast blend and Italian after-dinner roast). *For Mushrooms —* dry Madeira wine; paprika. *For Celery* —1 beef bouillon cube; Worcestershire sauce; 1 lemon. Suggest buying sweet butter.

Wine: 1 or 2 bottles Sancerre (a white Loire).

or

1 or 2 bottles Riesling (a white Alsatian).

See page 111 for correct wine service and alternate selections.

what to do

Several hours before dining, chill wine.

30 minutes before serving first course

1. Remove veal, ham, butter, mushrooms, celery and needed frozen foods from refrigerator. Unwrap veal.
2. Wipe fresh mushrooms with damp paper towel. Do not wash or peel. Discard dry ends of stems. Slice caps evenly down through stems directly into saucepan.

   Or: Open canned mushrooms. Drain well; place in saucepan.
3. Place frozen patty shells in 400° oven. Will take about 25 minutes to bake and brown.
4. Rinse hearts of celery quickly in running cold water to remove sand. Cut off most of leafy tops; stalk should be no more than 4½ in. long.

   Or: Make 4 celery clumps from 2 large bunches of celery: Remove outside stalks, leaving 2 large center clumps. Cut 4½ in. long; split in half. Wash thoroughly to remove sand; trim bases if needed.
5. Lay celery hearts (or clumps) flat in large skillet. Add 3-in. lump of butter. Cover; cook gently 6 to 8 min-

utes to soften.
6. Add 2-in. lump of butter to mushrooms. Cook gently, stirring as you do. Salt lightly; stir in 1 scant Tbsp. flour. Sliver in ham slice. Mix well; cook gently until all is limp, about 6 minutes. Add more butter if needed.
7. Butter rolls while mushrooms cook: Partially open segments and lay in butter. Lay on pan, ready to heat.
8. Into mushrooms, stir ½ cup heavy sweet cream and 3 Tbsp. dry Madeira. Cook gently 2 or 3 minutes so mixture thickens into a nice creamy sauce.
9. Turn off celery clumps; add 2 Tbsp. Worcestershire sauce. Swish around and taste. You may want more salt, a dash of lemon juice, or possibly 1 beef bouillon cube dissolved in a little boiling water. Cover; do not cook more now.

5 minutes before serving first course

10. Remove small circles of pastry from centers of baked patty shells.

    Or: Place bakery patty shells in a 450° oven for 4 to 5 minutes.

    Or: Cut crusts off 4 slices white bread; toast.
11. Taste mushroom sauce; adjust seasoning if necessary. If sauce thickens too much, stir in a little more cream or Madeira.
12. Cut each cutlet in half; lightly salt and flour both sides of all pieces.
13. Place warm patty shells (or buttered

toast) on individual plates; heap creamed mushrooms over and around. Sprinkle paprika over all.
14. If baking frozen strudel, place in 400° oven now. Will take about 30 minutes to bake and brown.

    Or: If serving bakery strudel, turn oven very low. Place strudel on pan to warm well for serving.

serve first course

Open chilled wine. Do not serve over ice. Fill glasses a little over halfway. Keep bottle cool.

assemble main course

1. In large skillet melt 3-in. lump of butter. Do not brown. Lay in veal; cook 4 or 5 minutes over medium flame. Baste occasionally with butter. Do not brown.
2. Reheat celery; cook gently until ready to serve.
3. Fill coffeemaker: Suggest combining half breakfast blend and half Italian after-dinner roast for hearty flavor.
4. Turn veal over. Add more butter if necessary. There should always be enough to bubble in skillet. Baste butter over veal often to keep it succulent. Cook about 5 minutes more.
5. Place rolls in oven to warm.
6. Place 1 large and 1 small platter, and dinner plates, in oven to warm.
7. Taste sauce around celery for final seasoning; adjust if necessary. Prick 1 clump of celery with fork; if soft in center, turn off heat and keep cov-

ered until serving. Otherwise, cover and cook gently a few more minutes.

8. Examine veal for doneness. Make small cut in center of 1 piece. For tenderest eating, should be faintly pink inside, not white.
   IMPORTANT:
   Place veal on warm platter the moment it is ready, or the heated skillet will continue to cook it. Pour pan juices over.
9. Place celery clumps on second warm platter. Sprinkle lavishly with slivered almonds; pour pan juices over.
10. If baking frozen strudel, turn off oven. Prick center with a fork to see if apples and pastry are baked. If so, remove from oven. If not, leave inside to finish baking with oven turned off.

serve main course

Place warmed rolls in basket, covered with napkin.
Pour more wine.

assemble dessert course

1. Slide warm strudel onto serving platter. Cut into 3-in. portions. Empty sour cream into separate bowl.
2. Turn off oven if necessary.
3. Turn on coffeemaker.

45   **serve dessert course**

serve after-dinner coffee

If coffee was not started earlier, make last-minute coffee in a saucepan. (See page 118.)

17 *menu for 4*

Scallops à la Poulette

Breasts of Chicken Tarragon
Asparagus with Drawn Butter

Large Fresh Blueberries
with
Heavy Sweet Cream

Coffee

WINE:

Chablis

Another superb dinner in the French tradition. Ideally, one should use fresh tarragon for the chicken. Dry tarragon, although aromatic, results in a completely different flavor. Either way, the chicken is delicious. On page 98 you will find five marvelous variations, each using the same cooking method, but different accompanying ingredients. Result: a total of six entirely different chicken dinners.

TO SUBSTITUTE:

If large fresh blueberries are not available, substitute strawberries Romanoff.

what to buy

Everything except the fresh scallops, bread and patty shells may be purchased the previous day, if more convenient.

1 lb. fresh or frozen scallops: Bay scallops are smaller, more tender — and more expensive — than sea scallops. Refrigerate.

1 *large bunch fresh asparagus:* You need about 2 lbs. Buy only crisp green stalks with young compact tips. Refrigerate. *If not available,* buy 2 or 3 packages frozen asparagus spears.

1 *fresh loaf French or Italian bread.* Or 1 package of partially baked French bread.

4 *puff-pastry patty shells:* Buy frozen, or from a good bakery. Or substitute 4 slices white bread.

4 *large chicken breasts:* Have butcher split in half to make 8 pieces. If you wish, substitute 2 young broilers, each 2¼ to 2½ lbs., cut up. Thighs and drumsticks may also be used; but, being less tender, they require 20 minutes of extra cooking.

2 *medium-sized white onions:* You need 1 for scallops and 1 for chicken.

1 *bunch fresh tarragon:* Refrigerate in sealed plastic bag. *If not available,* substitute the most aromatic dry tarragon you can find.

1 *or 2 boxes perfect fresh blueberries:* Get largest possible. Refrigerate.

If substituting strawberries Romanoff, buy 2 (1 lb.) cartons frozen whole strawberries. Do not keep in freezer. You will also need 1 pt. vanilla ice cream and ¼ cup Cointreau.

1 *small (3 or 4 oz.) can of sliced mushrooms:* For scallops.

1 *pt. heavy sweet cream:* You will need half for scallops, half for fresh blueberries or strawberries Romanoff.

Extras: Salt; pepper; 1 lb. butter; sugar and cream for coffee; drip grind coffee (breakfast blend and Italian after-dinner roast). *For Scallops* — flour; 2 eggs; 1 lemon; Worcestershire sauce; paprika. *For Asparagus* — seasoned bread crumbs. Suggest buying sweet butter.

Wine: 1 or 2 bottles Chablis (a white *Burgundy*).

NOTE: You will need ½ cup of this white wine for cooking, unless you wish to substitute dry French vermouth.

See page 111 for correct wine service and alternate selections.

what to do

Several hours before dining, chill wine.

30 minutes before serving
first course

1. Remove chicken, scallops, butter and needed frozen foods from refrigerator. Unwrap scallops and chicken. If using frozen whole strawberries, open cartons to hasten thawing.

2. Start chicken dish:
   In attractive casserole large enough for 8 chicken breasts, melt 3-in. lump of butter over gentle flame on top of stove. (If casserole is earthenware, prevent cracking by using asbestos pad over flame.)

   Peel 1 medium-sized onion. Sliver directly into casserole. Cook gently about 3 minutes, until soft and golden. Stir occasionally. Do not brown.

   Salt chicken lightly on both sides; lay into casserole, skin side down. Cook gently until skin side is golden brown. Add extra butter as needed.

3. Place frozen patty shells in 400° oven. Will take about 25 minutes to bake and brown.

4. Trim fresh asparagus. Quickest way is to cut about 2 in. off bottom of all stalks, while still tied in a bunch. Separate stalks; rinse quickly in running cold water. Do not remove scales unless they are blemished. Place in large skillet. Pour on boiling water to cover. Salt lightly. Cover; cook actively 7 or 8 minutes.

   Or: Place frozen asparagus spears in large skillet. Add ½ cup salted water. Do not cook yet.

5. When chicken is light golden brown on skin side, turn pieces over; brown other side. Add extra butter as needed.

6. Rinse scallops quickly in running cold water; pat dry with paper towels. If using sea scallops, cut each in half. Salt and flour lightly.

7. Baste chicken with juices in casserole. If using *dry* tarragon, scatter 2½ tsp. over chicken now. If using fresh tarragon, add just before serving.

8. Cover casserole; use heavy aluminum foil if you have no cover that fits. Cook gently until serving time. Baste

2 or 3 times while preparing first course. Add more butter if needed.

9. Test asparagus with fork. If still quite firm, cook a few more minutes. If starting to soften, turn off heat.

10. Start first course:
In skillet slowly melt 3-in. lump of butter. Do not brown.

Peel 1 medium-sized onion; sliver directly into skillet. Cook gently 3 minutes to soften. Do not brown.

Open canned mushrooms. Drain well; stir into skillet. Mix scallops into skillet. Add more butter if needed. Cook gently 2 or 3 minutes. Add ½ cup white wine from the bottle you are serving. (Or substitute dry French vermouth.) Cook about 4 minutes.

11. Fill coffeemaker: Suggest combining half breakfast blend and half Italian after-dinner roast for hearty flavor.

12. Stir scallops. In a large cup beat up 2 egg yolks with a fork; mix in 1 cup heavy sweet cream. Blend into skillet. Cover; cook very gently 4 or 5 minutes so mixture thickens into a nice creamy sauce.

5 minutes before serving first course

13. Remove small circles of pastry from centers of baking patty shells.

Or: Place bakery patty shells in 400° oven for 5 minutes to warm.

Or. Cut crusts off 4 slices white bread; toast.

14. Slice bread: If a long loaf, cut into 2-in. chunks. If a round loaf, cut into ½-in. slices, then cut loaf in half. Butter slices well on one side. Then put all slices in form of loaf on bake-pan, ready to heat.

15. Taste scallop sauce. Add more salt, or a dash of lemon juice or Worcestershire sauce if needed. If sauce thickens too much, stir in a little more cream or wine.

16. Place warm patty shells (or buttered toast) on individual plates; heap hot scallop mixture over and around. Sprinkle with paprika.

17. If using partially baked bread, turn oven to 450°; place bread inside. Takes about 15 minutes to bake and brown.

Or: If using fresh bread, turn off oven. Do not put bread inside yet.

18. Baste chicken frequently. Test with fork. If tender, turn off heat and reheat before serving.

serve first course

Open chilled wine. Do not serve over ice. Fill glasses a little over halfway. Keep bottle cool.

assemble main course

1. Look at fresh asparagus; add a little more water if needed. Cover; cook gently until serving main course.

Or: Cook frozen asparagus spears until serving main course.

2. Look at partially baked bread. If browning too fast, remove from oven for a few minutes, or turn oven off.

Or: Place fresh bread in oven for 5 to 8 minutes to warm.

3. Baste chicken with juices in casserole. Cover; continue cooking until time to serve.

4. Place platter for asparagus and dinner plates in oven to warm.

5. Prepare drawn butter for asparagus: Melt ¼ lb. butter in saucepan over gentle heat. Continue heating after butter has melted. Stir constantly until butter is a dark brown.

6. Test asparagus with a fork: Prick lower part of 1 stalk; should be tender but not mushy. If ready, lift stalks out gently so as not to break tips; lay on warm platter. Scatter bread crumbs over 2 in. or so of the tip ends. Pour drawn butter over tips; leave bottom ends of stalks unbuttered so they can be picked up for eating.

7. Turn off chicken. If using fresh tarragon, scatter 1 heaping Tbsp. fresh leaves over chicken. Baste with juices in casserole. Do not cook further. (Although dry tarragon can take any amount of cooking, fresh tarragon immediately loses all flavor when cooked.)

8. Turn off oven if necessary.

9. Taste strawberries. If defrosted, place cartons in refrigerator.

serve main course

Chicken is served in casserole; asparagus on warmed platter.

Place warmed bread in basket, covered with napkin.
Pour more wine.

assemble dessert course

1. Empty blueberries directly into serving bowl. If they are prime, and covered with cellophane, they need no washing. However, if you wish, rinse them quickly under running cold water; pat dry with paper towels.

   Or: Prepare strawberries Romanoff: Place ice cream in large bowl; break apart with spoon. Let soften 1 or 2 minutes.

   Meanwhile: Whip remaining 1 cup heavy sweet cream until it stands in soft peaks when beater is lifted.

   Work ice cream with a spoon so it is smooth and firm but not soupy. (It will soften more as you add other ingredients.) Fold in whipped cream. Add strawberries with all juice, and ¼ cup Cointreau. Mix gently but thoroughly. Taste; add more Cointreau if desired. Transfer to dessert bowl.
2. Turn on coffeemaker.

serve dessert course

Pitcher of heavy sweet cream and a bowl of sugar are needed at table if you are serving blueberries.

serve after-dinner coffee

If coffee was not started earlier, make last-minute coffee in a saucepan. (See page 118.)

Baked Stuffed Mushroom Caps
Petti di Pollo
Buttered Asparagus Tips

Fruit Medley:
California Oranges and
Fresh Red Raspberries

Coffee

WINE:

Soave

An impressive, yet easy, dinner. Petti di Pollo means breasts of chicken. In this recipe the uncooked flesh is sliced into thin "cutlets," then simmered in butter. Just before serving, slices are dressed with heavy sweet cream and cognac. The whole dish takes less than 10 minutes because slices are so thin and tender.

TO SUBSTITUTE:

You may have to substitute another fruit combination. Fresh raspberries are not always in the market. Nor are California navel oranges.

what to buy

Everything except the fresh bread may be purchased the previous day, if more convenient.

1 fresh loaf Italian or French bread.

16 medium or large fresh mushrooms: Should be uniform in size; pure white with an unbroken membrane connect-ing stem and cap. Refrigerate in original bag. *If not available,* buy 2 (6 oz.) cans of button mushrooms.

2 slices pre-cooked ham: For mushrooms. Should be only ⅛-in. thick, about 4 in. square. Or buy 1 small (2¼ oz.) can deviled ham.

16 or 20 slices of chicken breast: Should be cut ⅛-in. thick. Buy enough chicken breasts to provide these slices. Have butcher cut them for you.

¼ lb. shallots: You will need 5 for mushrooms. *If not available,* buy 2 medium-sized white onions.

1 small bunch fresh parsley: You will need ⅓ cup, cut fine.

2 large California navel oranges: Refrigerate.

2 pt. boxes fresh red raspberries: If necessary, substitute 1 qt. box of large ripe strawberries with fresh green hulls. Refrigerate. *If neither is available,* buy 2 (1 lb.) cartons of frozen whole strawberries. Do not keep in freezer. For frozen berries you will also need ⅓ cup Cointreau.

2 or 3 packages frozen asparagus spears.

½ pt. heavy sweet cream: For Petti di Pollo.

Extras: 1 lemon (½ for mushrooms, ½ for Petti di Pollo); salt; pepper; 1 lb. butter; sugar and cream for coffee; drip grind coffee (breakfast blend and Italian after-dinner roast). For *Mushrooms* — olive oil; ½ cup seasoned bread crumbs. For *Petti di Pollo* — flour; cognac. For *Dessert* — sugar. Suggest buying sweet butter.

Wine: 1 or 2 bottles Soave (an Italian white).

See page 111 for correct wine service and alternate suggestions.

what to do

Several hours before dining, chill wine.

30 minutes before serving first course

1. Remove chicken, ham, butter, mushrooms and needed frozen foods from refrigerator. If using frozen whole strawberries, open cartons to hasten thawing.
2. Start first course:

   Wipe fresh mushrooms with damp paper towel. Do not wash or peel. Remove stems completely. Use stems for stuffing.

   Or: Open canned mushrooms. Drain well; pat dry with paper towels. Remove stems.

   In large skillet heat ½ cup olive oil. Add mushroom caps; cook gently. Squeeze a little lemon juice over caps. Peel 5 shallots (or 2 medium-sized onions); sliver into skillet. Sliver mushroom stems into skillet. Salt all lightly. Lift out mushroom caps; place in attractive shallow baking dish, stem side up. Dot bottom of baking dish with butter.

   Add finely cut (or canned deviled) ham to skillet. Simmer 3 or 4 minutes.

Cut washed parsley quite fine with kitchen scissors. You need ⅓ cupful. Mix ½ cup seasoned bread crumbs into skillet. Taste; add more salt or lemon juice if needed.

Turn off heat; stir in cut parsley. Mixture should be fairly "solid."

With fingers, quickly mound mixture into each mushroom cap.

Do not bake yet.

3. Slice bread: If a round loaf, cut into ½-in. slices, then cut loaf in half. If a long loaf, cut into 2-in. chunks. Butter slices well on one side. Then put all slices in form of loaf on bakepan, ready to heat.

6 minutes before serving first course

4. Place baking dish of mushroom caps on middle rack of 450° oven.
5. Place bread on bottom rack of 450° oven for 5 or 6 minutes to warm.
6. Salt and flour chicken slices lightly on both sides.
7. Baste mushrooms with butter in baking dish. Add more butter if needed. Continue baking.
8. Fill coffeemaker: Suggest combining half breakfast blend and half Italian after-dinner roast for hearty flavor. Or use all Italian after-dinner roast.
9. Baste mushrooms with butter in baking dish. Turn off oven.

serve first course

Place warmed bread in basket, covered

with napkin.

Open chilled wine. Do not serve over ice. Fill glasses a little over halfway. Keep bottle cool.

assemble main course

1. Place asparagus spears in a large skillet. Add 3-in. lump of butter. Salt lightly. Cover; cook gently 7 or 8 minutes.
2. In large skillet melt 3-in. lump of butter over gentle flame. Lay in chicken. Cook first side gently 2 or 3 minutes over medium flame. Do not brown.
3. Place serving platter and dinner plates in oven to warm.
4. Turn chicken over. Add more butter if needed; skillet should not be dry. Cook another 2 or 3 minutes.
5. Mound fresh raspberries in center of dessert bowl. (Should not need washing if protected by cellophane wrapping in market.) Sugar if necessary. Refrigerate.

   Or: Prepare large fresh strawberries: Wash quickly in running cold water. Do not hull; just pat dry with paper towels. Mound in center of dessert bowl. Sugar if necessary. Refrigerate.

   Or: Prepare frozen strawberries: Empty into dessert bowl, juice and all. Add ⅓ cup Cointreau. If fully defrosted, refrigerate.

6. To chicken, add 1 cup heavy sweet cream. Stir to blend; cook gently 3 minutes so mixture thickens into a nice creamy sauce.

49

7. Test asparagus with a fork: Prick lower part of 1 stalk; should be tender but not mushy. If ready, turn off heat. Leave covered until serving.
8. To chicken, add 1 to 2 Tbsp. cognac for special flavor. Taste sauce. Add salt or dash of lemon juice if necessary.
9. Place chicken slices on warm platter; pour sauce over.
10. Arrange asparagus spears in clumps around chicken.

serve main course

Pour more wine.

assemble dessert course

1. Wash and wipe 2 navel oranges; do not peel. Slice into ¼-in. rounds. Dip both sides of each slice into granulated sugar. Lay in overlapping arrangement around raspberries or strawberries in dessert bowl.
2. Turn on coffeemaker, or put water on to boil.

serve dessert course

serve after-dinner coffee

If coffee was not started earlier, make last-minute coffee in a saucepan. (See page 118.)

19 *menu for 4*

Boula
Broiled Chicken
Baked Acorn Squash
Belgian Endive and Water Cress Salad
Cherries Jubilee
Coffee

WINE:

Tavel

This dinner is exceptional, if done as described. Boula is a fine rich soup not frequently encountered. It combines green turtle soup with purée of green pea soup. Although broiled chicken is encountered frequently, I have yet to taste any as delicious as this. Diligent basting is the secret.

TO SUBSTITUTE:

If acorn squash is not in season, substitute any fresh or frozen vegetable that appeals to you. Nearly any vegetable goes well with broilers. Fresh young stringless green beans are delicious cooked whole, and require practically no preparation. If fresh young peas are in the market, you have plenty of time to shell them. If fresh water cress is not available, serve Belgian endive with blue cheese dressing.

what to buy

Everything except the fresh bread may be purchased the previous day, if more convenient.

1 *fresh loaf French or Italian bread:* Or 1 package of partially baked French bread.

1 *(1 pt. 3½ oz.) can of green turtle soup:* For Boula.

1 *(13 oz.) can purée of green pea soup:* For Boula.

2 *fresh broiling chickens:* Each should weigh 2½ to 2¾ lbs. Have butcher split in half.

2 *medium-sized acorn squash:* Should be firm, and uniform in size. *If not available,* substitute any vegetable you choose.

1 *large bunch of fresh parsley:* You will need 1 cup, cut fine.

2 *or 3 fresh Belgian endive:* Stalks should be tightly closed; white with light green tips. Refrigerate.

1 *large bunch of crisp water cress: If not available,* buy 2 more Belgian endive and ¼ lb. Danish blue, Roquefort or Gorgonzola cheese.

2 *(1 lb.) cans pitted dark sweet cherries.*

Extras: Salt; pepper; ½ lb. butter; sugar and cream for coffee; drip grind coffee (breakfast blend and Italian after-dinner roast). *For Boula* — ¼ cup dry sherry wine. *For Chicken* — 1 lemon. *For French Dressing* — paprika; dry mustard; 1 clove of garlic; olive oil; vinegar. *For Cherries* — ½ cup rum or Cointreau. Suggest buying sweet butter.

Wine: 1 bottle Tavel (a Rhone rosé).

See page 111 for correct wine service and alternate selections.

what to do

1. Several hours before dining, chill wine.
2. As early as possible (if not done before storing), wash parsley, endive and water cress: Do not separate endive leaves. Rinse quickly in running cold water. Remove any discolored leaves and edges. Shake well; wrap in paper towels to absorb extra moisture. Seal wrapped in plastic bag, and refrigerate until needed.

30 minutes before serving first course

1. Remove chicken, butter and parsley from refrigerator. Unwrap chicken.
2. Mix French dressing for chicken and salad: Peel and split 1 clove garlic; place in small deep bowl with ½ tsp. paprika, ½ tsp. dry mustard, ½ tsp. salt and 3 Tbsp. vinegar. Mix well. Slowly stir in 6 Tbps. olive oil. Taste; add more oil or vinegar for perfect balance.
3. Start chicken:
   Wipe split halves with damp paper towels; do not wash. Salt lightly on both sides. Tuck wing tips under wings to prevent them from scorching.
   Lay in shallow pan, skin side up. Pour 3 or 4 Tbsp. French dressing over all;

dot each broiler half with 2 or 3 small lumps of butter.
Do not broil yet.

4. Wash and wipe acorn squash. Do not peel. Cut in half; remove seeds and stringy portion. Salt insides lightly; press small lump of butter into each. Place cut side down on shallow pan.
5. Turn oven control to "broil." Place pan with squash on middle rack of oven; bake until serving main course (about 30 minutes).
6. Slice bread: If a long loaf, cut into 2-in. chunks. If a round loaf, cut into ½-in. slices, then cut loaf in half. Butter slices well on one side. Then put all slices in form of loaf on bake-pan, ready to heat.
7. Place pan with chicken 4 in. below high broiler flame. Broil 12 minutes, or until skin is a dark golden brown. Do not scorch. Baste every few minutes with pan juices; add more butter if necessary.

15 minutes before serving first course

8. If using partially baked bread, place on bottom rack of oven now. Takes about 15 minutes to bake and brown.
9. Cut washed parsley quite fine with kitchen scissors. You need 1 cupful for the chicken.
10. Fill coffeemaker: Suggest combining half breakfast blend and half Italian after-dinner roast for hearty flavor.
11. Baste chicken.

12. Start endive and water cress salad: Starting at the base, cut several 1-in. sections from each endive stalk directly into salad bowl. Separate upper leaves. Cut off excess water cress stems; place cress in bowl. Refrigerate without dressing.
    Or: Start endive salad: Quarter stalks lengthwise directly into salad bowl. Do not separate leaves. Crumble blue cheese over the top. Refrigerate without dressing.
13. Baste chicken.
14. Move partially baked bread to top rack of oven to finish browning.
    Or: Place fresh bread on bottom rack of oven for 5 to 8 minutes to warm.
15. Blend green turtle soup and green pea soup together in saucepan. Heat gently.
16. Look at chicken. If nicely browned, turn over. Baste well with pan juices, filling the cavities. Add more butter if needed. Squeeze lemon juice over all. Broil about 15 minutes more.
17. Add ¼ cup dry sherry to soup; ladle into soup plates.
18. Turn oven control down almost halfway so broiling of chicken is less intense. Go by the size of the flame, since every stove has a different intensity of heat. You want chicken to keep cooking, but at a slower pace so it does not dry out while you eat. Repeated basting keeps it succulent.

serve first course

Place warmed bread in basket, covered

with napkin.

assemble main course

1. Place serving platter and dinner plates in oven to warm.
2. Baste chicken. Test with fork; if tender, turn off broiler.
3. Prick center of 1 squash with fork. If soft, remove pan from oven.
4. Arrange chicken crosswise on platter, skin side up, one half partially overlapping the other. Sprinkle with cut parsley. Pour pan juices over.
5. Place acorn squash, cut side up, at ends of platter. Place small lump of butter in each cavity.

serve main course

Open chilled wine. Do not serve over ice. Fill glasses a little over halfway.

assemble salad course

1. Salt salad lightly.
2. Toss with 4 or 5 Tbsp. French dressing, or just enough to moisten all leaves. Do not include split garlic.
3. If using endive, crumble in pieces of blue cheese.

serve salad course

assemble dessert course

1. In a saucepan, heat 2 (1 lb.) cans of pitted dark sweet cherries with half of their syrup.

2. *Meanwhile:* In a smaller, attractive saucepan, heat ½ cup rum or Cointreau. Do not boil.
3. Turn on coffeemaker.
4. When both cherries and liquor are hot, pour cherries into dessert bowl.

serve dessert course

Bring bowl of cherries, pan of steaming liquor, and dessert dishes to table. Pour liquor over cherries; light at once with a match. Spoon into dessert dishes while still flaming.

serve after-dinner coffee

If coffee was not started earlier, make last-minute coffee in a saucepan. (See page 118.)

Black Bean Soup
Broiled Lamb Chops
Tiny Peas with Fresh Mint
Sliced Tomatoes with Fresh Dill
Chocolate Mousse
Coffee

WINE:

Beaujolais

Lamb, when not overcooked, makes a marvelous dinner. The French value lamb greatly, and they always cook it rare. "A pointe," they say, which means just to the point of perfection. Once you taste lamb cooked like this you'll probably never want it any other way either. The dessert is one of my favorites — a lovely, creamy mousse with a very special flavor. And it's no trick at all to make!

TO SUBSTITUTE:

With the exception of the fresh herbs, which are not essential to the dinner, all ingredients should be readily available. However, if you think you would prefer mocha mousse to chocolate, see the recipe on page 109.

what to buy

Everything except the fresh bread may be purchased the previous day, if more convenient. I suggest buying the heavy sweet cream 2 or 3 days ahead, if possible; it will thicken in your refrigerator, and make a richer dessert.

1 *fresh loaf French or Italian bread:* Or 1 package of partially baked French bread.

2 *(10½ oz.) cans of black bean soup.*

1 *(10½ oz.) can of clear beef consommé.*

8 *loin or rib lamb chops:* Should be cut 1¼-in. thick. Or use 4 English chops, cut 2-in. thick. (An English chop is a loin chop which has a lamb kidney skewered to the tail.) Have butcher remove most fat.

2 *or 3 packages frozen tiny peas:* Sometimes these are labeled "Baby Peas" or "Petite Peas." (Unless labeled thus, peas will probably be large and not too sweet.) Canned baby peas are good eating but lack fresh green color.

1 *small bunch fresh mint:* Refrigerate in sealed plastic bag. *If not available,* buy 1 bunch fresh parsley.

1 *bunch fresh dill:* Do not wash. Refrigerate in sealed plastic bag. *If not available,* substitute fresh parsley or dry oregano.

3 *or 4 large firm tomatoes, ripe for slicing:* Beefsteak tomatoes are best. Refrigerate.

1 *fresh orange:* For mousse. Get a California navel orange if possible; you need the grated peel.

1 *(8 oz.) package unsweetened baking chocolate:* For mousse.

1 *(4 oz.) package unsweetened cocoa:* For mousse. "Droste's Dutch" is especially good.

53 1 *pt. heavy sweet cream.*

Extras: Salt; pepper; ¾ lb. butter; sugar and cream for coffee; drip grind coffee (breakfast blend and Italian after-dinner roast). *For Soup* — cayenne pepper; powdered cloves; 1 lemon; 2 eggs; ¼ cup dry sherry wine. *For Lamb* — dry thyme. *For French Dressing* — paprika; dry mustard; 1 clove of garlic; olive oil; vinegar. *For Mousse* — 1¼ cups sugar; ⅓ cup Cointreau. Suggest buying sweet butter.

Wine: 1 bottle Beaujolais (a red Burgundy).

See page 111 for correct wine service and alternate selections.

what to do

1. Several hours before dining, if possible, de-cork wine. Leave open, at room temperature, to breathe.
2. If using parsley, wash and dry in paper towel as early as possible (if not done before storing).

30 minutes before serving first course

1. Remove lamb, butter, 2 eggs, tomatoes and frozen peas from refrigerator. Unwrap lamb.
2. Start dessert:
Half-fill lower part of double boiler with warm water. Bring to active boil as you place top in position and break ½ lb. unsweetened baking

chocolate into it. Need not be broken small; heat and coffee will melt lumps.

Make 1 cup strong black coffee: In small saucepan, bring 1¼ cups fresh cold water to a near boil. Stir in 1 heaping Tbsp. drip grind coffee (breakfast blend or after-dinner roast). Let boil up to top of pan; turn off heat.

Quickly pour coffee through a fine sieve over the chocolate in top of double boiler. Stir in 1 cup sugar and dash of salt.

When fully melted, chocolate should look smooth and glossy. If granular, stir in water, a little at a time, until chocolate shines.

Remove top of double boiler from bottom. Grate outer skin of 1 orange into chocolate. Stir in ⅓ cup Cointreau. Taste; add more salt or Cointreau if desired.

Place chocolate mixture in refrigerator to cool for about 10 minutes.

3. Place 2 eggs in small saucepan; cover with cool water. (Warm water may make chilled eggs crack.) Cover; bring to boil. Boil gently just 12 minutes (14 minutes if eggs are very large). Then plunge into cold water for 3 or 4 minutes.

4. Slice bread: If a long loaf, cut into 2-in. chunks. If a round loaf, cut into ½-in. slices, then cut loaf in half. Butter slices well on one side. Then put all slices in form of loaf on bakepan, ready to heat.

15 minutes before serving
first course

5. If using partially baked bread, place in 450° oven now. Takes about 15 minutes to bake and brown.
6. Finish making dessert:
Whip ¾ pt. (1½ cups) heavy sweet cream until firm but not dry. (Should stand in soft peaks when beater is lifted.) Add ¼ cup sugar; beat just enough to blend in.
Fold whipped cream into cooled chocolate mixture. (Lift spoon from bottom to top. Do not stir around and around.)
When all is smooth-textured, transfer to soufflé dish or dessert bowl. Place in coldest part of refrigerator, but not in freezing compartment.
7. Slice tomatoes thin. Carefully overlap slices on flat round platter. Refrigerate.
8. Mix French dressing for lamb chops and salad: Peel and split 1 clove garlic; place in small deep bowl with ½ tsp. paprika, ½ tsp. dry mustard, ½ tsp. salt and 3 Tbsp. vinegar. Mix well. Slowly stir in 6 Tbsp. olive oil. Taste; add more oil or vinegar for perfect balance. Do not refrigerate.
9. Look at partially baked bread. If browning too fast, remove from oven for a few minutes, or turn oven down.
Or: Place fresh bread in 450° oven for 5 or 6 minutes to warm.
10. Blend black bean soup and beef consommé together in saucepan. Taste; you may wish to add a dash of cay-

enne pepper and ½ tsp. powdered cloves. Heat gently.
11. If substituting parsley for fresh mint and/or fresh dill, cut quite fine now with kitchen scissors. You need 1 cupful for peas, ½ cupful for tomatoes.
12. Slice 2 thin rounds of lemon; cut in half.
13. Shell eggs; cut whites and yolks into small bits directly into cup or small bowl. Mix well.
14. Ladle soup into soup plates. Add 1 Tbsp. dry sherry to each serving. Decorate top with a spoonful of minced eggs and ½ slice of lemon.

serve first course

Place warmed bread in basket, covered with napkin.

assemble main course

1. Lay lamb chops in shallow pan. Do not salt. Pour on 3 Tbsp. French dressing, including the split clove of garlic. Sprinkle on scant ½ tsp. dry thyme. (Too much thyme creates a bitter taste.) Dot each chop with small lump of butter.
2. Turn oven control to "broil"; place lamb pan 3 to 3½ in. below high flame. Broil first side 3 minutes (5 minutes if using English chops) to brown.
3. Rinse several sprigs of fresh mint in running cold water. Break 1 or 2 into saucepan. Add peas, a large lump of

butter and dash of salt. Cover; cook gently until ready to serve.
4. Turn chops over; baste with pan juices. Broil only 2 to 3 minutes (4 to 5 minutes if using English chops).
5. Place serving platter and dinner plates in oven to warm.
6. Fill coffeemaker: Suggest combining half breakfast blend and half Italian after-dinner roast for hearty flavor.
7. Examine chops for rareness: Make small cut in center of 1 chop. If too raw, cook only another minute; look again. (Lamb chops must be pink inside — "à pointe" as the French say — to be worth eating. Like beef, lamb can overcook and become grey in half a minute. So watch carefully.)
IMPORTANT:
Remove pan from broiler the moment chops are ready, or they will continue to cook even if broiler is turned off.
8. Lay chops attractively in center of warm platter, ends towards the middle. Lay small bunch fresh mint or parsley in center for good looks. Pour some of pan juices over chops. Do not include split garlic.
9. Remove cooked mint from peas. Arrange peas around chops.
10. Remove mousse from refrigerator so it will not be served ice cold. Tastes best when only slightly chilled.

serve main course

Pour wine. Fill glasses a little over halfway.

assemble salad course

1. Salt tomatoes lightly. Decorate with freshly cut dill, cut parsley, or dry oregano.
2. Pour 3 or 4 Tbsp. French dressing over all.

serve salad course

assemble dessert course

1. Cover chocolate mousse with a ¼-in. layer of unsweetened cocoa. Do not add sugar.
2. Turn on coffeemaker.

serve dessert course

serve after-dinner coffee

If coffee was not started earlier, make last-minute coffee in a saucepan. (See page 118.)

Consommé Bellevue

Sautéed Veal Kidneys
Tiny Peas and Whole String Beans
with
Balls of Foie Gras

Hearts of Palm Salad

Fruit Tart

Coffee

WINE:

Muscadet
or
Chablis

This dinner is a continuous procession of specialties. Nothing is particularly extravagant, yet it is hard to imagine a more engaging light dinner. Consommé Bellevue combines clam juice and clear chicken consommé, and is spiked lightly with dry sherry. Veal kidneys fixed this way are superb. Canned hearts of palm, a Brazilian import, makes a marvelous salad.

TO SUBSTITUTE:

Unfortunately only shops in large cities bother to get canned hearts of palm. They are not wildly expensive. In the meantime, see page 114 for other excellent salad suggestions. If you cannot buy a fine fruit tart locally, substitute frozen fruit turnovers.

what to buy

Everything except the fresh bread and fruit tart may be purchased the previous day, if more convenient.

1 fresh loaf French or Italian bread: Or 1 package of partially baked French bread.

1 medium-sized fresh fruit tart: Buy the particular kind your pastry shop makes best: apple, cherry, apricot, peach, blueberry, etc.
If substituting frozen fruit turnovers, buy 1 package of 4. You will also need some powdered sugar, and possibly some heavy sweet cream.

2 (10½ oz.) cans of clear chicken consommé: Be sure there is no rice in it.

1 (8 oz.) bottle or can of clear clam broth.

4 fresh veal kidneys: Have butcher remove outside fat casing and thin membrane.

½ lb. medium-sized fresh mushrooms: For kidneys. Should be pure white with an unbroken membrane connecting stem and cap. Refrigerate in original bag. *If not available,* buy 2 (3 or 4 oz.) cans of sliced mushrooms.

½ pt. heavy sweet cream: You will need a little for the consommé, the rest for the kidneys.

1 package frozen whole string beans.

2 packages frozen tiny peas: Sometimes these are labeled "Baby Peas" or "Petite Peas." (Unless labeled thus, peas will probably be large and not too sweet.) Canned baby peas are good eating but lack fresh green color.

1 small (2 or 3 oz.) can paté de foie gras: Get a nice but inexpensive variety.

2 (14 oz.) cans of hearts of palm. Refrigerate. *If not available,* substitute any salad of your choice. See page 114 for suggestions.

Extras: Salt; pepper; ¾ lb. butter; sugar and cream for coffee; drip grind coffee (breakfast blend and Italian after-dinner roast). *For Consommé —* ⅓ cup dry sherry wine. *For Veal Kidneys —* flour; dry tarragon; ⅓ cup cognac or bourbon; 1 lemon. *For French Dressing —* paprika; dry mustard; 1 clove of garlic; olive oil; vinegar. Suggest buying sweet butter.

Wine: 1 or 2 bottles Muscadet (a white Loire).
or
1 or 2 bottles Chablis (a white Burgundy).
NOTE: You will need ½ cup of this white wine for cooking, unless you wish to substitute dry French vermouth. See page 111 for correct wine service and alternate selections.

what to do

1. Several hours before dining, chill wine and hearts of palm.
2. If using salad greens instead of hearts of palm, wash as early as possible (if not done before storing).

30 minutes before serving first course

1. Remove veal kidneys, butter, mushrooms and frozen vegetables from refrigerator. Unwrap kidneys.
2. Wash kidneys quickly in running cold water; dry with paper towels. Cut across, into ⅛-in. thick slices. Salt and flour slices lightly on both sides.
3. Mix French dressing: Peel and split 1 clove garlic; place in small deep bowl with ½ tsp. paprika, ½ tsp. dry mustard, ½ tsp. salt and 3 Tbsp. vinegar. Mix well. Slowly stir in 6 Tbsp. olive oil. Taste; add more oil or vinegar for perfect balance. Set aside for salad course; do not refrigerate.
4. Fill coffeemaker: Suggest combining half breakfast blend and half Italian after-dinner roast for hearty flavor.
5. Slice bread: If a long loaf, cut into 2-in. chunks. If a round loaf, cut into ½-in. slices, then cut loaf in half. Butter slices well on one side. Then put all slices in form of loaf on bake-pan, ready to heat.

15 minutes before serving first course

6. If using partially baked bread, place in 450° oven now. Takes about 15 minutes to bake and brown.
7. Start kidney dish:
   In large skillet slowly melt 3-in. lump of butter. Do not brown. Add kidney slices; cook gently 4 or 5 minutes. Do not brown.

Wipe fresh mushrooms with damp paper towel. Do not wash or peel. Discard dry ends of stems. Slice caps evenly down through stems.
Or: Open canned mushrooms: drain well.

Stir mushrooms into skillet. Add more butter if needed; there should always be enough to bubble in skillet. Cook gently 1 or 2 minutes.

Crumble in 1 heaping tsp. dry tarragon. Stir in ⅓ cup cognac or bourbon. Cook about 2 minutes.

When liquor is hot, put a lighted match to its surface to flame sauce.

When flame dies, add ½ cup dry white wine from the bottle you are serving. (Or substitute dry French vermouth.)

Turn off heat. Finish just before serving.

8. Look at partially baked bread. If browning too fast, remove from oven for a few minutes, or turn oven down
   Or: Place fresh bread in 450° oven for 5 or 6 minutes to warm.
9. Blend chicken consommé and clam broth together in saucepan. Heat gently.
10. Place string beans in saucepan with 3-in. lump of butter and ¼ tsp. salt. Cover; cook gently until serving main course.
11. Add ⅓ cup dry sherry to consommé; ladle into soup plates or cups. Float a little heavy sweet cream on each serving, by holding a teaspoon on surface, rounded side up, and pour

ing cream carefully and slowly over it. Do not mix cream in.

12. Turn off oven. Turn off string beans.

serve first course

Place warmed bread in basket, covered with napkin.

assemble main course

1. Reheat kidneys over gentle flame. Taste sauce; you may want to add a dash of lemon juice or salt to bring out flavor. Stir in ½ cup heavy sweet cream. Cook 3 or 4 minutes so mixture thickens into a nice creamy sauce.
2. Add peas to saucepan with string beans. Cover; cook gently until ready to serve.
3. Place serving platter and dinner plates in oven to warm.
4. Open can of paté de foie gras.
5. Turn off kidneys. If sauce gets too thick, add a little more cream, or white wine or vermouth.
6. Place kidneys on warm platter; pour sauce over. Decorate top with nice red paprika.
7. Turn off vegetables. Cut small pieces of foie gras into pan. Do not cook more or foie gras will dissolve. Arrange vegetables around kidneys.
8. If baking fruit turnovers, place in 400° oven now. Will take about 20 minutes to bake and brown.

serve main course

Open chilled wine. Do not serve over ice.

Fill glasses a little over halfway.

assemble salad course

1. Open chilled cans of hearts of palm. Arrange hearts on 4 individual plates. Spoon 2 or 3 Tbsp. French dressing over each serving.
2. If baking turnovers, turn off oven. If well browned, remove from oven. Otherwise, leave inside to finish baking with oven turned off.

serve salad course

assemble dessert course

1. Place fruit tart on tray. Do not cut into servings.
   Or: Arrange hot turnovers on tray. Dust with powdered sugar.
2. Turn on coffeemaker.

serve dessert course

serve after-dinner coffee

If coffee was not started earlier, make last-minute coffee in a saucepan. (See page 118.)

22 *menu for 4*

Seafood Salad

Broiled Fresh Fish

Asparagus with Hollandaise Sauce

*Ripe Mango Halves
filled with
Raspberry Ice*

Coffee

WINE:

*Chablis
or
Muscadet
or
Graves*

This is an excellent fish dinner. Broiling is one of the finest ways to prepare fish, providing it is not allowed to dry out. Vegetables acquire a fishy taste when served with fish. So I suggest you serve the vegetable after the fish course, using new plates. Asparagus is an ideal choice because it is a nice course to serve separately, and can double as a salad as well.

TO SUBSTITUTE:

If you prefer, serve oysters or clams on the half shell instead of seafood salad. If fresh mangoes are not available, substitute ripe Manilla papayas dressed with orange ice. Manilla papayas are small, just slightly larger than a pear.

what to buy

Everything except the fresh seafood, fish,

asparagus and bread may be purchased the previous day, if more convenient.

1 freshly boiled lobster: For seafood salad. Should weigh 2 lbs. Have dealer split in half, remove meat from body and claws, and place in separate container. Be sure to ask for the emptied half shells. Refrigerate. *If fresh lobster is not available,* buy 1 (1 lb.) can of frozen lobster meat, or 2 frozen rock lobster tails. Do not keep in freezer.

1 lb. medium-sized freshly boiled shrimp: For seafood salad. Have dealer shell and clean, if necessary. Refrigerate. *If not available,* substitute 1 lb. shelled and cleaned frozen boiled shrimp. Do not keep in freezer.

½ lb. fresh crabmeat: For seafood salad. This is flown in cans to fine stores and fish dealers from the southeast coast. Flavor is superior to frozen. Insist on large lumps. Refrigerate. *If not available,* substitute 1 (6 oz.) package of frozen Alaska king crabmeat. Do not keep in freezer.

1 large fresh fish: Should weigh about 3½ lbs. Or 2 smaller fish, each weighing 1¾ to 2 lbs. Must be fresh catch of the day; eyes should be bright and clear, not clouded. Good broiling fish are sea bass, striped bass, whitefish, bluefish, boned shad, and red snapper. Have dealer clean and split in half; do not have him skin. Most of tail should be cut off. I like to leave head on, both for looks and for eating by those who like it. But do as you please. Store in coldest part of refrigerator, but do not freeze.

1 large bunch fresh asparagus: You need about 2 lbs. Buy only crisp green stalks with young compact tips. Refrigerate. *If not available,* buy 2 or 3 packages frozen asparagus spears.

1 fresh loaf French or Italian bread: Or 1 package of partially baked French bread.

1 large bunch of crisp water cress: For seafood salad. *If not available,* buy extra parsley.

1 large bunch fresh parsley: You will need about 1 cup, cut fine. (Get extra if you cannot buy water cress.)

2 large ripe mangoes: Should be soft and juicy. Refrigerate.

If substituting papaya halves with orange ice, buy 2 ripe small papayas and 1½ pts. orange ice. Refrigerate.

1½ pts. raspberry ice: For mangoes.

½ pt. sour cream: You will need only 1½ to 2 heaping Tbsp. for first course. Remainder will keep for days in refrigerator.

Extras: 4 lemons (½ for seafood salad, 3 for fish, ½ for hollandaise); salt; pepper; ¾ lb. butter; sugar and cream for coffee; drip grind coffee (breakfast blend and Italian after-dinner roast). *For Seafood Salad* — ½ cup mayonnaise; Worcestershire sauce. *For Fish* — dry tarragon. *For Hollandaise* — 3 eggs; cayenne pepper. Suggest buying sweet butter.

Wine: 1 or 2 bottles Chablis (a white Burgundy).
or
1 or 2 bottles Muscadet (a white Loire).
or
1 or 2 bottles Graves (a white Bordeaux).
See page 111 for correct wine service and alternate selections.

what to do

1. Several hours before dining, chill wine.
2. As early as possible (if not done before storing), wash parsley and water cress: Cut off most of stems. Rinse quickly in running cold water. Remove discolored leaves. Shake well; wrap in paper towels to absorb extra moisture. Seal in plastic bag, and refrigerate until needed.
3. If using frozen seafood, remove from refrigerator in plenty of time to defrost before using.

30 minutes before serving
first course

1. Remove seafood, fish, butter, and asparagus from refrigerator.
2. Trim fresh asparagus. Cut about 2 in. off bottom of all stalks, while still tied in a bunch. Separate stalks; rinse quickly in running cold water. Do not peel. Place in a large skillet. Cover with cold water. Do not cook yet.

   Or: Place frozen asparagus spears in a large skillet. Do not cook yet.
3. Start first course:

Mix Seafood Sauce: Combine 3½ to 4 heaping Tbsp. mayonnaise with half as much sour cream, a dash of salt, 1 Tbsp. lemon juice and 1 Tbsp. Worcestershire sauce. Taste. Should be slightly pungent, but not too lemony. If so, add mayonnaise or sour cream.

Separate crabmeat with fingers, keeping lumps large. Eliminate any bits of bone you feel. Mix in some Seafood Sauce carefully, so as not to break up lumps.

Mix cooked shrimp with same sauce. Keep separate.

Mix some Seafood Sauce into lobster meat.

Arrange in separate mounds on a large round platter with clusters of water cress. Refrigerate until serving time.

4. Prepare fish for broiling:
Lay 4 small pieces of butter in large shallow pan.

Rinse fish quickly in running cold water. Pat dry with paper towels. Salt lightly on both sides. Lay in pan on top of butter, flesh side up.

Pour over the juice of 1 lemon, and 1 Tbsp. French dressing (page 116). Crumble on 1 heaping tsp. dry tarragon. Dot in 4 or 6 places with butter, depending on size of fish.

Do not broil yet.

5. Slice bread: If a long loaf, cut into 2-in. chunks. If a round loaf, cut into ½-in. slices, then cut loaf in half. Butter slices well on one side. Then put all slices in form of loaf on bakepan, ready to heat.

just before serving
first course

6. Turn oven control to "broil"; place fish pan 2½ in. below high flame. Fish must be broiled close to high flame; otherwise it will exude moisture and be ruined. Broil about 15 to 18 minutes. Baste 2 or 3 times with pan juices. Add butter if needed. Do not turn fish; it will break.

   If broiling 2 small fish instead of 1 large one, watch them more closely and baste more often. They take about 12 minutes and tend to dry out faster than a large fish. Partially baked bread can go in oven when you begin broiling fish. Bread can finish baking while you transfer fish to platter.

7. Remove seafood platter from refrigerator. Decorate with clusters of parsley, if lacking water cress, thus separating each mound of seafood.

8. If using partially baked bread, place in oven now. Takes about 15 minutes to bake and brown.

9. Baste fish with pan juices after serving first course (but before eating it). Add more butter if needed. If browning too fast, lower pan slightly or turn flame down. But do not turn down too much.

serve first course

Open chilled wine. Do not serve over ice.

Fill glasses a little over halfway. Keep bottle cool.

assemble main course

1. Remove partially baked bread from oven if golden brown.
   Or: Place fresh bread in oven for 5 or 6 minutes to warm.

2. Warm serving platter and plates at same time.

3. Baste fish again to keep succulent. Add extra butter if needed. Turn broiling flame low if fish is getting too brown.

4. Cut washed parsley quite fine with kitchen scissors. You need 1 cupful for the fish.

   IMPORTANT:
   Remove pan from broiler the second fish is ready, or it will continue to cook even if broiler is turned off. Turn off oven.

5. Run metal spatula under fish and slide carefully to warm platter. Scatter on cut parsley; pour pan juices over. Place 8 quarters, or 4 halves, of lemon on edge of platter.

6. Half-fill lower part of double boiler with water. Heat gently.

7. Cook fresh asparagus 12 minutes while eating first course.

serve main course

Place warmed bread in basket, covered with napkin.

Pour more wine.

assemble vegetable course

1. Place 4 individual plates for asparagus in oven to warm.
2. Make hollandaise sauce:

   Separate 3 eggs; place yolks in upper part of double boiler.

   Turn off heat under lower part of double boiler. Place upper part on top. Beat eggs briskly with wire whisk or fork. Do not let egg yolks get too hot or sauce will curdle.

   Leave top of double boiler in position while you beat in about ¼ lb. softened butter, 1½-in. pieces at a time. Let mixture thicken slightly after each addition. Be sure to beat mixture on bottom and sides of pan. When all butter is beaten in and mixture is the consistency of medium thick cream sauce, add dash of cayenne pepper, a little salt, and a good squeeze of lemon juice. Taste; should be slightly piquant. Add more lemon juice if needed. Whole process takes about 8 minutes.

   IMPORTANT:

   If sauce is slow in blending, you may need to reheat the water below for a minute or two. (But do not let it boil.) Then turn heat off, or very, very low. Remember, egg yolks cannot stand sustained heat.

   If sauce gets too thick, add 1 Tbsp. of hot water from the asparagus.
3. Test asparagus with fork: Prick lower part of 1 stalk; should be tender but not mushy. If ready, lift stalks out gently so as not to break tips; lay on 4 individual plates.

4. Spoon hollandaise sauce over tips and centers of stalks.

serve vegetable course

Pour more wine.

assemble dessert course

1. Fill coffeemaker: Suggest combining half breakfast blend and half Italian after-dinner roast for hearty flavor.
2. Wash and dry mangoes. Cut in half around pit. (They are difficult to split apart because flesh clings tenaciously to center pit.) Working over a bowl to save juice, use a curved grapefruit knife to work around pit until you can pry halves loose. Place halves on individual plates; fill cavities with juice in bowl and raspberry ice.

   Or: Prepare papayas: Wash and dry. Cut in half; remove seeds. Place halves on individual plates; fill with orange ice.
3. Turn on coffeemaker.

serve dessert course

serve after-dinner coffee

If coffee was not started earlier, make last-minute coffee in a saucepan. (See page 118.)

23 *menu for 4*

Broiled Shrimp

Hamburgers Light and Juicy
Hearts of Artichokes
Potato Chips

Apples Flambée

Coffee

BEER, OR WINE:
*Tavel
or
Mateus*

This is a casual dinner, not intended for high occasions, but very good eating. The shrimp are cooked like the famous Italian scampi, a magnificent dish. And these hamburgers never fail to bring enthusiastic compliments because they are marvelously light and juicy — not at all like conventional hamburgers.

TO SUBSTITUTE:

No substitutions should be necessary. However, if tangy fresh apples are temporarily unavailable, buy a frozen apple strudel. Or the best fresh fruit in the market. In hot weather you may wish to substitute ice cold vichysoisse for the broiled shrimp.

what to buy

Everything except the fresh shrimp, ground beef and fresh bread may be purchased the previous day, if more convenient.

2 lbs. large fresh shrimp: Fresh shrimp are more flavorsome than frozen, and generally less expensive. Have fish dealer shell and clean, ready for you to cook. Or buy 2 lbs. of shelled and cleaned frozen shrimp. Refrigerate.

2 lbs. freshly ground beef: Choose top sirloin or top round. Have butcher remove all fat and grind twice. (Do not buy previously ground beef or frozen patties.)

1 fresh loaf French or Italian bread: Or 1 loaf or large package of dark pumpernickel.

1 large bunch fresh chives: You will need ¼ cup, cut fine, for shrimp. Refrigerate in sealed plastic bag. *If not available,* buy 1 bunch scallions with good green stems, or 1 large Spanish or Bermuda onion. Refrigerate scallions.

1 large bunch fresh parsley: You will need 3 cups, cut fine.

4 or 5 medium-sized apples: Buy a tangy-flavored variety, such as McIntosh, Jonathans, greenings or Winesaps. Should be firm, with no soft spots. Refrigerate.

If substituting apple strudel, buy 1 frozen package. Do not keep in freezer. Sour cream is a delicious topping; suggest you buy some.

2 (9 oz.) cans or 2 packages frozen artichoke hearts.

1 large bag or box of potato chips.

Extras: 4 lemons (3 for shrimp, 1 for apples); salt; pepper; ¾ lb. butter;

sugar and cream for coffee; drip grind coffee (breakfast blend and Italian after-dinner roast). *For Shrimp* — 3 cloves of garlic; olive oil; capers. *For Hamburgers* — Bahamian or Dijon mustard; Worcestershire sauce. *For Apples* — ¾ cup sugar; ½ cup bourbon. Suggest buying sweet butter.

6 cans or bottles of beer.
or
Wine: 1 or 2 bottles Tavel (a Rhone rosé).
or
1 or 2 bottles Mateus (a Portuguese rosé).

See page 111 for correct wine service and alternate selections.

what to do

1. Several hours before dining, chill beer or wine.
2. As early as possible (if not done before storing), wash parsley: Rinse quickly in running cold water. Remove discolored leaves. Shake well; wrap in paper towels to absorb extra moisture. Seal in plastic bag, and refrigerate until needed.

30 minutes before serving first course

1. Remove apples, shrimp, butter, chives, parsley and needed frozen foods from refrigerator. Do not remove ground beef.

2. Start dessert:
   Wash and dry apples. Remove stems; do not peel or core. Cut across into ¼-in. slices. Leave core intact; it helps keep slice whole and is pretty as well.

   In skillet, melt 3-in. lump of butter over gentle flame; do not brown. Add apple slices; sprinkle with 2 Tbsp. lemon juice to retain color. Cover with ¾ cup sugar.

   Cook gently 5 minutes, or until soft but not mushy. Carefully move slices around so all cook evenly. Turn off heat; reheat just before serving.

3. Start first course:
   Rinse shrimp quickly in running cold water while apples cook. Remove all visible black cords. Pat dry with paper towels. Lay flat in shallow pan.

   Peel 2 or 3 cloves of garlic; sliver very fine directly over shrimp.

   Wash chives; dry in paper towels. With kitchen scissors, cut about ¼ cup directly over shrimp.

   Or: Clean scallions, cut about ¾ cup (white and green parts combined) directly over shrimp.

   Or: Peel 1 large Spanish or Bermuda onion; sliver directly over shrimp.
   Top shrimp with juice of 1 lemon, ⅓ cup olive oil and 1 Tbsp. capers. Salt lightly. Mix well. Do not broil yet.

4. Cut washed parsley quite fine with kitchen scissors. You need 3 cupfuls — 1 apiece for shrimp, hamburgers and artichokes.

10 minutes before serving first course

5. Turn oven control to "broil"; place shrimp pan 3 in. below high flame. Broil only 9 or 10 minutes.
6. Slice white bread; if a long loaf, cut into 2-in. chunks. If a round loaf, cut into ½-in. slices, then cut loaf in half. Butter slices well on one side. Then put all slices in form of loaf on bake-pan, ready to heat.

   Or: Cut loaf of pumpernickel into ½-in. slices. Butter generously. Lay flat on serving plate.
7. Stir shrimp so all cook evenly. Do not bunch them.
8. Place frozen artichokes (or drained canned artichokes) in saucepan with 2-in. lump of butter. Do not cook yet.
9. Baste shrimp.
10. Fill coffeemaker: Suggest combining half breakfast blend and half Italian after-dinner roast for hearty flavor.
11. Place serving platter and 4 first-course plates in oven to warm.
12. Taste shrimp sauce. Add more lemon juice if needed. Broil shrimp 1 or 2 minutes more if not quite cooked. But watch closely; if cooked too long shrimp toughen.

    IMPORTANT:

    Remove pan from broiler the moment shrimp are ready or they will continue to cook even if broiler is turned off.
13. Mix 1 cup cut parsley into shrimp. Transfer to warm platter, sauce and all. Garnish with 4 halves of lemon.
14. If baking apple strudel, turn oven to 400°; place strudel inside. Will take about 30 minutes to bake and brown.

serve first course

Put warmed white bread in basket, covered with napkin.

Or: Bring in plate of buttered pumpernickel.

Open chilled wine. Do not serve over ice. Fill glasses a little over halfway. Keep bottle cool. Or pour chilled beer into glasses.

assemble main course

1. Start hamburgers:

   In large skillet slowly melt 3-in. lump of butter while you season ground beef with 1½ tsp. salt and 2 Tbsp. Bahamian or Dijon mustard. Mix very lightly with fork or fingers; handle as little as possible or hamburgers will be tough. Taste; add more salt if needed. Lightly form 4 hamburgers into the shape of a large sweet potato. Do not pack meat; it will not be as juicy when cooked. Top each with a small lump of butter.

   Add 2 Tbsp. Worcestershire sauce to melted butter. Lay hamburgers carefully into butter so they keep their shape. Cook 8 to 10 minutes over medium heat, basting constantly. Add more butter if needed so skillet is never dry.
2. Cover artichokes; cook over gentle flame until serving time. Look occa-sionally; add more butter if needed.
3. Spread potato chips in shallow pan; place in oven to warm. Improves them greatly.
4. Place dinner plates in oven to warm.
5. Baste hamburgers. Do not attempt to turn over; they might fall apart. Constant basting will cook them so they are hot inside although still rare. Peek at center occasionally. Do not over-cook; they must be a little rare to be juicy.
6. Turn off artichokes. Salt lightly; add cup of cut parsley.
7. As soon as hamburgers are cooked, lift onto warm plates with two large spoons. Top with cup of cut parsley; pour pan juices over. Surround with artichokes and warm potato chips.
8. If baking strudel, turn off oven. Prick center with a fork to see if apples and pastry are baked. If so, remove from oven. If not, leave inside to finish baking with oven turned off.

serve main course

Pour more wine.

assemble dessert course

1. Place serving platter in oven to warm.
2. Turn on coffeemaker.
3. Reheat apple slices.

   Meanwhile: In a small attractive sauce-pan heat ½ cup bourbon.

   When both apples and liquor are hot, slide apples onto warm platter and top with sauce in skillet. Pan of hot liquor is brought to table separately for flaming.

Or: Prepare apple strudel: Slide onto warm platter. Cut into 3-in. portions. Empty sour cream into bowl.

serve dessert course

Bring platter of apples, pan of heated liquor, and dessert dishes to table. Pour liquor over apples; light at once with a match. Serve when flame dies.

Or: If serving apple strudel, bring to table with bowl of chilled sour cream.

serve after-dinner coffee

If coffee was not started earlier, make last-minute coffee in a saucepan. (See page 118.)

24 *menu for 4*

Vichysoisse

Steak Tartare

Caesar Salad

French Dessert Cheese

Coffee

WINE:

Tavel
or
Mateus

This dinner is not suitable for all guests, but those who love raw ground beef find it delicious in hot weather. Steak tartare is often successfully served as a cocktail or buffet specialty. With it good black bread is imperative. A large green salad is essential.

For fun you might end the dinner with one of the coffee variations suggested on page 118.

TO SUBSTITUTE:

Ideally the salad should be made with romaine lettuce. However, if none is available you may combine iceberg lettuce and escarole. There should be no need for other substitutions.

what to buy

Everything except the ground beef and fresh bread may be purchased the previous day, if more convenient.

2 lbs. freshly ground beef: Choose lean top sirloin or top round. Have butcher remove every trace of fat; tell him it is not for hamburgers, it is to be eaten raw. Should be ground 2 times. (In a pinch, this meat can be bought the previous day. But do not expose to air until just before serving.)

1 or 2 fresh loaves black bread: Or 2 packages of the darkest pumpernickel you can find. Remember, you will need some for dessert course.

3 (13 oz.) cans vichysoisse: Plan to refrigerate several hours before serving, or buy already chilled. Must be served ice cold, but never placed in freezing compartment or against cooling coils.

1 small bunch fresh chives: For vichysoisse. Refrigerate in sealed plastic bag. *If not available,* substitute some green stems of scallions, or cut-up parsley mixed with minced onion. (Vichysoisse needs a green topping for contrast, and some manner of onion flavor.)

1 bunch fresh scallions: For steak tartare. Stems should be firm and green. Refrigerate. *If not available,* buy 1 large Spanish or Bermuda onion.

1 large bunch fresh parsley: You will need 1 cup, cut fine. (Cut 1½ cups if you have neither chives nor scallions.)

1 large or 2 small heads of crisp romaine lettuce: If not available, substitute 1 head of iceberg lettuce and 1 head of escarole.

1 or 2 (2 oz.) cans of rolled or flat anchovies: For steak tartare.

¾ *lb. black Greek olives:* For steak tartare. These are oil-cured; slightly salty. Best are sold by weight at delicatessen counters. Also available dried in jars; these need to be soaked in warm water about ½ hour to expand. *If not available,* substitute 1 (12 oz.) jar domestic black olives—pitted, if possible. Refrigerate.

1 *small (1¾ oz.) jar grated Parmesan cheese:* For Caesar salad.

½ *pt. heavy sweet cream:* You may need a little for vichysoisse.

½ *lb. whipped sweet butter.*

French dessert cheese: Choose any ripe soft-type French cheese, imported or domestic. (See page 117 for specific suggestions and cheese-buying and serving tips.) Buy a whole or a half cheese if practical; it makes a more handsome appearance than individual portions. Do not refrigerate. Must be served at room temperature. A cheese I greatly enjoy is Crema Danica. Though Danish, it resembles French brie, without being quite so acid.

Extras: 6 or 10 eggs (4 or 8 eggs for meat, 2 eggs for salad); salt; peppercorns for pepper mill; sugar and cream for coffee; drip grind coffee (breakfast blend and Italian after-dinner roast). *For Salad* — 4 or 5 slices white bread; paprika; dry mustard; 2 cloves of garlic; olive oil; vinegar.

Wine: 1 or 2 bottles Tavel (a Rhone rosé). or
1 or 2 bottles Mateus (a Portuguese rosé).

Remember you will need wine for the dessert course.

See page 111 for correct wine service and alternate selections.

what to do

1. Several hours before dining, chill vichysoisse and wine.
2. As early as possible (if not done before storing), wash parsley and salad greens: Separate leaves; rinse quickly in running cold water. Remove discolored leaves and edges. Shake well; wrap in paper towels to absorb extra moisture. Seal in plastic bag, and refrigerate until needed.
3. If using dried black Greek olives, place in warm water 1 hour before dinner. They need ½ hour to expand, and another ½ hour to chill before serving.

30 minutes before serving first course

1. Remove butter, parsley, chives and scallions from refrigerator. Do not remove ground beef. (The beauty of fine steak tartare is its fresh red color, and ground beef darkens quickly once it is exposed to air.)
2. Make croutons for salad: Cut crusts from 4 or 5 slices white bread; then cut into ¼-in. cubes. Scatter in shallow pan and brown lightly in 350° oven about 10 minutes. Stir frequently so they brown evenly; remove those that brown quickest so none scorch.
3. Clean scallions. Cut fine: white parts in one bowl; green stems in another. You need 1 cup of each for steak tartare. If you have no chives, cut an extra ¼ cup of green stems for vichysoisse.

   Or: Peel 1 large Spanish or Bermuda onion; cut quite fine.
4. Stir croutons.
5. Cut washed parsley quite fine with kitchen scissors. You will need 1 cupful for steak tartare. If you have neither chives nor scallions, cut an extra ½ cup for vichysoisse.
6. Stir croutons.
7. Fill coffeemaker: Suggest combining half breakfast blend and half Italian after-dinner roast for hearty flavor.
8. Remove croutons as soon as ready; they need not be warm for salad. Turn off oven.
9. Open vichysoisse; empty into bowl and taste. May need salt, and a little heavy whipped sweet cream to enrich it. Return to refrigerator at once to keep ice cold.
10. Cut bread into ½-in. slices if in loaf. Butter generously. Lay flat on serving plate. Or butter sliced bread well.
11. Peel 2 cloves of garlic; split in half. Rub around salad bowl or mix into French dressing.
12. Mix French dressing: Place garlic in small deep bowl with ½ tsp. paprika, ½ tsp. dry mustard, ½ tsp. salt and 3 Tbsp. vinegar. Mix well. Slowly stir in 6 Tbsp. olive oil. Taste; add more oil or vinegar for perfect balance. Set aside for salad course; do not refrigerate.

13. Cut Greek olives free of pit, keeping pieces as large as possible. Or serve whole.

    Or: Drain domestic olives; slice into rings.

just before serving
first course

14. Pour vichysoisse into 4 deep individual bowls.
15. With scissors snip a clump of washed chives into center of each serving.

    Or: Center 1 Tbsp. cut green stems of scallions on each serving.

    Or: Mix about 3 Tbsp. cut onion with enough cut parsley to give a dominant green color; center some on each serving.

serve first course

assemble main course

1. Salt chilled ground beef to taste; 1½ tsp. salt should be about right. Mix lightly with fork or fingers. Divide into 4 equal portions. Center each on individual dinner plates, and lightly shape to resemble a bird's nest. (Hollow in center should be large enough to hold 1 whole egg or 2 egg yolks.)
2. Break (or separate) each egg into a cup, then pour into place. Top each yolk with 2 rolled anchovies, or 2 flat anchovies across whole egg.
3. Surround meat with clumps of the various trimmings: cut parsley, black olives, cut green stems of scallions, and finely cut scallion tips (or cut-up onion).

serve main course

Have salt and pepper mill at table so each guest can flavor his meat as he mixes all ingredients.

Bring more buttered bread if needed.

Open chilled wine. Do not serve over ice. Fill glasses a little over halfway. Keep bottle cool.

assemble salad course

1. Coddle 2 eggs: Place 2 unbroken eggs in small saucepan with cool water. Bring to a boil; remove eggs after 1-2 minutes. Do not cook. (This will slightly coagulate whites.)
2. Break lettuce leaves into salad bowl while eggs are coddling; pieces should be approximately 2½ in. long. Salt lightly.
3. Add croutons to bowl; break eggs over all. Toss lightly.
4. Pour on 4 or 5 Tbsp. French dressing, or just enough to moisten all leaves. Do not include split garlic. Toss well.
5. Sprinkle in all of grated Parmesan cheese; toss just enough to mix in.

serve salad course

assemble dessert course

1. Turn on coffeemaker.
2. Place cheese and cheese knife on cheese tray or large plate.
3. Have buttered black bread at table.

serve dessert course

Pour more wine.

serve after-dinner coffee

If coffee was not started earlier, make last-minute coffee in a saucepan. (See page 118.) Or make one of the variations on page 118.

25 *menu for 4*

Fresh Crabmeat with Water Cress

Mixed Grill:
Beefsteak, Calves' Liver, Pork Sausages
and Bacon
Potato Chips

Sliced Tomatoes with Oregano

Bananas Flambée

Coffee

WINE:

Riesling
or
Gewurztraminer

Mixed Grill combinations can vary. Another good combination: loin lamb chops, lamb kidneys, calves' liver and bacon. Still another is a Mongolian grill which is made up of thin slices of beef, veal, chicken breast, eggplant, sweet potato, onion and green pepper, and split Belgian endive. (See page 102 for recipes for these two combinations.)

TO SUBSTITUTE:

If good fresh water cress is not available, serve avocado halves stuffed with crabmeat or tiny canned shrimp. If you wish, you may substitute beef frankfurters for the pork sausages.

what to buy

Everything except the fresh crabmeat and fresh bread may be purchased the previous day, if more convenient.

1 lb. fresh crabmeat: This is flown in cans to fine stores and fish dealers from the southeast coast. Flavor is superior to frozen. Insist on large lumps. Refrigerate. *If not available*, substitute 2 (6 oz.) packages of frozen Alaska king crabmeat. Or 4 or 5 (3 oz.) jars of tiny shrimp.

1 fresh loaf or large package dark rye or pumpernickel.

4 slices beef tenderloin: This is not the expensive filet mignon. Should be cut ½ in. thick.

4 slices fresh calves' liver: Should be cut ½ in. thick. Have butcher remove thin membrane from edge of each slice, and any bits of hard fiber inside. *If not available*, substitute ¾ lb. fresh chicken livers.

8 pre-cooked pork sausages: A ½-lb. package holds about 10. *If you prefer*, substitute 4 fairly plump beef frankfurters. For these you will need prepared mustard when serving.

8 or 12 slices bacon; thick cuts are superior.

1 large sack or box of potato chips.

2 large bunches of crisp water cress: If not available, substitute 2 large ripe avocados, and buy only ½ lb. of fresh crabmeat. (Or only 1 package of frozen crabmeat, or 2 jars of tiny shrimp.) Refrigerate.

3 or 4 large firm tomatoes, ripe for slicing: Beefsteak tomatoes are best. Refrigerate.

4 medium-sized all-yellow bananas: Should have no soft spots.

½ pt. sour cream: You will need only 1½ to 2 heaping Tbsp. for first course. Remainder will keep for days in refrigerator.

Extras: Salt; pepper; ½ lb. butter; sugar and cream for coffee; drip grind coffee (breakfast blend and Italian after-dinner roast). *For Crabmeat* — 1 lemon; ½ cup mayonnaise; Worcestershire sauce. *For Mixed Grill* — dry thyme; flour. *For French Dressing* — paprika; dry mustard; 1 clove of garlic; olive oil; vinegar. *For Tomatoes* — fresh or dry oregano. *For Bananas* — brown sugar; ⅓ cup bourbon or rum. Suggest buying sweet butter.

Wine: 1 or 2 bottles Riesling (a white Alsatian).
or
1 or 2 bottles Gewurztraminer (a white Alsatian).

See page 111 for correct wine service and alternate selections.

what to do

1. Several hours before dining, chill wine.
2. As early as possible (if not done before storing), wash water cress: Cut off most of stems. Rinse quickly in running cold water. Remove discolored leaves. Shake well; wrap in paper towels to absorb extra moisture. Seal in plastic bag, and refrigerate until needed.

30 minutes before serving
first course

1. Remove meats, butter, mayonnaise, sour cream and tomatoes from refrigerator. Unwrap meats.
2. If using frozen crabmeat, take out of carton. Leave in wrapper; immerse in cool water for about 25 minutes to thaw. If defrosted in less time, place in a bowl and refrigerate until needed.
3. Mix Seafood Sauce for crabmeat (or shrimp). Cut these amounts in half if using avocados instead of water cress: Combine 3½ to 4 heaping Tbsp. mayonnaise with half as much sour cream, a dash of salt, 1 Tbsp. lemon juice and 1 Tbsp. Worcestershire sauce. Taste. Should be slightly pungent, but not too lemony. If so, add more mayonnaise or sour cream. Refrigerate until needed.
4. Slice tomatoes thin. Carefully overlap slices on flat round platter. Sprinkle a little oregano over top. Refrigerate.
5. Mix French dressing for mixed grill and salad: Peel and split 1 clove garlic; place in small deep bowl with ½ tsp. paprika, ½ tsp. dry mustard, ½ tsp. salt and 3 Tbsp. vinegar. Mix well. Slowly stir in 6 Tbsp. olive oil. Taste; add more oil or vinegar for perfect balance. Set aside until needed; do not refrigerate.
6. Cut bread into ½-in. slices if necessary; butter generously and replace in loaf. Or butter packaged sliced bread.

7. Fill coffeemaker: Suggest combining half breakfast blend and half Italian after-dinner roast for hearty flavor.
8. Lay slices of beef and sausages (or frankfurters) in shallow pan. Lightly salt and flour liver; lay in pan. Pour 2 Tbsp. French dressing over all; sprinkle with a scant ½ tsp. dry thyme. Do not broil yet.

just before serving
first course

9. Separate crabmeat with fingers; keep lumps large. Eliminate any bits of bone you feel.
   Or: Open jars of shrimp; drain well.
10. Mix crabmeat (or shrimp) into Seafood Sauce gently so as not to break.
11. If using avocados, wash and cut in half lengthwise. Twist halves in opposite directions to separate. Remove pit and thin skin surrounding it. Salt flesh lightly; sprinkle with lemon juice to retain color.
12. Place crabmeat (or shrimp) mixture in center of round platter and surround with a thick garland of water cress.
   Or: Heap mixture into cavities of split avocados; place on 4 individual plates.

serve first course

Open chilled wine. Do not serve over ice. Fill glasses a little over halfway. Keep bottle cool.

assemble main course

1. Put 8 or 12 slices of bacon in large skillet; fry over low heat until crisp but not brittle. Drain off grease as it collects.
2. Turn oven control to "broil"; place meat pan 3 in. below high flame. Broil only 3 minutes on first side.
3. Place serving platter and dinner plates in oven to warm.
4. Spread potato chips in shallow pan.
5. Turn bacon over; watch closely from now on. Drain cooked bacon on paper towels.
6. Turn meats over; broil 3 minutes more. If cooking too fast, turn broiler flame down a bit; beef and liver should be served rare.
7. Put potato chips in oven to warm; improves them greatly.
8. Remove pan from broiler the moment beef and liver are ready or they will continue to cook even if broiler is turned off. Turn off oven.
9. Arrange meats attractively on warm platter. Pour all pan juices over. Lay bacon slices over meats. Place warm potato chips at each end.

serve main course

Pour more wine.

If serving frankfurters, pass prepared mustard.

assemble salad course

1. Salt tomatoes lightly; pour 3 or 4 Tbsp.

French dressing over all. Do not include split garlic.

2. Place platter in oven to warm for dessert course.

serve salad course

assemble dessert course

1. Melt 3-in. lump of butter in skillet while you peel 4 bananas and slice in half lengthwise. Add bananas to skillet; sprinkle with brown sugar. Cook gently 3 or 4 minutes, spooning butter over. Do not try to turn them; they break easily.

   Meanwhile: In a small attractive saucepan heat ⅓ cup bourbon or rum.

   When bananas are cooked and liquor is hot but not boiling, slide bananas onto warm platter and top with sauce in skillet.

2. Turn on coffeemaker.

serve dessert course

Bring platter of bananas, pan of steaming liquor, and dessert plates to table. Pour liquor over bananas; light at once with a match. Allow flame to die.

serve after-dinner coffee

If coffee was not started earlier, make last-minute coffee in a saucepan. (See page 118.)

26 *menu for 4*

Spaghetti with Clam Sauce

Veal Meat Balls
Vegetable Medley:
Asparagus Spears, Frenched String Beans and Tiny Peas

White Pears Baked in Wine

Coffee

WINE:

Chianti Antinori

Another tasty Italian dinner! Note that none of these dishes features the tomato sauce so often associated with Italian cooking. These meat balls have an unusually fine flavor. If you like, include them in your next hot buffet — they're always very popular. The baked pears are a good hot buffet dish, too, especially if cavities are filled with crushed macaroons, and if a bowl of freshly whipped cream stands alongside.

TO SUBSTITUTE:

No substitutions should be necessary.

what to buy

Everything except the fresh bread may be purchased the previous day, if more convenient.

1 fresh loaf Italian or French bread: Or 1 package of partially baked French bread.

1 lb. spaghetti.

1 (7½ oz.) can minced clams.

1½ lbs. freshly ground veal: Choose a piece of veal rump or shoulder. Have butcher remove all fat and grind twice.

1 package frozen asparagus spears.

1 package frozen Frenched string beans.

1 package frozen tiny peas: Sometimes these are labeled "Baby Peas" or "Petite Peas." (Unless labeled thus, peas will probably be large and not too sweet.) Canned baby peas are good eating but lack fresh green color.

1 large (6 or 8 oz.) jar grated Parmesan cheese: For spaghetti and for meat balls. Keeps well in refrigerator.

1 (3 oz.) can tomato paste: For meat balls.

2 (1 lb. 4 oz.) cans premium quality Bartlett pear halves: Each can will contain 5 to 7 pear halves; you need at least 8.

1 large bunch fresh parsley: You will need 2 cups, cut fine.

¼ lb. shallots: You will need 4 for clam sauce. *If not available,* buy 1 bunch scallions with good green stems, or 2 small white onions.

½ pt. heavy sweet cream: You will need a little for meat balls; serve the rest with coffee.

Extras: Salt; pepper; ¾ lb. butter; sugar and cream for coffee; drip grind coffee (breakfast blend and Italian after-dinner roast). *For Clam Sauce —* olive oil; 1 clove of garlic. *For Veal —* dry Marsala wine; dry basil (or oregano); 2 eggs; flour. *For Pears —* brown sugar;

1 lemon; ⅓ cup port, or dry Marsala, or dry Madeira wine. Suggest buying sweet butter.

Wine: 1 or 2 bottles Chianti Antinori (an *Italian red*).

See page 111 for correct wine service and alternate selections.

what to do

As early as possible (if not done before storing), wash parsley: Rinse quickly in running cold water. Remove discolored leaves. Shake well; wrap in paper towels to absorb extra moisture. Seal in plastic bag, and refrigerate until needed.

30 minutes before serving first course

1. Remove veal, butter, parsley, 2 eggs and frozen vegetables from refrigerator. Unwrap veal.
2. Cut washed parsley quite fine with kitchen scissors. You need 2 cupfuls — ½ cup for clam sauce, ½ cup for meat balls and 1 cup for vegetables.
3. Start meat balls:
   With a fork, lightly mix ground veal with salt, pepper, ½ cup grated Parmesan cheese, 1 Tbsp. tomato paste, 1 Tbsp. dry Marsala wine; ½ tsp. dry basil (or oregano) and 2 eggs. Taste; adjust flavor if necessary.

   Lightly shape meat into balls the size of a walnut, flouring your hands as you roll each one. Place on waxed paper until ready to cook.

20 minutes before serving first course

4. For spaghetti, put 6 qts. water and 2 Tbsp. salt in large kettle. Bring to an active boil.
5. In large skillet slowly melt 3-in. lump of butter. Do not brown. Lay in meat balls. Add butter as needed, and keep flame very low, so meat balls do not fry hard. Cover; cook gently about 5 minutes.
6. Slice bread: If a round loaf, cut into ½-in. slices, then cut loaf in half. If a long loaf, cut into 2-in. chunks. Butter slices well on one side. Then put all slices in form of loaf on bakepan, ready to heat.
7. Carefully turn meat balls with two spoons so they do not break. Add more butter if necessary so skillet is never dry. Cover; cook another 5 minutes; then turn off heat.
8. When water is boiling hard, take whole sheaf of spaghetti in your hand and push down against bottom of kettle. Sheaf becomes limp in 1 or 2 minutes. Never break spaghetti. (Broken spaghetti looks like leftovers.)
9. Stir spaghetti. Cook actively until done, anywhere from 7 to 9 minutes, depending on thickness.
10. Make clam sauce:
    In small saucepan slowly melt 3½ Tbsp. butter. Add 2 Tbsp. olive oil.
    Peel 4 shallots (or 2 small white onions) and 1 clove garlic; sliver directly into pan. Cook gently 3 minutes, or until golden. Do not brown.

Drain minced clams; save ½ cup broth. Add clams to saucepan; cook gently 2 or 3 minutes.

Add clam broth. Simmer gently until sauce comes to a boil. Taste; adjust seasoning if necessary.

Turn off heat. Mix in ½ cup cut parsley.

11. When spaghetti has boiled 7 minutes, taste: To be right, it must be cooked "al dente," as the Italians say. (Firm to the bite, but not hard.) If too hard the first time, keep tasting every minute or two until it is ready. (Watch carefully; overcooking makes spaghetti pasty and slimy.)

IMPORTANT:
The moment spaghetti is ready, drain entire kettle into a colander waiting in the sink. Never run cold water over spaghetti "to wash off starchiness," as some cookbooks suggest. (If properly cooked, there is no such starchiness.)

12. Let spaghetti drain about 1 minute; then return it to kettle, but do not cook.
13. Measure out ½ cup grated Parmesan; place the rest in small serving bowl.
14. Add clam sauce to spaghetti. With large fork and spoon, gently lift spaghetti high, then let it fall, to blend all ingredients. Continue mixing in this way, gradually adding the ½ cup grated Parmesan. Mix gently but quickly, so spaghetti does not cool too much: takes less than 2 minutes to blend all.

15. Quickly transfer spaghetti to serving bowl.
16. If using partially baked bread, place in 450° oven now. Takes about 15 minutes to bake and brown.

serve first course

Bring bowl of spaghetti to table with bowl of grated Parmesan cheese. Give each guest a soup spoon which he can use to help roll up the spaghetti on his fork. One should never cut spaghetti into small pieces.

Pour wine. Fill glasses a little over halfway.

assemble main course

1. Look at partially baked bread. If browning too fast, remove from oven for a few minutes, or turn oven down. *Or: Place fresh bread in 450° oven for 5 to 8 minutes to warm.*
2. Combine asparagus spears, Frenched string beans and tiny peas in large saucepan. Add 3-in. lump butter and ¼ tsp. salt. Cover; cook gently about 7 minutes. Look occasionally; add more butter if needed.
3. Reheat meat balls. Turn again. There should be plenty of sauce for serving, so add more butter, or 1 to 2 Tbsp. Marsala, or heavy sweet cream, or some of each. Taste sauce; adjust flavor if needed. Simmer another 5 minutes.
4. Place serving platter, bowl and dinner plates in oven to warm.

5. Open canned pears; arrange 8 halves, cavity side up, in attractive shallow baking dish. Pour half of syrup from can into baking dish.
6. Spoon meat balls onto warm platter. Mix ½ cup cut parsley into sauce; pour over meat.
7. Test vegetables with fork. If done, turn off heat. Mix in rest of cut parsley. Spoon into warm bowl.
8. Place baking dish with pears on middle rack of 450° oven.

serve main course

Place warmed bread in basket, covered with napkin.
Pour more wine.

assemble dessert course

1. Crumble brown sugar into cavities of baking pear halves. Pour on ⅓ cup port, or dry Marsala, or dry Madeira wine. Bake 1 or 2 minutes more to melt sugar.
2. Fill coffeemaker: Suggest combining half breakfast blend and half Italian after-dinner roast for hearty flavor.
3. Turn on coffeemaker.
4. Turn off oven. Taste sauce in baking dish. Season with more wine or a dash of lemon juice, if necessary.

serve dessert course

Bring baking dish and dessert dishes to table. Baste sauce in baking dish over pears when you serve.

serve after-dinner coffee

If coffee was not started earlier, make last-minute coffee in a saucepan. (See page 118.)

Mushrooms Lyonnaise

*Sautéed Calves' Liver
Mashed Potatoes*

*Sliced Tomato and
Whole String Bean Salad*

Fresh Figs

Coffee

WINE:

*Beaujolais
or
Muscadet*

Those who like calves' liver find this a delicious dinner. If the slices are the correct thickness, the manner of cooking assures you tender, delectable results. However, never serve liver unless you are absolutely sure your guests like it and are allowed to eat it.

TO SUBSTITUTE:

If fresh figs are not available, substitute canned figs heated with rum, and served with heavy sweet cream. Or the best fresh fruit in the market.

what to buy

Everything except the fresh bread may be purchased the previous day, if more convenient.

1 fresh loaf French or Italian bread: Or 1 loaf or large package of the darkest pumpernickel you can find.

1 lb. medium-sized fresh mushrooms: Should be pure white with an unbroken membrane connecting stem and cap. Refrigerate in original bag. *If not available,* buy 4 small (3 or 4 oz.) cans of sliced mushrooms.

1 large bunch fresh parsley: You will need 2½ cups, cut fine.

1 large bunch fresh chives: You will need ¼ cup, cut fine, for mushrooms. Refrigerate in sealed plastic bag. *If not available,* buy 1 bunch scallions with good green stems, or 1 large Spanish or Bermuda onion. Refrigerate scallions.

3 large firm tomatoes, ripe for slicing: Beefsteak tomatoes are best. Refrigerate.

8 large fresh figs: Should be soft. Kadota figs should be greenish yellow. Black Mission figs should be dark purple. Refrigerate. *If not available,* buy 2 (8 oz.) cans whole figs; you will also need ½ cup rum and ½ pt. heavy sweet cream.

1 large juicy orange: For fresh figs. Refrigerate.

4 slices fresh calves' liver: Should be cut ½-in. thick. Have butcher remove thin membrane from edge of each slice, and any bits of hard fiber inside.

1 package instant mashed potatoes: Buy milk if brand requires it.

1 package frozen whole string beans.

1 (6 oz.) can tomato paste: For mushrooms.

1 (10½ oz.) can of clear beef consommé: For mushrooms.

Extras: Salt; pepper; 2 cloves of garlic (1 for mushrooms, 1 for French dressing); ¾ lb. butter; sugar and cream for coffee; drip grind coffee (breakfast blend and Italian after-dinner roast). *For Mushrooms* — bay leaves; whole cloves; 4 slices white bread. *For Liver* — flour. *For French Dressing* — paprika; dry mustard; olive oil; vinegar. Suggest buying sweet butter.

*Wine: 1 bottle Beaujolais (a red Burgundy).
or
1 or 2 bottles Muscadet (a white Loire).*
See page 111 for correct wine service and alternate selections.

what to do

1. Several hours before serving, de-cork Beaujolais. You need not lay in wine basket because Beaujolais, being a young wine, has no sediment. Leave open, at room temperature, to breathe and expand. If serving white Chilean wine instead, chill well; open just before pouring.

2. As early as possible (if not done before storing), wash parsley: Rinse quickly in running cold water. Remove discolored leaves. Shake well; wrap in paper towels to absorb extra moisture. Seal in plastic bag, and refrigerate until needed.

30 minutes before serving first course

1. Remove liver, butter, frozen string beans and needed fresh vegetables from refrigerator. Unwrap liver.
2. Start salad:

   Place string beans in saucepan with 2 Tbsp. water, 1 Tbsp. butter and ¼ tsp. salt. Cover; bring to boil. Cook gently 5 or 6 minutes.

   Slice tomatoes thin. Carefully overlap slices on flat round platter, leaving room on edge for string beans. Refrigerate.

   Cut washed parsley quite fine with kitchen scissors. You need 2½ cupfuls — 1 cup for mushrooms, 1 cup for liver and potatoes and ½ cup for salad.

   Drain beans if necessary. Empty into bowl. Refrigerate.

   Mix French dressing: Peel and split 1 clove garlic; place in small deep bowl with ½ tsp. paprika, ½ tsp. dry mustard, ½ tsp. salt and 3 Tbsp. vinegar. Mix well. Slowly stir in 6 Tbsp. olive oil. Taste; add more oil or vinegar for perfect balance. Set aside until needed; do not refrigerate.
3. Start first course:

   Wipe fresh mushrooms with damp paper towel. Do not wash or peel. Discard dry ends of stems. Slice caps evenly down through stems.

   Or: Open canned mushrooms; drain well.

   In saucepan, slowly melt 2-in. lump of butter. Do not brown. Peel and split 1 clove garlic; add to saucepan with 1 bay leaf and 2 whole cloves. Cook gently 5 minutes.
4. Slice French or Italian bread: If a long loaf, cut into 2-in. chunks. If a round loaf, cut into ½-in. slices, then cut loaf in half. Butter slices well on one side. Then put all slices in form of loaf on bakepan, ready to heat.

   Or: Cut pumpernickel into ½-in. slices if necessary. Butter generously. Lay flat on serving plate.
5. Remove garlic pieces and spices from saucepan. Add sliced mushrooms; salt lightly. Cook gently 5 minutes to soften.
6. Wash chives; dry in paper towels. With kitchen scissors, cut about ¼ cup directly over mushrooms.

   Or: Clean scallions; cut about ¾ cup (white and green parts combined) directly over mushrooms.

   Or: Peel 1 large Spanish or Bermuda onion: sliver directly over mushrooms.
7. Fill coffeemaker: Suggest combining half breakfast blend and half Italian after-dinner roast for hearty flavor.

just before serving first course

8. Finish first course:

   To mushrooms, add 1 Tbsp. tomato paste and ½ cup beef consommé. Mix well; simmer gently 2 or 3 minutes.

   Cut crusts off 4 slices white bread; toast.

   Taste sauce; adjust seasoning if needed. Add 2 Tbsp. butter.

   Turn off heat; stir in a generous ¾ cup cut parsley.

   Butter toast; place on individual plates. Spoon mushroom mixture on top. Garnish with rest of parsley.

serve first course

Pour wine. Fill glasses a little over halfway. Keep white wine cool.

assemble main course

1. If serving French or Italian bread, place in 450° for 5 to 8 minutes to warm.
2. Start preparing instant mashed potatoes as directed on package.
3. Start liver:

   In large skillet (or two skillets if necessary), melt 2-in. lump of butter. Do not brown.

   Lightly salt and flour both sides of all liver slices. Lay into skillet; they should lie flat. Cook first side gently 3 minutes. Add more butter as needed, and keep flame very low, so liver does not fry hard.
4. Place large round serving platter and dinner plates in oven to warm.
5. Turn liver over; baste with pan juices. Cook gently only 3 minutes more.
6. Finish preparing instant mashed potatoes. Cover to keep warm.
7. Examine liver for rareness: Cut small gash in center of 1 slice. If too raw, cook another minute or less; look again. (Calves' liver is delicious, ten-

der and succulent if served somewhat pink inside. Overcooking dries and toughens it. So watch closely.)

IMPORTANT:

Place liver in center of warm platter the moment it is ready or the heated skillets will continue to cook it. Pour pan juices over.

8. Arrange mashed potatoes around liver; sprinkle cut parsley over all.

serve main course

Place warmed white bread in basket, covered with napkin.

Or: Bring in plate of buttered pumpernickel.

Pour more wine.

assemble salad course

1. Arrange string beans in even bunches around tomato slices. Sprinkle cut parsley generously over tomatoes.
2. Salt all lightly. Pour 4 or 5 Tbsp. French dressing over all. Do not include split garlic.

serve salad course

assemble dessert course

1. Wash and dry 8 fresh figs. Cut in half; place 4 halves on each of 4 individual plates. Squeeze fresh orange juice over all.

   Or: Prepare canned figs. Empty 2 (8 oz.) cans whole figs into saucepan.

Add ½ cup rum; heat gently. Spoon into 4 dessert dishes.

2. Turn on coffeemaker.

serve dessert course

Pass a pitcher of heavy sweet cream for canned figs.

serve after-dinner coffee

If coffee was not started earlier, make last-minute coffee in a saucepan. (See page 118.)

28 *menu for 4*

Vichysoisse

*Ratatouille Provençale
with
Pork Sausages*

*Avocado, Belgian Endive and
Water Cress Salad*

French Dessert Cheese

Coffee

WINE:

*Riesling
or
Gewurztraminer*

This is a simple, inexpensive dinner for casual entertaining. Ratatouille is a vegetable stew from Provence, in southern France. It is generally served without sausages. However, they are a good addition for a complete dish. They not only taste perfect with ratatouille; they also retain its charming provincial character. You should also know that ratatouille makes a fine vegetable specialty for hot buffets.

TO SUBSTITUTE:

Except for the salad ingredients, no substitutions should be necessary. The only seasonal ingredient in the dinner is eggplant, and you cannot make ratatouille without it. For other tasty salad combinations, see page 114.

what to buy

Everything except the fresh bread may be

purchased the previous day, if more convenient.

1 or 2 fresh loaves French or Italian bread: Or 2 packages of partially baked French bread. Remember, you will need some for dessert course.

3 (13 oz.) cans vichysoisse: Most people like generous servings. Plan to refrigerate several hours before serving, or buy already chilled. Must be served ice cold, but never placed in freezing compartment or against cooling coils.

1 small bunch fresh chives: For vichysoisse. Refrigerate in sealed plastic bag. *If not available,* substitute 1 bunch scallions with good green stems, or 1 bunch fresh parsley and 1 small white onion. (Vichysoisse needs a green topping for contrast, and some manner of onion flavor.)

1 large eggplant, or 2 small ones: For ratatouille. Choose firm ones with shiny purple skins and no rust spots. Refrigerate.

3 medium-sized fresh zucchini: For ratatouille. Should be firm, with no dark spots. Refrigerate. *If not available,* buy 2 packages frozen zucchini.

2 large green peppers: For ratatouille. Should be firm and crisp. Refrigerate.

2 large yellow onions: For ratatouille.

1 large ripe avocado: Should be soft enough to yield readily to gentle pressure from palms of hands. Refrigerate.

2 or 3 large fresh Belgian endive: Stalks should be tightly closed: white with light green tips. Refrigerate.

1 large bunch of crisp water cress.

2 (½ lb.) packages pre-cooked pork sausages: For ratatouille. Refrigerate.

1 (8 oz.) can peeled Italian plum tomatoes: For ratatouille. Get those seasoned with basil, if possible. *If not available,* buy 1 (8 oz.) can of peeled whole tomatoes.

½ pt. heavy sweet cream: You may need a little for vichysoisse.

French dessert cheese: Choose any ripe soft-type French cheese, imported or domestic. (See page 117 for specific suggestions and cheese-buying and serving tips.) Buy a whole or a half cheese if practical; it makes a more handsome appearance than individual portions. Do not refrigerate. Must be served at room temperature.

Extras: Salt; pepper; 4 cloves of garlic (3 for ratatouille, 1 for French dressing); ¼ lb. butter, sugar for coffee; drip grind coffee (breakfast blend and Italian after-dinner roast). *For Ratatouille—* olive oil; dry thyme; dry oregano. *For French Dressing —* paprika; dry mustard; olive oil; vinegar. Suggest buying sweet butter.

Wine: 1 or 2 bottles Riesling (a white Alsatian).
or
1 or 2 bottles Gewurztraminer (a white Alsatian).
Remember you will need wine for the dessert course.

See page 111 for correct wine service and alternate selections.

what to do

1. Several hours before dining, chill vichysoisse and wine.
2. As early as possible (if not done before storing), wash endive and water cress, and parsley if using it: Do not separate endive leaves. Rinse quickly in running cold water. Remove any discolored leaves and edges. Shake well; wrap in paper towels to absorb extra moisture. Seal in plastic bag, and refrigerate until needed.

30 minutes before serving first course

1. Remove sausages, butter and main course vegetables from refrigerator.
2. Start ratatouille:
In attractive casserole, heat ½ cup olive oil over medium flame on top of stove. (If casserole is earthenware, prevent cracking by using an asbestos pad over flame.)

Slice vegetables directly into casserole in this order, so each gets required amount of cooking. Mix with spoon as you go along.

Peel 2 large yellow onions and 3 cloves garlic; slice very fine.

Peel eggplant if you wish; it's not essential. Cut into 1½ in. cubes.

Wash and dry peppers; remove stems and seeds. Cut into 1 in. strips.

Wash and dry zucchini; remove stems. Do not peel. Cut into slices a good ¼ in. thick.
Or: Add frozen zucchini; do not cut up more.

Drain canned tomatoes; save juice in case you need to add liquid to casserole later. Add tomatoes to casserole. Salt and pepper all well. Stir in ½ tsp. dry thyme and ½ tsp. dry oregano.

Taste for flavor; adjust if necessary. Add a little extra olive oil if not velvety enough.

Stir in 16 or 20 pre-cooked sausages. (If you are compelled to use uncooked pork sausages, you must simmer them in water for 10 minutes to dispose of fat before adding them to casserole. Do not allow skins to break.)

Cover casserole; use heavy aluminum foil if you have no cover that fits. Cook over medium flame about 15 minutes more, stirring occasionally.

3. Slice bread: If a long loaf, cut into 2 in. chunks. If a round loaf, cut into ½ in. slices, then cut loaf in half. Butter slices well on one side. Then put all slices in form of loaf on bakepan, ready to heat.

5 minutes before serving first course

4. Open vichysoisse; taste. May need salt, and a little heavy whipped sweet cream to enrich it. Pour into 4 deep individual bowls.
5. With scissors snip a clump of washed chives into center of each serving.
   Or: Cut 1 Tbsp. washed green stems of scallions over center of each serving.
   Or: Peel 1 small white onion, cut very fine. Mix with enough cut parsley to give a dominant green color; center some on each serving.
6. If using partially baked bread, place in 450° oven now. Takes about 15 minutes to bake and brown.
7. Stir ratatouille. Prick eggplant with fork. If soft, turn off casserole; reheat before serving. Should not be mushy.

serve first course

assemble main course

1. Look at partially baked bread. If browning too fast, remove from oven for a few minutes, or turn oven off.
   Or: Place fresh bread in 450° oven for 5 or 6 minutes to warm.
2. Turn on casserole if necessary. Taste sauce; adjust if necessary.
3. Place dinner plates in oven to warm.
4. Mix French dressing: Peel and split 1 clove garlic; place in small deep bowl with ½ tsp. paprika, ½ tsp. dry mustard, ½ tsp. salt and 3 Tbsp. vinegar. Mix well. Slowly stir in 6 Tbsp. olive oil. Taste; add more oil or vinegar for perfect balance. Set aside for salad course; do not refrigerate.
5. Turn off oven; leave oven door closed.

serve main course

Place warmed bread in basket, covered with napkin.

Open chilled wine. Do not serve over ice. Fill glasses a little over halfway.

assemble salad course

1. Prepare salad:

Starting at base, cut several 1 in. sections from each endive stalk directly into salad bowl. Separate upper leaves.

Cut off excess water cress stems; place leaves in bowl.

Slit skin of avocado in 4 places; strip it off. Cutting towards center pit, slice flesh into thin crescents directly into bowl.

Salt salad lightly. Toss carefully with 4 or 5 Tbsp. French dressing, or just enough to moisten all leaves. Do not include split garlic.

2. Place extra bread in oven to warm for salad and cheese courses. Much better than crackers.

serve salad course

assemble dessert course

1. Place cheese and cheese knife on cheese tray or large plate.
2. Fill coffeemaker: Suggest combining half breakfast blend and half Italian after-dinner roast for hearty flavor.
3. Turn on coffeemaker.

serve dessert course

Refill bread basket with warm bread. Pour more wine.

serve after-dinner coffee

If coffee was not started earlier, make last-minute coffee in a saucepan. (See page 118.)

Cold Vegetables Vinaigrette

Zuppa di Pesce

Peaches Sultanes

Coffee

WINE:

Soave

or

Muscadet

This informal dinner is a delight to fish lovers. Zuppa di pesce is a stew of mixed fishes—an Italian version of French bouillabaisse. As in bouillabaisse, combinations of fish may vary, but certain ingredients are a must. In zuppa di pesce, mussels seem essential. Peaches sultanes combines pistachio ice cream, canned sliced peaches, and slivered almonds into a delectable dessert.

TO SUBSTITUTE:

No major substitutions should be necessary. However, if you do not wish to serve peaches sultanes, why not substitute an Italian cheese such as mellow Bel Paese or tangy Gorgonzola. See page 117 for cheese-buying and serving advice, and a listing of other appropriate dessert cheeses.

what to buy

Everything except the fresh fish, eel, mussels and bread may be purchased the previous day, if more convenient.

4 slices young cod (scrod): Should be 1½ in. thick.

4 slices young halibut: Should be 1½ in. thick.

1 striped bass, black bass or sea bass: Should weigh about 2½ lbs. Have dealer remove head; then clean and cut into 4 chunks.

4 fresh fish heads: For fish bouillon. Dealer will give them to you; just ask for them.

1 eel: Should be skinned and cut in 2½-in. chunks. (Eel has a sweet flavor and nice texture, but do not include it if you are prejudiced.)

16 to 20 fresh mussels: Shells should be tightly closed. Have dealer scrape very clean.

1 or 2 fresh loaves Italian or French bread: Or 2 packages of partially baked French bread. People tend to eat more bread with this dinner.

2 (4 oz.) jars marinated artichoke hearts: For first course. These are packed in olive oil, vinegar and spices. *If not available,* buy 1 (9 oz.) can of artichoke hearts packed in own liquid. Refrigerate.

1 (5½ oz.) jar marinated button mushrooms: For first course. *If not available,* buy 2 small (3 or 4 oz.) cans of button mushrooms packed in own liquid, not in a butter sauce. Refrigerate.

1 (10½ oz.) jar or can of asparagus tips: For first course. Refrigerate.

1 (8 oz.) can tomato sauce: For zuppa di pesce.

1 (1 lb. 13 oz.) can of premium sliced peaches: For peaches sultanes. Refrigerate. Or 2 boxes frozen sliced peaches.

1 large bunch fresh parsley: You will need 1 cup, cut fine.

1 small bunch fresh chives: For sauce vinaigrette. Refrigerate in sealed plastic bag. *If not available,* substitute 1 small white onion.

2 large yellow onions: For zuppa di pesce.

1 red or green pepper: For zuppa di pesce.

1½ pts. pistachio ice cream: For peaches sultanes.

1 small package of slivered toasted almonds: For peaches sultanes.

Extras: Salt; pepper; olive oil; 5 cloves of garlic (1 for sauce vinaigrette, 4 for zuppa di pesce); ¼ lb. butter; sugar and cream for coffee; drip grind coffee (breakfast blend and Italian after-dinner roast). *For Sauce Vinaigrette* — vinegar; paprika; dry mustard; fresh or dry tarragon; fresh or dry chervil. *For Zuppa di Pesce* — dry oregano; dry basil; bay leaves; 3 lemons. Suggest buying sweet butter.

Wine: 1 or 2 bottles Soave (an Italian white).

or

1 or 2 bottles Muscadet (a white Loire).

NOTE: You will need ½ cup of this white wine for cooking, unless you wish to substitute dry French vermouth.

See page 111 for correct wine service and alternate selections.

what to do

1. Several hours before dining, chill wine.
2. As early as possible (if not done before storing), wash parsley: Rinse quickly in running cold water. Remove discolored leaves. Shake well; wrap in paper towels to absorb extra moisture. Seal in plastic bag, and refrigerate until needed.

30 minutes before serving first course

1. Remove fish, eel, butter and needed vegetables from refrigerator.
2. Wash all fish, and eel, quickly in running cold water. Rewrap chunks of solid fish and eel; refrigerate until needed.
3. Make a fish bouillon: Place washed fish heads in saucepan; cover with water. Add 2 tsp. salt, 2 bay leaves, a little dry oregano and dry basil, and 1 large yellow onion, split in half. Bring to boil; cook actively for 15 minutes.
4. Prepare first course:
   Open and drain artichoke hearts, mushrooms and asparagus tips. Arrange on deep-centered platter: asparagus tips in center, artichoke hearts on one side, mushrooms on the other. Cover with 1 or 2 tsp. of artichoke or mushroom marinade to keep vegetables moist while chilling. Refrigerate until ready to serve.
   Make sauce vinaigrette (which is really a variation of French dressing): Peel and split 1 clove garlic; place in small deep bowl with ½ tsp. paprika, ½ tsp. dry mustard, ½ tsp. salt and 3 Tbsp. vinegar. Mix well. Slowly stir in 6 Tbsp. olive oil. Taste. Vinegar flavor should be slightly dominant; add more if necessary. Add 1 Tbsp. cut fresh chives (or 1½ Tbsp. finely cut onion), 1 Tbsp. cut parsley, 1 tsp. fresh or dry tarragon and 1 tsp. fresh or dry chervil. Mix well. Taste again; adjust flavor if necessary. Set aside until serving first course; do not refrigerate.
5. Slice bread: If a round loaf, cut into ½-in. slices then cut loaf in half. If a long loaf, cut into 2-in. chunks. Butter slices well on one side. Then put all slices in form of loaf on bakepan, ready to heat.

15 minutes before serving first course

6. If using partially baked bread, place in 450° oven now. Takes about 15 minutes to bake and brown.
7. Start zuppa di pesce:
   In very large attractive casserole, heat ½ cup olive oil over medium flame on top of stove. (If casserole is earthenware, prevent cracking by using asbestos pad over flame.)

   Peel 1 large yellow onion and 4 cloves garlic; remove stem and seeds from 1 pepper. Sliver all into casserole. Cook slowly, stirring occasionally, until foods are soft. Do not brown.

   Add 3 Tbsp. tomato sauce, salt and freshly ground pepper; then crumble in 1 tsp. each of oregano and basil. Mix well. Taste; sauce should have pronounced herb flavor.

   Slowly add about 2 cups hot fish bouillon, cooking and stirring constantly. After 1½ cups are added, taste to see whether sauce is a perfect blend — not too oily, not too thin and watery. Add more oil or bouillon, whichever is needed, until you have a very tasty sauce in which to cook fish.
8. Look at partially baked bread. If browning too fast, remove from oven for a few minutes, or turn oven off.
   Or: Place fresh bread in 450° oven for 5 to 8 minutes to warm.
9. Finish Zuppa di pesce:
   Lightly salt fish and eel. Squirt with lemon juice and lay into casserole, heaviest chunks on the bottom.

   Add ½ cup white wine from the bottle you are serving. (Or substitute dry French vermouth.)

   Cover casserole; use heavy aluminum foil if you have no cover that fits. Cook quite actively about 6 minutes.

   Wash mussel shells thoroughly.

   Taste sauce. With a baster, baste sauce in bottom of casserole over top layer of fish. You need plenty of sauce for serving. If necessary, combine remaining fish bouillon with a little tomato sauce, olive oil and wine. Season with pepper, oregano and basil. Taste. When flavor pleases you, add to casserole.

Lay mussels on top of fish. Cover casserole well so mussels will steam open; this takes about 12 minutes.
10. Stir sauce vinaigrette to blend well. Spoon generously over platter of chilled vegetables. Include all of cut greens, but not split garlic.
11. Turn off oven.

serve first course

Place warmed bread in basket, covered with napkin.

Open chilled wine. Do not serve over ice. Fill glasses a little over halfway. Keep bottle cool.

assemble main course

1. Place dinner plates in oven to warm.
2. Cut washed parsley quite fine with kitchen scissors. You need 1 cupful for zuppa di pesce.
3. Look at zuppa di pesce. If all mussels have steamed open, dish is ready to serve. Otherwise, recover, turn up heat and cook a few more minutes.
4. Cut 2 lemons in half; place on serving plate.
5. Taste sauce in casserole. Adjust if necessary. Sprinkle cut parsley over top.

serve main course

Bring casserole to table with plate of 4 lemon halves. With two large spoons, serve portions in the largest soup plates you have. Give each guest a portion of every kind of fish. Pile some mussels on top; then ladle over as much sauce as soup plate will hold. Each guest should have a soup spoon and fork, and a separate bowl in which to put fish bones and mussel shells.

Pour more wine.

assemble dessert course

1. Fill coffeemaker: Suggest combining half breakfast blend and half Italian after-dinner roast for hearty flavor.
2. Turn on coffeemaker.
3. Spoon ice cream attractively into dessert bowl. Pour on sliced peaches and juice. Scatter slivered almonds over top.

serve dessert course

serve after-dinner coffee

If coffee was not started earlier, make last-minute coffee in a saucepan. (See page 118.)

30 *menu for 4*

Deviled Crabs
Shashlik
Rice

Boston Lettuce Salad

Baked Rhubarb with Sour Cream

Coffee

WINE:
Tavel

Shashlik (lamb and vegetables on skewers) is now an internationally famous dish. For correct presentation, you should have four 12- or 14-in. skewers. However, if you do not have them, shashlik can be broiled just as well in a shallow pan.

TO SUBSTITUTE:

If fresh or frozen deviled crabs are not available, substitute any soup of your choice. Cream of pea soup spiked with a little dry Madeira wine is very nice. If Boston lettuce is not in the market, buy romaine, or any lettuce that looks choice. If good fresh rhubarb is not to be had, serve a fresh fruit tart. Or apples flambée.

what to buy

Everything except the fresh deviled crabs and fresh bread may be purchased the previous day, if more convenient.

4 deviled crabs: Buy fresh, from a good specialty shop if possible. Refrigerate. Otherwise, buy 4 large (or 8 small) frozen deviled crabs. Do not keep in freezer.

If substituting cream of pea soup, buy 2 (10½ oz.) cans of pea soup and 1 (10½ oz.) can of clear beef consommé, or ½ pt. milk. You will also need ¼ cup dry Madeira wine.

1 fresh loaf French or Italian bread: Or 1 package of partially baked French bread.

24 cubes of fresh lamb: Should be cut 1½ in. square, without fat. They are most tender when cut from leg of lamb. (Suggest buying a leg. Have top chops cut off; do not buy unless you want them. If some meat is left at shank end, roast it for ½ hour next day; this meat is most tender and flavorsome, so use every bit.)

1 large bunch fresh parsley: You will need 1 cup, cut fine.

4 medium-sized, firm, ripe tomatoes: For shashlik. Refrigerate.

2 large green peppers: For shashlik. Should be firm and crisp. Refrigerate.

12 small white onions. For shashlik. Should be uniform in size.

8 small fresh mushrooms: For shashlik. Very good, but not essential. Should be uniform in size; pure white with an unbroken membrane connecting stem and cap. Refrigerate in original bag.

2 heads of crisp young Boston lettuce: Or 1 head of romaine lettuce.

2 bunches fresh crisp rhubarb: Refrigerate.

If substituting a fresh fruit tart, buy the kind your pastry shop makes best. One medium-sized tart will serve 4.

If substituting apples flambée, buy 4 or 5 medium-sized tangy-flavored apples (McIntosh, Jonathans, greenings or Winesaps); should be firm, with no soft spots. Refrigerate. You will also need sugar, 1 lemon and ½ cup bourbon.

½ pt. sour cream: For baked rhubarb.

1 (14 oz.) package instant rice.

Extras: Salt; pepper; ½ lb. butter; sugar and cream for coffee; drip grind coffee (breakfast blend and Italian after-dinner roast). *For Crabs* — dry sherry wine. *For Shashlik* — dry thyme. *For French Dressing* — paprika; dry mustard; 1 clove of garlic; olive oil; vinegar. *For Rhubarb* — 1 cup sugar. Suggest you buy sweet butter.

Wine: 1 or 2 bottles Tavel (a Rhone rosé).

See page 111 for correct wine service and alternate selections.

what to do

1. Several hours before dining, chill wine.
2. As early as possible (if not done before storing), wash parsley and salad greens: Separate leaves; rinse quickly in running cold water. Remove discolored leaves and edges. Shake well; wrap in paper towels to absorb extra moisture. Seal in plastic bag, and refrigerate until needed.

30 minutes before serving first course

1. Remove frozen deviled crabs, lamb, butter, needed vegetables and rhubarb (or apples) from refrigerator. Unwrap lamb.
2. Mix French dressing for shashlik and salad: Peel and split 1 clove garlic; place in small deep bowl with ¾ tsp. paprika, ¾ tsp. dry mustard, ¾ tsp. salt and 5 Tbsp. vinegar. Mix well. Slowly stir in 10 Tbsp. olive oil. Taste; add more oil or vinegar for perfect balance.
3. Start shashlik:
Put lamb cubes in large bowl. Add each vegetable as it is prepared:

Peel 12 small white onions; do not cut up.

Wash 4 medium-sized tomatoes; cut in quarters.

Wash 2 large green peppers; cut into quarters, discarding seeds and stems.

Wipe 8 small fresh mushrooms with damp paper towel. Do not wash or peel. Cut stems even with caps. Refrigerate stems for another meal; add caps to bowl.

Salt all lightly. Scatter in ½ tsp. dry thyme. (Use no more; too much thyme creates a bitter taste.) Pour on more than half of French dressing. Mix well with spoon so all foods are well saturated. Let stand in marinade as long as possible.

Cut washed parsley quite fine with kitchen scissors. You need 1 cupful for shashlik.

4. Slice bread: If a long loaf, cut into 2-in. chunks. If a round loaf, cut into ½-in. slices, then cut loaf in half. Butter slices well on one side. Then put all slices in form of loaf on bake-pan, ready to heat.

15 minutes before serving first course

5. If using partially baked bread, place in 450° oven now. Takes about 15 minutes to bake and brown.
6. If using frozen deviled crabs, lay in shallow pan. Place on middle rack of oven; bake about 15 minutes.
7. Start dessert:
Cut green tops and dried ends off rhubarb stalks. Do not peel. Rinse quickly in running cold water; do not dry. Cut pieces to fit across an oblong baking dish; or cut them half the diameter of a large pyrex pie plate and arrange like spokes of a wheel. Cover with 1 generous cup sugar. Do not bake yet.

Or: Prepare apples for flaming: Wash and dry 4 or 5 apples. Remove stems; do not peel or core. Cut across into ¼-in. slices. Leave core intact; it helps keep slice whole and is pretty as well. In skillet, melt 3-in. lump of butter over gentle flame; do not brown. Add apple slices; sprinkle with 2 Tbsp. lemon juice to retain color. Cover with ¾ cup sugar. Cook gently 5 minutes, or until soft but not mushy. Carefully move slices around so all cook evenly. Turn off heat; re-

heat just before serving.

8. If using fresh deviled crabs, place on shallow pan. Put small lump of butter and ½ tsp. dry sherry wine into center of each. Turn oven control to "broil." Place pan 3½ in. below high broiler flame. Broil about 10 minutes. Watch so they do not dry out; add more butter if needed.

Or: Add small lump of butter and ½ tsp. dry sherry to each deviled crab baking in oven.

9. String foods on 4 long skewers, alternating them in appetizing arrangement: tomato, lamb, onion, pepper, lamb, mushroom, etc. Suspend skewers over shallow pan; pour on all of French dressing in bowl.

Or: If you have no skewers, arrange foods in shallow pan and pour all of French dressing in bowl over them.

10. Look at partially baked bread. If browning too fast, remove from oven for a few minutes.

Or: Place fresh bread in oven for 5 to 8 minutes to warm.

11. Look at deviled crabs; add more butter if needed.

Or: Blend 2 cans pea soup with can beef consommé or ½ pt. milk. Heat gently.

12. Fill coffeemaker: Suggest combining half breakfast blend and half Italian after-dinner roast for hearty flavor.
13. Arrange deviled crabs on 4 individual plates.

Or: Ladle soup into soup plates. Add 1 Tbsp. dry Madeira wine to each serving.

14. Turn off oven; leave oven door closed.

serve first course

Place warmed bread in basket, covered with napkin.

Open chilled wine. Do not serve over ice. Fill glasses a little over halfway. Keep bottle cool.

assemble main course

1. Turn oven control to "broil"; place shashlik pan 3 in. below high flame. Broil 4 minutes.
2. Start preparing 1⅔ cups instant rice as directed on package.
3. Turn skewers over; baste with pan juices. Broil 4 more minutes.

Or: Mix foods broiling in pan with a spoon. Broil 4 more minutes.

4. Finish preparing instant rice. Cover to keep warm.
5. Place serving platter and dinner plates in oven to warm.
6. Examine lamb for rareness: Look at 1 piece. If too raw, broil 1 minute or less; look again. (Lamb must be pink inside for tenderest eating.)
IMPORTANT:
Remove pan from broiler the moment lamb is ready, or it will continue to cook even if broiler is turned off.
7. Lay a bed of cooked rice on warm platter; arrange skewers (or foods in pan) attractively on top. Scatter parsley over all.
8. Spoon some of pan juices over lamb. Pour the rest into gravy boat. (If all

were poured over platter, rice would absorb all, leaving none for lamb.)
9. Turn off oven; leave oven door closed.

serve main course

Each guest takes 1 skewer and some rice; then, with his dinner fork, he pushes foods off skewer and onto his plate.
Pour more wine.

assemble salad course

1. If baking rhubarb, turn oven to 400°. Place baking dish on middle rack; bake 15 to 20 minutes. Rhubarb should be soft but not mushy.

   Or: Place serving platter for apples in oven to warm.
2. Place Boston lettuce in salad bowl; keep leaves whole if possible.

   Or: Break romaine leaves into 2½-in. lengths.
3. Salt salad lightly. Toss with 4 or 5 Tbsp. French dressing, or just enough to moisten all leaves. Do not include split garlic.

serve salad course

assemble dessert course

1. Turn off oven. Taste rhubarb. Add more sugar if needed. Empty sour cream into a bowl.

   Or: Reheat apple slices for flaming.
   Meanwhile: In a small attractive saucepan heat ½ cup bourbon. When both apples and liquor are hot, slide apples onto warm platter and top with sauce in skillet. Serve immediately.
2. Turn on coffeemaker.

serve dessert course

Serve rhubarb hot in its bake dish. Bring in bowl of sour cream separately.

Or: Serve apples flambée: Bring platter of apples, pan of steaming liquor, and dessert dishes to table. Pour liquor over apples; light at once with a match. Let flame die.

serve after-dinner coffee

If coffee was not started earlier, make last-minute coffee in a saucepan. (See page 118.)

Recipes

spaghetti alfredo

4 servings

1 lb. spaghetti
2 tablespoons salt
2½ cups (or 8 oz. jar) grated Parmesan
   cheese
5 tablespoons butter
½ cup heavy sweet cream

PREPARATION TIME:

10 minutes (for water to boil)

COOKING TIME:

7 to 9 minutes, depending on thickness
of spaghetti

1. In large kettle bring 6 qt. water and salt to a rolling boil.
2. When water is boiling hard, take whole sheaf of spaghetti in your hand and push down against bottom of kettle. Sheaf becomes limp in 1 or 2 minutes. Never break spaghetti. (Broken spaghetti looks like leftovers.)
3. Stir; cook actively until spaghetti is done, anywhere from 7 to 9 minutes.
4. After 7 minutes, taste: To be right, it must be cooked "al dente," as the Italians say. (Firm to the bite, but not hard.) If too hard the first time, keep tasting every minute or two until it is ready. (Watch carefully; overcooking makes spaghetti pasty and slimy.)
5. The moment spaghetti is ready, drain kettle into a standing colander waiting in your sink. Never run cold water over spaghetti to "wash away starchiness," as some cookbooks suggest. (If properly cooked, there is no such starchiness.)
6. Let spaghetti drain about 1 minute; then return it to kettle, but do not cook.
7. Add ½ cup grated Parmesan cheese and the butter which should be cut into 3 or 4 pieces. With large fork and spoon, gently lift spaghetti high, then let it fall, to blend all ingredients. Continue mixing in this way, gradually putting in all of heavy sweet cream and another ½ cup grated Parmesan. Mix gently but quickly so spaghetti does not cool too much.
8. Quickly transfer to warm bowl. Carry to table with bowl of additional grated Parmesan.

NOTE:

This same recipe is also successfully prepared with broad noodles instead of spaghetti. Another wonderful pasta Italians frequently use is fettuccine; do try it if you can get it at your grocer.

spaghetti with clam sauce

4 servings

1 lb. spaghetti
3½ tablespoons butter
2 tablespoons olive oil
1 clove of garlic
4 shallots
   (Or: 2 small white onions)
1 (7½ oz.) can minced clams
½ cup finely cut parsley
1¾ cups (or 8 oz. jar) grated Parmesan
   cheese

PREPARATION TIME:

10 minutes (for spaghetti water to boil)

COOKING TIME:

7 to 9 minutes, depending on thickness of spaghetti

1. Cook spaghetti as directed in Steps 1 through 5 in recipe for Spaghetti Alfredo.
2. While spaghetti cooks, slowly melt butter in small saucepan; add olive oil.
3. Peel garlic and shallots (or onions); sliver directly into pan. Cook gently 3 minutes, or until golden; do not brown.
4. Drain minced clams; save ½ cup broth. Add clams to saucepan; cook gently 2 or 3 minutes.
5. Add clam broth. Simmer gently until sauce comes to a boil.
6. Taste; adjust seasoning if necessary. Turn off heat; mix in parsley.
7. Return drained cooked spaghetti to kettle, but do not cook. Add clam sauce. With large fork and spoon, gently lift spaghetti high, then let it fall, to blend all ingredients. Continue mixing in this way, gradually adding ½ cup grated Parmesan cheese. Mix gently but quickly, so spaghetti does not cool too much. Quickly transfer to warm bowl. Carry to table with bowl of additional grated Parmesan.

NOTE:

Steps 2 through 5 may be done well in advance of serving.

cold vegetables vinaigrette

4 servings

2 (4 oz.) jars marinated artichoke hearts

(Or: 1 (9 oz.) can of artichoke hearts in own liquid)

1 (5½ oz.) jar marinated button mushrooms

(Or: 2 small (3 or 4 oz.) cans of button mushrooms in own liquid)

1 (10½ oz.) jar or can of asparagus tips

1 clove of garlic

½ teaspoon paprika

½ teaspoon dry mustard

½ teaspoon salt

3 tablespoons vinegar

6 tablespoons olive oil

1 tablespoon freshly cut chives

(Or: 1½ tablespoon finely cut onion)

1 tablespoon finely cut parsley

1 teaspoon freshly cut tarragon (or crumbled dry tarragon, if necessary)

1 teaspoon freshly cut chervil (or crumbled dry chervil, if necessary)

1 hard-boiled egg (optional)

PREPARATION TIME:

about 8 minutes

1. Open and drain artichoke hearts, mushrooms and asparagus tips. Arrange on deep-centered platter: asparagus tips in center, artichoke hearts on one side, mushrooms on the other. Cover with 1 or 2 tsp. of artichoke or mushroom marinade to keep vegetables moist while chilling. Refrigerate until serving.

2. Make sauce vinaigrette (which is really a variation of French dressing): Peel and split garlic; place in small deep bowl with paprika, dry mustard, salt and vinegar. Mix well. Slowly stir in olive oil.

Taste; vinegar flavor should be slightly dominant. Add more if necessary.

Add chives (or onion), parsley, tarragon and chervil. Mix well. Taste again; adjust if necessary. Set aside until serving time.

3. When ready to serve, stir sauce vinaigrette to blend well. Spoon generously over vegetables; be sure to include all of cut-up greens, but not split garlic. Crumble hard-boiled egg yolk over top, if you wish.

NOTE:

Steps 1 and 2 should be done well in advance of serving.

SUGGESTION:

This is a great addition to a buffet table, particularly a summer buffet with cold poached fresh salmon accompanied by a mayonnaise sauce.

eggplant parmigiana

4 servings

½ cup olive oil

2 cloves of garlic

1 large eggplant, or 2 small ones

Salt and pepper

1 (1 lb.) can peeled Italian plum tomatoes: should be seasoned with basil

½ teaspoon dry basil (or oregano)

1 cup seasoned bread crumbs

1 cup finely cut parsley

1 cup (or 3 oz. jar) grated Parmesan cheese

4 tablespoons butter

1 large Mozzarella cheese: should weigh about 1 lb.

PREPARATION TIME:

2 minutes

COOKING TIME:

about 28 minutes

1. Pre-heat oven to 450°.

2. In attractive casserole, heat a generous ¼ cup olive oil over gentle flame on top of stove. (If casserole is earthenware, use an asbestos pad over flame.)

3. While oil heats, peel garlic cloves; sliver directly into casserole.

4. Peel eggplant; cut into ⅛-in. slices. Salt and pepper; lay into casserole. Move slices around so all cook evenly until soft, about 3 minutes on each side.

5. While eggplant cooks, open tomatoes; drain well.

6. Move most of softened eggplant slices to one side. Leave only a single layer on bottom of casserole. Keep cooking as you layer on several tomatoes, a little basil (or oregano), parsley, grated Parmesan cheese and bread crumbs. Salt lightly; moisten all with 1 tsp. olive oil and dots of butter.

7. Add another identical layer, and another, each time starting with eggplant and ending with bread crumbs. Dot top layer here and there with butter and 1 or 2 Tbsp. olive oil.

8. Place on middle rack of oven. Bake for about 10 minutes.

9. Cover entire top of casserole with ¼-in. slices of Mozzarella cheese. Bake 5 minutes more to melt cheese.

into a creamy blanket. (Do not bake longer, or cheese will toughen.)

10. Serve directly from casserole, with plenty of warm French or Italian bread.

NOTE:

Steps 2 through 7 may be done well in advance of serving. However, you must allow extra baking time if casserole has cooled.

SUGGESTION:

This makes a very special buffet dish, particularly since it is not frequently encountered. Serve with tasty hot sausages or a large platter of prosciutto (thin Italian ham) and good Italian salami.

tomatoes à la provençale

4 servings

5 tablespoons olive oil
4 fairly large, firm ripe tomatoes
Salt and pepper
2 cloves of garlic
1 small bunch fresh chives
   (Or: 1 small Spanish or Bermuda onion)
½ cup seasoned bread crumbs
¼ cup finely cut parsley
1 teaspoon dry basil
¼ teaspoon dry thyme
4 teaspoons butter

PREPARATION TIME:

about 10 minutes

BAKING TIME:

15 minutes

1. Pre-heat oven to 400°.
2. Put 2 Tbsp. olive oil in an attractive shallow baking dish.
3. Wash and dry tomatoes; do not peel. Cut in half horizontally. Lay halves into baking dish, cut side up. Gash each surface with a knife to make a recess in center. Salt and pepper lightly.
4. Peel garlic cloves; sliver very finely directly into tomatoes. (Noticeable garlic flavor is good.)
5. Wash chives; dry in paper towels. With kitchen scissors, cut about 3 Tbsp. directly into a bowl.

   Or: Peel 1 small Spanish or Bermuda onion; sliver directly into a bowl.
6. Add bread crumbs, parsley, basil and thyme to cut chives (or onion). Mix well; stir in 3 Tbsp. olive oil.
7. Stuff tomatoes with bread crumb mixture. Dot each tomato half with ½ tsp. butter.
8. Place baking dish on middle rack of oven; bake 15 minutes, or until crumbs are golden, basting every 5 minutes.
9. Carry to table in baking dish. Baste juices in dish over tomatoes when serving. Pass warm French bread; juices are worth dipping up.

NOTE:

Steps 2 through 7 may be done well in advance of serving.

SUGGESTION:

In some of the French provinces, men often order this as a main luncheon dish. It is followed by a nice green salad, and cheese with French bread and fresh fruit in season.

To serve 4 for luncheon, I suggest you buy 2 extra tomatoes, and increase all other ingredients proportionately.

baked stuffed mushroom caps

4 servings

16 medium or large fresh mushrooms
   (Or: 3 small (3 or 4 oz.) cans of button mushrooms)
½ cup olive oil
1 juicy lemon
5 shallots
   (Or: 2 medium-sized white onions)
Salt
4 tablespoons butter
2 slices pre-cooked ham: only ⅛ in. thick, about 4 in. square
   (Or: 1 small (2¼ oz.) can deviled ham)
½ cup seasoned bread crumbs
⅓ cup finely cut parsley

PREPARATION TIME:

4 or 5 minutes

COOKING TIME:

about 16 minutes

1. Wipe fresh mushrooms with damp paper towel; do not wash or peel. Remove stems completely, to make a recess.
   Or: Open canned mushrooms; drain well. Remove stems.
2. In large skillet heat olive oil. Add mushroom caps; cook gently.

Squeeze a little lemon juice over caps.

3. Peel shallots (or onions); sliver into skillet. Sliver mushroom stems into skillet. Salt all lightly.
4. Pre-heat oven to 450°.
5. Continue cooking contents of skillet as you lift out mushroom caps and place them in attractive shallow baking dish, stem side up. Dot bottom of baking dish with butter.
6. Add finely cut (or canned deviled) ham to skillet; simmer 3 or 4 minutes.
7. Mix bread crumbs into skillet.
8. Taste; add more salt or lemon juice if necessary. Turn off heat; stir in parsley. Mixture should be fairly "solid."
9. With spoon, quickly mound mixture into each mushroom cap.
10. Place baking dish on middle rack of oven. After 3 minutes baste mushrooms with butter in dish. Add more butter if needed. Bake 3 minutes more.
11. Carry to table in baking dish. Serve warm French bread.

NOTE:

Steps 1 through 9 may be done well in advance of serving.

mushrooms lyonnaise

4 servings

¼ lb. butter
1 clove of garlic
1 dry bay leaf
2 whole cloves

1 lb. medium-sized fresh mushrooms
 (Or: 4 small (3 or 4 oz.) cans of sliced or button mushrooms)
Salt
1 bunch fresh chives
 (Or: 1 bunch fresh scallions, or 1 large onion)
1 tablespoon tomato paste
½ cup beef consommé
4 puff-pastry patty shells
 Buy already baked, or bake frozen patty shells ahead according to package directions.
 (Or: 4 slices white toast)
1 cup finely cut parsley

PREPARATION TIME:

1 minute

COOKING TIME:

about 13 minutes

1. In saucepan slowly melt 4 Tbsp. butter. Do not brown. Peel and split garlic; add garlic, bay leaf and cloves to pan. Cook gently 5 minutes.
2. Meanwhile, wipe fresh mushrooms with damp paper towel; do not wash or peel. Discard dry ends of stems. Slice caps evenly down through stems.
 Or: Open canned mushrooms; drain well.
3. Remove garlic and spices from butter. Add sliced mushrooms; salt lightly. Cook gently 5 minutes to soften.
4. Wash chives; dry in paper towels. With kitchen scissors, cut about ¼ cup directly over mushrooms.
 Or: Wash scallions; cut ½ cup of

green stems directly over mushrooms. Or: Peel 1 large onion; sliver directly over mushrooms.
5. Add tomato paste and consommé. Mix well; simmer gently 2 or 3 minutes.
6. Taste sauce; adjust seasoning if needed. Add 2 Tbsp. butter. Turn off heat; stir in a generous ¾ cup of parsley. If too thin, dust with flour.
7. Place warm patty shells (or buttered toast) on individual plates; fill and surround with hot mushroom mixture. Garnish with rest of parsley.

NOTE:

Steps 1 through 5 may be done well in advance of serving.

creamed mushrooms in patty shells

4 servings

¼ lb. butter
½ lb. medium-sized fresh mushrooms
 (Or: 2 small (3 or 4 oz.) cans of sliced or button mushrooms)
1 slice pre-cooked ham: only ⅛-in. thick about 4 in. square
Salt
1 scant tablespoon flour
½ cup heavy sweet cream
3 tablespoons dry Madeira wine
½ teaspoon freshly grated nutmeg
4 puff-pastry patty shells
 Buy already baked, or bake frozen patty shells ahead according to package directions.
 (Or: 4 slices white toast)
Paprika

6 minutes

COOKING TIME:
about 10 minutes

1. In saucepan slowly melt 4 Tbsp. butter. Do not brown.
2. Wipe fresh mushrooms with damp paper towel; do not wash or peel. Discard dry ends of stems. Slice caps evenly down through stems directly into saucepan.
   Or: Open canned mushrooms. Drain well; place in saucepan.
3. Salt mushrooms lightly; sprinkle in flour. Sliver in ham slice. Mix well; cook gently until all is limp, about 6 minutes. Add more butter if needed.
4. Stir in heavy sweet cream and Madeira. Grate in fresh nutmeg if you can; the powdered has no flavor so is useless. Cook gently 2 or 3 minutes so mixture thickens slightly into a nice creamy sauce.
5. Taste sauce; adjust seasoning if necessary. If sauce thickens too much, stir in a little more cream or Madeira.
6. Place warm patty shells (or buttered toast) on individual plates; fill and surround with hot creamed mushrooms. Sprinkle paprika over all.

NOTE:
Steps 1 through 4 may be done well in advance of serving.

SUGGESTION:
This is a good main dish for a summer luncheon. Follow with a water cress and Belgian endive salad, and ices or good seasonal fruit for dessert.
To serve 4 for luncheon, double quantities of everything.

seafood salad

4 servings

1 large bunch fresh water cress
1 cup (or ½ pt. jar) mayonnaise
½ cup sour cream
Salt
1 juicy lemon
2 tablespoons Worcestershire sauce
½ lb. fresh crabmeat: insist on
  large lumps
  (Or: 1 (6 oz.) package of frozen Alaska king crabmeat)
1 lb. medium-sized freshly boiled shrimp: shelled and cleaned
  (Or: 1 lb. boiled, shelled and cleaned frozen shrimp)
1 freshly boiled lobster: should weigh 2 lbs.
  Have dealer remove meat from body and claws, and place in separate container. Ask for emptied half-shells.
  (Or: 1 (2 lb.) frozen lobster, or 2 frozen rock lobster tails)

PREPARATION TIME:
about 10 minutes (once frozen foods are defrosted)

1. Cut off most of water cress stems before unfastening bunch. Separate into small handfuls; wash in running cold water. Discard injured and discolored parts. Shake well; wrap loosely in paper towels, then seal in a plastic bag. Refrigerate thus wrapped until serving.
2. Mix seafood sauce: Blend together mayonnaise, sour cream, salt, the juice of ½ lemon, and Worcestershire sauce. Taste; should be slightly pungent, but not too lemony. If so, add more mayonnaise or sour cream.
3. Separate crabmeat with fingers, keeping lumps large. Eliminate any bits of bone you feel. Mix in some seafood sauce carefully, so as not to break up lumps.
4. Rinse shrimp quickly under running cold water. Remove all visible black cords; pat dry with paper towels. Mix with some seafood sauce.
5. Mix some seafood sauce into lobster meat.
6. Heap all three mixtures tastefully into lobster shells centered on an oval platter. Chill well.
7. Just before serving, lay a wide ribbon of water cress between shells. Very attractive, and very tasty, with seafood.

NOTE:
Steps 1 through 6 may be done well in advance of serving. If you prefer, refrigerate the three mixtures separately. At serving time, arrange in separate clumps on a large round platter. Lay water cress tastefully between.

SUGGESTION:
This salad makes a splendid main course for luncheon on hot summer days. Follow

with chilled melon and iced coffee.

To serve 4 for luncheon, buy 1 extra pound of shrimp and ½ lb. more of crabmeat. There is sufficient lobster.

broiled shrimp

4 servings

2 lbs. large fresh shrimp: shelled and cleaned, but not cooked
  (Or: 2 lbs. uncooked shelled and cleaned frozen shrimp)
1 large bunch fresh chives
  (Or: 1 bunch fresh scallions, or 1 large onion)
2 or 3 cloves of garlic
3 juicy lemons
⅓ cup olive oil
1 tablespoon capers
Salt
1 cup finely cut parsley

PREPARATION TIME:
10 minutes

BROILING TIME:
10 minutes

1. Rinse shrimp quickly in running cold water. Remove all visible black cords. Pat dry with paper towels. Lay flat in shallow pan.
2. Wash chives; dry in paper towels. With kitchen scissors, cut about ¼ cup directly over shrimp.
   Or: Wash scallions; cut about ¾ cup of white and green parts combined, directly over shrimp.

Or: Peel 1 large onion; sliver directly over shrimp.
3. Peel garlic cloves; sliver very fine directly over shrimp.
4. Top shrimp with juice of 1 lemon, olive oil and capers. Salt lightly. Mix well.
5. Begin broiling only 10 minutes before serving. Place pan 3 in. below high flame of broiler. Broil 10 minutes, stirring every 3 minutes so all cooks evenly.
6. After 9 minutes taste sauce; add more lemon juice if needed. Broil shrimp 1 or 2 minutes more if not quite cooked. (But watch closely; if cooked too long shrimp toughen.)
7. Before serving, mix in parsley. (Do not cook; it will lose color.)
8. Transfer to warm platter, sauce and all. Serve with 8 quarters of lemon and warm French bread. Sauce is worth dipping up.

NOTE:
Steps 1 through 4 may be done well in advance of serving.

SUGGESTION:
You can serve this as the main course in a light summer dinner. Follow with a large fresh green salad and a cool dessert.

To serve 4 for dinner, buy 1 extra pound of shrimp and increase all other ingredients proportionately.

clams casino

4 servings

1 box of coarse salt
24 fresh cherry-stone clams on half shell
  Have dealer open clams as near dinner time as possible and pack on half shells over crushed ice.
3 juicy lemons
5 or 6 shallots
  (Or: 1 bunch fresh scallions, or 3 small white onions)
2 large green peppers
1 small (2oz.) jar or can of pimientos
Salt
1 tablespoon Worcestershire sauce
3 slices lean bacon

PREPARATION TIME:
16 minutes

BROILING TIME:
3 or 4 minutes

1. In a large attractive shallow baking pan, make a bed of salt ½ in. deep. Place clams on the half shell on top in a tasteful pattern. Flavor each clam with less than ½ tsp. lemon juice.
2. Peel shallots (or onions).
   Or: Clean white and green parts of all scallions.
3. Wash and dry peppers; remove stems and seeds.
4. Open pimientos; drain well.
5. Chop shallots (or substitute), peppers and pimientos together rather fine. Salt lightly; add Worcestershire sauce. Taste for pleasant flavor;

should not be very salty. (Bacon will provide extra salt.)

6. Mound some of mixture on each clam. Lay a small square of bacon atop each.
7. Begin broiling only 4 minutes before serving. Place baking dish 4 in. below medium high flame of broiler. Broil 2 minutes.
8. Turn baking dish around, if necessary, so all bacon cooks evenly. Broil another minute.
9. Look at bacon. If still raw, broil another minute or less; look again. (Bacon scorches quickly.)
10. When bacon is nice and crisp, but not charred, remove baking dish immediately. Place 8 quarters of lemon on bed of salt. Carry baking dish to table.

NOTE:

Steps 1 through 6 may be done well in advance of serving. If more convenient, you may put the baking dish in a 500° oven for 8 or 9 minutes.

TO SERVE CLAMS CASINO:

With his fingers, each guest lifts 6 clams and 2 lemon wedges to his plate. He does not take any salt.

scallops à la poulette

4 servings

1 lb. fresh or frozen scallops: bay scallops are more choice than sea.

Salt
Flour
¼ lb. butter
1 medium-sized white onion
1 small (3 or 4 oz.) can of sliced, not chopped, mushrooms
½ cup dry white wine or dry vermouth
2 egg yolks
½ pt. heavy sweet cream
1 juicy lemon
Worcestershire sauce
4 puff-pastry patty shells
Buy already baked, or bake frozen patty shells ahead according to package directions.

(Or: 4 slices white toast)
¼ cup finely cut parsley
Paprika

PREPARATION TIME:

about 6 minutes

COOKING TIME:

about 15 minutes

1. Rinse scallops quickly in running cold water; pat dry with paper towels. If using sea scallops cut each in half. Salt and flour lightly.
2. In skillet slowly melt 4 Tbsp. butter. Do not brown. Peel onion; sliver directly into skillet. Cook gently 3 or 4 minutes to soften. Do not brown.
3. Open mushrooms; drain well. Stir into skillet.
4. Mix scallops into skillet. Add more butter if needed. Cook gently 2 or 3 minutes.
5. Add white wine or vermouth. Cook

4 minutes.

6. Meanwhile, in a large cup beat up egg yolks with fork. Mix in most of cream, then blend all into skillet.
7. Cover; cook very gently 4 or 5 minutes so mixture thickens slightly into a nice creamy sauce.
8. Taste for flavor; add more salt, or a dash of lemon juice or Worcestershire sauce if needed. If sauce thickens too much, stir in a little more cream or wine.
9. Place warm patty shells (or buttered toast) on individual plates; fill and surround with hot scallop mixture. Garnish with parsley and paprika.

NOTE:

Steps 1 through 7 may be done well in advance of serving.

SUGGESTION:

This is an excellent main course for luncheon. Follow with a fresh green salad and a light dessert.

To serve 4 for luncheon, double quantities of everything.

sautéed oysters

4 servings

24 fresh oysters in their own liquor
(Or: 2 (8 oz.) cans small oysters)
¼ lb. butter
Salt
Cayenne pepper
1 tablespoon flour

1 tablespoon lemon juice
1 tablespoon Worcestershire sauce
½ cup heavy sweet cream
⅓ cup dry Madeira wine
4 puff-pastry patty shells
  Buy already baked, or bake frozen patty
  shells ahead according to package directions
  (Or: 4 slices white toast)
1 cup finely cut parsley
Paprika

PREPARATION TIME:

3 minutes

COOKING TIME:

10 minutes

1. Open oysters; drain well. Remove any
   bits of shell.
2. In skillet slowly melt 4 Tbsp. butter.
   Do not brown. Add oysters.
3. Salt lightly; shake on just a dash of
   cayenne pepper. Sprinkle on flour.
   Cook gently 4 or 5 minutes, until edges
   curl.
4. Stir in lemon juice and Worcestershire
   sauce. Add more butter if needed. Stir
   in heavy sweet cream and Madeira;
   cook gently 4 or 5 minutes so mixture
   thickens slightly into a nice creamy
   sauce.
5. Taste sauce; adjust seasoning if
   needed. If sauce thickens too much,
   stir in a little more cream or Madeira.
6. Turn off heat; stir in a generous ¾
   cup of parsley.
7. Place warm patty shells (or buttered
   toast) on individual plates; fill and

surround with hot oyster mixture. Garnish with rest of parsley and a sprin-
kling of paprika.

NOTE:

Steps 1 through 4 may be done well in
advance of serving.

SUGGESTION:

This makes a fine main course for a summer dinner, or an excellent hot buffet
dish. In either case, eliminate the patty
shells in favor of good French bread. Add
a large mixed salad, and serve cheese
and/or fresh fruit tarts for dessert.

To serve 4 for dinner, double the quantities.

For buffets, quantities would depend on
the number of guests. The dish is particularly handsome served in a large oblong
copper baking dish over alcohol burners
or an electric hot plate.

MAIN COURSE

filet of beef limousin

4 servings

2 lbs. filet of beef: same cut as filet mignon. Keep in 1 piece; do not have fat
  wrapped around.
¼ lb. pure white salt pork
  Have cut into ¼-in. strips, 2¼ in. long.
Salt
6 tablespoons butter
1 small (2 or 3 oz.) can paté de foie gras:
  least expensive variety.
  (Or: 1 small can liver paté)
¼ cup heavy sweet cream
½ cup dry Madeira wine

PREPARATION TIME:

7 minutes

ROASTING TIME FOR "RARE":

about 10 minutes

1. Pre-heat oven to 500°.
2. Lard filet on top side in 10 or 12
   places. Very easy; just make a 2-in.
   deep gash with a slim knife and slip
   in a strip of salt pork along knife
   blade. Salt filet lightly.
3. In roasting pan lightly brown butter
   on top of stove. Place filet in pan;
   then place pan on middle rack of
   oven. Roast 5 minutes.
4. While filet roasts, open can of paté
   and mash smooth with heavy sweet
   cream.
5. Stir Madeira into pan juices. Baste
   filet well; roast about 5 minutes
   more.
6. Meanwhile, blend some of pan juices

into paté to thin it to the consistency of very heavy cream.

7. Examine filet for rareness: Cut gash in center with small knife. If too raw, cook only another minute; look again. (There is no greater calamity than an overcooked filet.)
8. Remove filet from oven the moment it is ready. Let stand at room temperature a few minutes before carving.
9. Carve in pan, into slices ¼-in. thick.
10. Arrange on warm platter. Pour a little paté sauce around meat, not over it. Serve rest of sauce separately.

NOTE:
Steps 2 and 4 may be done well in advance of serving.

tournedos of beef
4 servings

¼ lb. butter
¼ lb. butter
6 shallots
   (Or: 1 bunch fresh scallions, or 3 small white onions)
Salt
4 filets of beef (filet mignon): each at least 1½ in. thick. Do not have fat wrapped around them. Ask; it may be less expensive to buy the filet in 1 piece and cut it yourself.
1 tablespoon Worcestershire sauce
4 tablespoons dry Madeira wine
1 heaping teaspoon dry tarragon
½ cup fine cut parsley

PREPARATION TIME:
8 minutes

COOKING TIME FOR "RARE":
5 or 6 minutes

1. Wipe mushrooms with damp paper towel; do not wash or peel. Cut stems even with caps so mushrooms retain shape while cooking; refrigerate stems. In small saucepan melt 2 Tbsp. butter; add mushroom caps. Cover; cook slowly about 8 minutes. Add more butter during cooking if necessary.
2. In large skillet slowly melt 3 Tbsp. butter. Do not brown.
3. Peel shallots (or onions); sliver directly into skillet.
   Or: Wash scallions: cut a good ½ cup of white and green parts combined, directly into skillet.
4. Cook shallots (or substitute) gently 3 or 4 minutes to soften. Do not brown.
5. Salt filets lightly on both sides; place in skillet.
6. Add Worcestershire sauce, and more butter if needed. (It is correct to continue adding butter as you go along; keeps butter from turning brown and makes foods succulent, not greasy.) Cook 3 minutes on first side.
7. Look at mushrooms; add 1 Tbsp. Madeira, and more butter if necessary.
8. Turn filets over; add 3 Tbsp. Madeira and the tarragon. Mix well. Baste filets with this sauce; cook 2 minutes more.

9. Examine for rareness: Make small cut in center of 1 filet. If too raw, cook only another minute; look again. (Beef can overcook in very little time.)
10. Place filets on warm platter the second they are ready, or the heated skillet will continue to cook them.
11. Taste sauce for flavor; adjust if necessary. Turn off heat; mix in parsley.
12. Top each filet with a mushroom cap; pour sauce over.

NOTE:
Steps 1 through 4 may be done well in advance of serving.

VARIATION:
TOURNEDOS ROSSINI: Instead of mushroom caps, top each filet with a slice of paté de foie gras. Very French, very good.

broiled porterhouse steak
4 servings

1 Porterhouse steak: nearly 2 in. thick, with a small tail. Have butcher remove tail, cut off fat and grind twice for use next day.
2 teaspoons Bahamian or Dijon mustard
⅓ cup Worcestershire sauce
2 tablespoons French dressing. (See page 116)
   (Or: 2 Tbsp. olive oil)
3 tablespoons butter
1 cup finely cut parsley

4 minutes

BROILING TIME FOR "RARE":

about 10 minutes

1. Remove steak from refrigerator several hours ahead of broiling if possible, so it can acquire room temperature.
2. Lay in shallow pan. Do not salt. Spread thin layer of mustard on both sides. Pour over Worcestershire sauce and French dressing (or olive oil). Dot in 4 or 5 places with small lumps of butter.
3. Begin broiling only 10 minutes before serving. Place pan 3½ in. below high flame of boiler. Broil first side 6 or 7 minutes to brown.
4. Turn steak over; baste with pan juices. Broil only 3 minutes. (If using the ground tail meat to supplement portions of the steak, place it under broiler now so it will not overcook. If necessary, it can continue cooking while you carve.)
5. Examine steak for rareness: Make small cut in center. If too raw, cook only 1 minute; look again. (Watch carefully; even 1 minute of extra cooking can make steak grey and tough.)
6. Remove from broiler the second it is ready or it will continue to cook even if broiler is turned off.
7. Carve steak in pan, then slide onto warm platter, bone and all, so shape of steak is retained. (If you prefer to carve at the table, remember knife cuts can ruin a silver platter.)
8. After transferring steak to platter, de-

corate with a thick ribbon of parsley. Pour pan juices over.

NOTE:

Steps 1 and 2 should be done well in advance of serving.

TO CARVE A PORTERHOUSE STEAK:

1. Use a sharp knife. Cut closely around bone to release both areas of meat: the small, which is the filet, and the large, called the contre filet.
2. Then, holding the knife slightly slanted away from you, cut each area crosswise (across the grain) into slices 1 in. thick.

TO SERVE A PORTERHOUSE STEAK:

1. Individual steak knives are a "must."
2. Each guest should be given a portion of the filet, the contre filet, and the ground tail meat, if you are serving it. Offer end slices to those who want steak less rare.
3. Ladle platter juices over each portion.

steak au poivre

4 servings

1 jar cracked black pepper
  (Or: 1 box black peppercorns)
Salt
4 large shell steaks: each only ½ in. thick.
  (Or: 4 small T-bone steaks, each only ½ in. thick)

¼ lb. butter
4 tablespoons olive oil
¼ cup dry vermouth
2 tablespoons cognac

PREPARATION TIME:

6 minutes

COOKING TIME FOR "RARE":

4 or 5 minutes

1. If using whole peppercorns instead of cracked pepper, place in small plastic bag, or between two dry paper towels, and press hard with rolling pin. Pieces should be larger than coarsest grinding of a pepper mill.
2. Salt steaks lightly. Press cracked pepper into both sides with heel of your hand.
3. In each of two skillets, melt 2 Tbsp. butter. Add 2 Tbsp. olive oil.
4. When oil is hot, lay in steaks. Cook over medium flame, about 2 minutes on first side.
5. Turn over. Add more butter if needed; skillets should not be dry. Cook 2 minutes more.
6. Add vermouth and cognac; blend well.
7. Examine for rareness: Make small gash in center of 1 steak. If too raw, cook 1 minute or less; look again. (Steak this thin cooks in very little time.)
8. Place steaks on warm platter the second they are ready, or the heated skillets will continue to cook them.
9. Taste sauce for flavor; adjust if necessary. Pour over steaks.

NOTE:

Steps 1 and 2 may be done well in advance of serving.

steak diane

4 servings

Salt and pepper
20 slices beef tenderloin: each should be
    ¼-in. thick.
¼ lb. butter
2 tablespoons Worcestershire sauce
½ cup bourbon or dry Madeira wine
1 cup finely cut parsley

PREPARATION TIME:

about 2 minutes

COOKING TIME:

4 or 5 minutes

1. Salt and pepper meat lightly on both sides.
2. In large skillet slowly melt 6 Tbsp. butter. Do not brown. Lay in meat; cook gently 3 or 4 minutes, turning slices over carefully. Add more butter as needed; skillet should not be dry.
3. Add Worcestershire sauce and bourbon or Madeira. Swish all around to blend well.
4. Taste sauce for flavor; adjust if necessary.
5. Place meat on warm platter; sprinkle with cut parsley. Pour sauce over.

NOTE:

Step 1 may be done well in advance of serving.

beef stroganoff

4 servings

Salt and pepper
1½ lbs. beef tenderloin; have cut into
    ½-in strips, 4½-in. long
Flour
¼ lb. butter
1 large onion
4 heaping tablespoons sour cream
1 juicy lemon
1 bunch fresh dill
    (Or: 1 bunch fresh parsley)

PREPARATION TIME:

2 or 3 minutes

COOKING TIME:

about 7 minutes

1. Salt and pepper beef strips; flour lightly all over.
2. In large skillet, slowly melt 6 Tbsp. butter. Do not brown.
3. Peel large onion; grate (do not sliver) directly into skillet. Lay in beef strips.
4. Cook gently 4 minutes, turning beef over with large spoon. Add more butter as needed: skillet should not be dry.
5. Stir in sour cream. With scissors snip fresh dill (or parsley) into skillet; stir to mix in. Cook gently 2 minutes more to blend well. Do not let cream boil.
6. Taste for flavor; adjust if necessary. You may wish to add salt or a squeeze of lemon juice.
7. Transfer all to warm platter; snip more fresh dill (or parsley) over top.

NOTE:

Step 1 may be done well in advance of serving.

hamburgers light and juicy

4 servings

2 lbs. freshly ground beef: top sirloin or
    top round
    Have butcher remove all fat; grind
    twice.
1½ to 2 teaspoons salt
2 tablespoons Bahamian or Dijon mustard
¼ lb. butter
2 tablespoons Worcestershire sauce
1 cup finely cut parsley

PREPARATION TIME:

6 minutes

COOKING TIME FOR "RARE":

8 minutes

1. Season ground beef with 1½ tsp. salt and the mustard. Mix very lightly with fork or fingers; handle as little as possible or hamburgers will be tough. Taste; add more salt if needed.
2. In large skillet, slowly melt almost 4 Tbsp. butter while you lightly form 4 hamburgers in the shape of a large sweet potato. Do not pack meat; it will not be as juicy when cooked. Stick a small lump of butter into top of each.
3. Add Worcestershire sauce to melted butter. Lay hamburgers carefully into butter so they keep their shape.

4. Cook over medium flame, basting constantly. Add butter as needed so skillet is never dry. Do not attempt to turn hamburgers over; they might fall apart. Constant basting will cook them so they are hot inside although still rare.
5. Peek at center occasionally. Do not overcook; they must be a little rare to be juicy.
6. When cooked, lift from skillet with two large spoons; top with parsley and pour pan juices over.

steak tartare

4 servings

¾ lb. black Greek olives: sold in bulk at delicatessen counters

(Or: 1 (8 oz.) jar or can pitted domestic black olives)

1 bunch fresh scallions with good green stems

(Or: 1 large Spanish or Bermuda onion, and ½ cup fresh celery leaves from center of the bunch)

2 lbs. freshly ground beef: top sirloin or top round

Have butcher remove every trace of fat; tell him meat is to be eaten raw. Should be ground twice.

4 whole eggs or 8 egg yolks

1 small can flat or rolled anchovies

1 cup finely cut parsley

PREPARATION TIME:

about 10 minutes

1. Cut Greek olives free of pit, keeping pieces as large as possible.
   Or: Drain domestic olives; slice into rings.
2. Wash scallions. Cut fine: white parts in 1 pile, slivered green stems in another. Wash celery leaves. Cut fine.
   Or: Peel onion; cut fine. Do not mix with celery leaves.
3. Divide chilled ground beef into 4 equal portions. Salt lightly. Center each portion on a dinner plate, gently shaping it to resemble a bird's nest. Hollow in center should be large enough to hold 1 whole egg or 2 egg yolks.
4. Break (or separate) each egg into a cup, then carefully pour into place. Top each yolk with 2 rolled anchovies, or 2 flat anchovies laid crisscross.
5. Surround meat with clumps of the various trimmings: parsley, sliced olives, cut green stems of scallions (or celery leaves) and cut scallion tips (or onion).
6. Have salt and a pepper mill on table so each guest can flavor his meat as he mixes all ingredients. Delicious served with well-buttered black bread or pumpernickel.

NOTE:

Steps 1 and 2 may be done well in advance of serving. Do *not* shape meat until just before serving; raw ground beef discolors quickly once it is exposed to air.

ham in cream sauce

4 servings

4 tablespoons butter

3 tablespoons flour

Salt

½ pt. light sweet cream, or 1 cup milk

1 teaspoon dry tarragon

¼ cup dry Madeira wine

2 center slices ready-to-eat ham: each ⅜ in. thick.

½ cup finely cut parsley

PREPARATION TIME:

about 5 minutes (to make cream sauce)

COOKING TIME:

about 10 minutes

1. In large skillet make a tasty cream sauce: Melt butter over gentle flame; do not brown. Turn flame very low; stir in flour and dash of salt to make a smooth paste. Slowly pour in cream or milk as you continue to stir to keep everything smooth. If mixture starts to lump, remove skillet from heat and work out lumps with spoon. Then continue as before.
2. When sauce has thickened slightly, crumble in tarragon and slowly stir in Madeira. Taste for flavor; adjust if necessary.
3. Cut each ham slice in half; lay into sauce. Cook very gently until ham is heated through, about 10 minutes. If sauce thickens too much, stir in more Madeira, or cream or milk.
4. Place ham on warm platter; pour

cream sauce over. Decorate with parsley.

NOTE:

Steps 1 and 2 may be done well in advance of serving.

sautéed veal cutlet

4 servings

2 slices milk-fed veal cutlet: each should
    be ½ in. thick
Salt
Flour
½ lb. butter

PREPARATION TIME:

1 minute

COOKING TIME:

about 11 minutes

1. Cut each cutlet in half; lightly salt and flour both sides of all pieces.
2. In large skillet slowly melt 6 Tbsp. butter. Do not brown. Lay in veal; cook first side 4 or 5 minutes over medium flame. Baste occasionally with butter. Do not brown.
3. Turn veal over. Add more butter if necessary. There should always be enough to bubble in skillet. Baste butter over veal often to keep it succulent. Cook about 5 minutes more.
4. Examine for doneness: Make small cut in center of 1 piece. For tenderest eating, veal should be faintly pink inside, not white.

5. Place on warm platter; pour pan juices over.

NOTE:

Step 1 may be done well in advance of serving.

veal parmigiana

4 servings

2 slices milk-fed veal cutlet: each should
    be ½- to ¾-in. thick
Salt
2 eggs
1 cup seasoned bread crumbs
*3 level tablespoons grated Parmesan
    cheese*
½ lb. butter
*1 large Mozzarella cheese: should weigh
    less than 1 lb.*

PREPARATION TIME:

5 minutes

COOKING TIME:

11 minutes

1. Cut each cutlet in half; lightly salt both sides of all pieces.
2. Break eggs into shallow bowl; with a fork, beat in 2 Tbsp. cold water until all is well mixed.
3. In small shallow pan, mix bread crumbs with 3 Tbsp. grated Parmesan cheese.
4. Dip each slice of veal into beaten egg to moisten both sides; then coat well with crumbs. Place on waxed paper

until ready to cook.
5. In large skillet slowly melt 6 Tbsp. butter. Do not brown. Lay in veal; cook first side 4 minutes over medium flame. Do not brown.
6. Turn veal over. Add more butter if necessary. There should always be enough to bubble in skillet, and bread crumbs absorb a great deal. Cook 4 minutes more.
7. Lay ¼-in. slices of Mozzarella cheese over veal, covering completely. Cover skillet; cook gently about 3 minutes to melt cheese into a creamy blanket. (Do not cook longer or Mozzarella will toughen.)
8. Serve directly from skillet, or slide entire contents to warm platter. Melted Mozzarella is very stringy and hard to cut apart.

NOTE:

Steps 1 through 4 may be done well in advance of serving.

veal scalloppine al marsala

4 servings

½ lb. medium-sized fresh mushrooms
    (Or: 2 small (3 or 4 oz.) cans of sliced,
    not chopped, mushrooms)
Salt
Flour
*20 slices milk-fed veal: each should be
    paper thin, about 2¼ in. square*
½ lb. butter
½ cup dry Marsala wine
1 cup finely cut parsley

PREPARATION TIME:

about 6 minutes

COOKING TIME:

5 minutes

1. Wipe mushrooms with damp paper towel; do not wash or peel. Discard dry ends of stems. Slice caps evenly down through stems.
   Or: Open canned mushrooms; drain well.
2. Salt and flour veal lightly on both sides.
3. In large skillet slowly melt 6 Tbsp. butter. Do not brown. Lay in veal; cook gently 2 minutes on first side.
4. Turn veal over; it should not be browned, but kept white for tenderness. Add more butter as needed; skillet should not be dry.
5. Stir in sliced mushrooms and Marsala; cover and cook gently about 2 minutes more.
6. Taste sauce for flavor; adjust if necessary. Turn off heat; mix in parsley.
7. Place veal on warm platter; pour sauce and mushrooms over.

NOTE:

Steps 1 and 2 may be done well in advance of serving.

NOTE:

Scallopine can be cut from the loin, the leg or the rump of the veal. First two cuts are much too costly. Country butchers may have only the rump which is perfectly good eating if veal is white and tender. Butcher cuts slices as thin as he can, lays them between sheets of butcher's paper, then beats them thin with flat side of his cleaver.

VARIATION:

Use only ¼ lb. fresh mushrooms, or 1 small can. Instead of the Marsala, add 4 heaping Tbsp. sour cream. Do not let cream boil. Just before serving, add a scant ⅓ cup cognac or bourbon, and perhaps a squeeze of lemon juice. Transfer to warm platter; sprinkle a little paprika here and there for good looks.

saltimbocca alla romana

4 servings

Salt
Flour
8 slices milk-fed veal: each should be ¼ in. thick, about 4 in. square
¼ lb. butter
½ teaspoon dry sage
8 slices pre-cooked ham: each should be ¼ in. thick, same size as veal
½ cup dry vermouth

PREPARATION TIME:

3 minutes

COOKING TIME:

7 minutes

1. Salt and flour veal lightly on both sides.
2. In large skillet slowly melt 6 Tbsp. butter. Do not brown. Lay in veal; cook gently 3 minutes on first side.
3. Turn veal over. Crumble a little sage over each slice.
4. Place ham slices into skillet; cook gently 2 minutes.
5. Turn ham slices over. Lay a veal slice on each ham slice. Baste with butter. Add more butter if needed; skillet should not be dry.
6. Pour in vermouth. Cover; cook gently 2 or 3 minutes more.
7. Taste sauce for flavor; adjust if necessary.
8. Transfer veal and ham combination to warm platter intact; pour sauce over.

NOTE:

Step 1 may be done well in advance of serving.

veal meat balls

4 servings

1½ lbs. freshly ground veal: should be from rump or shoulder. Have butcher remove all fat; grind twice.
Salt and pepper
½ cup (or 1¾ oz. jar) grated Parmesan cheese
1 tablespoon tomato paste
2 to 3 tablespoons dry Marsala wine
½ teaspoon dry basil (or oregano)
2 eggs
Flour
½ lb. butter
Heavy sweet cream (optional)
½ cup finely cut parsley

COOKING TIME:

about 15 minutes

1. With a fork, lightly mix ground veal with salt, pepper, ½ cup grated Parmesan cheese, tomato paste, 1 Tbsp. Marsala, basil (or oregano) and eggs. Taste; adjust flavor if necessary.
2. Lightly shape meat into balls the size of a walnut, flouring your hands as you roll each one. Place on waxed paper until ready to cook.
3. In large skillet, slowly melt 6 Tbsp. butter. Do not brown. Lay in meat balls. Add butter as needed, and keep flame very low so meat balls do not fry hard. Cover; cook gently about 5 minutes.
4. Carefully turn meat balls with two spoons so they do not break. Add more butter if necessary so skillet is never dry. Cover; cook another 5 minutes.
5. Turn meat balls again. There should be plenty of sauce for serving, so add more butter, or 1 to 2 Tbsp. Marsala, or heavy sweet cream, or some of each. Taste sauce; adjust flavor if needed. Simmer another 5 minutes.
6. Spoon meat balls onto warm platter. Mix parsley into sauce; pour over meat.

NOTE:

Steps 1 through 4 may be done well in advance of serving.

97

chicken à la vallée d'auge

4 servings

½ lb. butter
6 shallots
(Or: 3 small white onions)
Salt
Flour
4 large chicken breasts: have split in half, to make 8 pieces
(Or: 2 young broilers, cut up. Thighs and drumsticks may also be used; but, being less tender, they require 20 minutes of extra cooking.)
1 tsp. dry tarragon
½ cup Calvados or American applejack
(Or: ½ cup cognac)
3 medium-sized fresh mushrooms
(Or: 1 small (3 or 4 oz.) can of sliced or button mushrooms)
½ cup dry white wine or dry vermouth
½ pt. heavy sweet cream
1 cup finely cut parsley

PREPARATION TIME:

about 1 minute

COOKING TIME:

about 30 minutes

1. In attractive casserole, melt 6 Tbsp. butter over gentle flame on top of stove. (If casserole is earthenware, use an asbestos pad over flame.)
2. While butter melts, peel shallots (or onions); sliver directly into casserole. Cook gently 3 or 4 minutes to soften. Do not brown.
3. Salt and flour chicken lightly on all sides; lay into casserole, skin side down. Cook gently. When light golden brown, turn pieces over; brown other side. Add extra butter as needed; flour absorbs butter.
4. Scatter tarragon over chicken. Pour in Calvados or applejack (or cognac). Cognac will alter the flavor of the dish, but is a delicious substitute if necessary.
5. While liquor heats (will take about 2 minutes), wipe fresh mushrooms with damp paper towel; do not wash or peel. Discard dry ends of stems. Slice caps evenly down through stems. Add later.

Or: Open canned mushrooms; drain well.

6. Put a lighted match to surface of casserole. Hot liquor will flame; a delicious brandied apple flavor will remain.
7. When flame dies, add white wine or vermouth and mushooms. Mix well. Cover casserole; use heavy aluminum foil if you have no cover that fits. Cook gently about 5 minutes.
8. Stir in ½ cup heavy sweet cream. Continue cooking over very low flame about 10 minutes more.
9. Taste sauce; adjust flavor if necessary. Simmer a few minutes more.
10. Just before serving, sprinkle parsley over surface. Serve directly from casserole.

NOTE:

Steps 1 through 7 may be done well in advance of serving.

VEAL A LA VALLEE D'AUGE:

Instead of chicken, use 20 slices of milk-fed veal; each should be paper thin, about 2¼ in. square. Sautée shallots (or onions). Salt and flour veal. Cook veal only 2 minutes on each side; add mushrooms when you turn veal over. Proceed as for chicken in Steps 4 to 6. When flame dies, add white wine or vermouth. Stir in well; then add ½ cup heavy sweet cream. Simmer gently only a few minutes to blend flavors. Sprinkle parsley over surface. Serve directly from casserole. Entire dish takes only about 15 minutes to prepare, because these thin veal slices cook so quickly.

breasts of chicken tarragon

4 servings

4 large chicken breasts; have split in half, to make 8 pieces.

(Or: 2 young broilers, cut up. Thighs and drumsticks may also be used; but being less tender, they require 20 minutes of extra cooking.)

½ lb. butter
1 medium-sized white onion
Salt
1 heaping tablespoon fresh tarragon leaves

(Or: 2½ teaspoons dry tarragon, the most aromatic you can find)

PREPARATION TIME:
about 1 minute

COOKING TIME:
about 30 minutes

1. In attractive casserole, melt 6 Tbsp. butter over gentle flame on top of stove. (If casserole is earthenware, use an asbestos pad over flame.)
2. While butter melts, peel onion; sliver directly into casserole. Cook gently 3 or 4 minutes to soften. Do not brown.
3. Salt chicken lightly on all sides; lay into casserole, skin side down. Cook gently. When light golden brown, turn pieces over; brown other side. Add extra butter as needed.
4. If using dry tarragon, scatter over chicken. Do not add fresh tarragon yet.
5. Cover casserole; use heavy aluminum foil if you have no cover that fits. Cook gently about 15 minutes, basting occasionally with juices in bottom. Add extra butter if needed; casserole must not be dry.
6. If using fresh tarragon, scatter over chicken only after casserole has been removed from stove. Baste with juices in bottom. (Although dry tarragon can take any amount of cooking, fresh tarragon loses all flavor if cooked.)
7. Serve directly from casserole.

NOTE:

Steps 1 through 4 may be done well in advance of serving. If more convenient, you may put the casserole in a 400° oven after it is covered, and bake for 30 minutes. (Oven roasting is always slower than top-of-stove cooking.)

I. WITH BELGIAN ENDIVE: After chicken is golden brown, add 8 small whole endive, or 4 large endive split in half lengthwise. Omit all tarragon; add 2 Tbsp. Worcestershire sauce and ½ tsp. dry thyme. Roast as above. Just before serving, sprinkle on 1 cup finely cut parsley.

II. WITH MUSHROOMS, ARTICHOKES AND WATER CHESTNUTS: After chicken is golden brown, add 1 (6 oz.) can of drained button mushrooms, 1 (9 oz.) can of drained artichoke hearts, and 1 (5 oz.) can of drained water chestnuts. Add 1½ tsp. dry tarragon (instead of 2½ tsp.). Roast as above. Just before serving, sprinkle on 1 cup finely cut parsley.

III. WITH PAPRIKA AND SOUR CREAM: After chicken is golden brown, add about 2 tsp. paprika. Omit all tarragon. Roast as above. Ten minutes before serving, add 3 to 4 heaping Tbsp. sour cream; stir to make a sauce. Excellent served over boiled rice.

IV. WITH CELERY AND GREEN OLIVES: Use olive oil instead of butter. After chicken is golden brown, add ½ tsp. dry sage, 12 celery stalks 3 in. long, and 2 slices of uncooked lean bacon, cut in half. Omit all tarragon. Just before serving, drain 1 (6 oz.) jar of pitted, unstuffed green olives; add to casserole. Touch of Worcestershire sauce is good.

V. WITH VEAL AND CHICKEN LIVERS: Use only 2 breasts, split in half. After chicken is golden brown, add 4 slices of veal, cut ¼ in. thick, about 2¾ in. square. Sprinkle in 1 tsp. dry tarragon (instead of 2½ tsp.). Roast as above. Ten minutes before serving, add 4 chicken livers cut in half, then salted and floured. Keep chicken livers slightly rare for best eating. Five minutes of cooking at end is better than ten.

petti di pollo

4 servings

Salt
Flour
16 slices uncooked chicken breast: each only ⅛-in. thick. Buy enough breasts to provide these slices; have butcher cut them.
½ lb. butter
½ pt. heavy sweet cream
1 to 2 tablespoons cognac
1 juicy lemon

PREPARATION TIME:

about 3 minutes

COOKING TIME:

7 to 9 minutes

1. Salt and flour chicken slices lightly on both sides.
2. In large skillet slowly melt ¼ lb. butter. Do not brown. Lay in chicken. Cook first side 2 or 3 minutes over medium flame. Do not brown.
3. Turn chicken over. Add more butter if needed; skillet should not be dry. Cook another 2 or 3 minutes.
4. Add heavy sweet cream. Stir to blend; cook gently 3 minutes to thicken.

5. Stir in 1 Tbsp. cognac for special flavor.
6. Taste sauce for seasoning. Add salt, or dash of lemon juice, or more cognac if necessary.
7. Place chicken on warm platter; pour sauce over.

NOTE:

Step 1 may be done well in advance of serving.

luscious broiled chicken

4 servings

2 fresh broilers: each should weight 2½ to 2¾ lbs. Have butcher split in half.
Salt
3 or 4 tablespoons French dressing (See page116)
½ lb. butter
1 juicy lemon
1 cup finely cut parsley

PREPARATION TIME:

about 4 minutes

BROILING TIME:

about 30 minutes

1. Salt chicken lightly on both sides. Tuck wing tips under wings to prevent them from scorching.
2. Lay in shallow pan, skin side up. Pour French dressing over all; dot each broiler half with 2 or 3 small pieces of butter.
3. Begin broiling 25 to 30 minutes before serving. Place pan 4 in. below high

broiler flame. Broil 12 minutes, or until skin is a dark golden brown. Do not scorch. Baste every few minutes with pan juices; add more butter if necessary.
4. Turn chicken over; baste well with pan juices, filling the cavities. Add more butter if needed. Squeeze lemon juice over all. Broil 5 to 7 minutes more.
5. Reduce heat almost in half so broiling is less intense. Go by the size of the flame, since every stove has a different intensity of heat. You want chicken to keep cooking, but at a slower pace so it does not dry out.
6. Broil only 10 minutes more, basting every few minutes to keep chicken juicy. Lower heat if still cooking too fast.
7. Place chicken on warm platter, skin side up; pour pan juices over. Decorate with parsley.

NOTE:

Steps 1 and 2 may be done well in advance of serving.

broiled butterfly lamb

4 servings

1 fresh leg of spring lamb
Top chops must be cut off; do not buy unless you want them. Have butcher cut rest of leg open its full length, remove bone, and lay meat out in butterfly shape.
6 tablespoons French dressing. (See page 116)

Scant ½ teaspoon dry thyme. (Too much thyme creates a bitter taste.)
¼ lb. butter
1 cup finely cut parsley

PREPARATION TIME:

2 minutes

COOKING TIME FOR "RARE":

about 9 minutes

1. Spread lamb flat in shallow pan, cut side up. Do not salt. Pour French dressing over; sprinkle on thyme. Dot in 4 or 5 places with small pieces of butter.
2. Begin broiling only 12 minutes before serving. Place pan 3 in. below high flame of broiler. Broil first side 5 or 6 minutes to brown. Watch closely so it doesn't scorch.
3. Turn lamb over; baste with pan juices. Broil only 3 minutes.
4. Examine for rareness: Make a small cut in thickest part. It should be pink; remember that ends and thinner areas will be cooked more. If too raw, cook only 1 minute more; look again. (This boned leg of lamb takes less time to broil than a thick steak. And like steak, it must be rare for really superb eating.)
5. Remove pan from broiler the second lamb is ready or it will continue to cook even if broiler is turned off.
6. Carve in pan. Cut in half, down the center; then cut each half crosswise (against the grain) into slices ½ in. thick.
7. Slide all onto warm platter; slices should overlap. Lay a strip of cut parsley down the center. Pour pan juices over.

NOTE:

Step 1 may be done well in advance of serving.

broiled lamb chops

4 servings

8 loin or rib lamb chops; each should be 1¼ in. thick

(Or: 4 English lamb chops; each should be 2 in. thick. These are loin chops, each with a lamb kidney skewered into its tail.)
3 tablespoons French dressing (see page 116)
Scant ½ teaspoon dry thyme (Too much thyme creates a bitter taste.)
¼ lb. butter

PREPARATION TIME:

2 minutes

BROILING TIME FOR "RARE":

5 to 10 minutes, depending on thickness

1. Lay chops in shallow pan. Pour on French dressing, including the split clove of garlic. Sprinkle on thyme. Dot each chop with small piece of butter.
2. Begin broiling only 6 minutes before serving loin or rib chops (11 minutes before serving English chops). Place pan 3 to 3½ in. below high flame of broiler. Broil first side 3 minutes (5 minutes if English chops) to brown.
3. Turn chops over; baste with pan juices. Broil only 2 to 3 minutes (4 to 5 minutes if English chops).
4. Examine chops for rareness: Make small cut in center of 1 chop. If too raw, cook only another minute; look again. (Lamb chops must be pink inside—"à pointe" as the French say—to be worth eating. Like beef, lamb can overcook and become grey in half a minute. So watch closely.)
5. Place chops on warm platter the moment they are ready or they will continue to cook even if broiler is turned off. Pour some of pan juices over; do not include split garlic.

NOTE:

Step 1 may be done well in advance of serving.

shashlik

4 servings

1 clove of garlic
¾ teaspoon paprika
¾ teaspoon dry mustard
¾ teaspoon salt
5 tablespoons vinegar
10 tablespoons olive oil
24 cubes of fresh lamb: each 1½ in. square, without fat. They are most tender when cut from leg of lamb. (Suggest buying a leg. Have top chops cut off; do not buy unless you want them. If some meat is left at shank end, roast it ½ hour the next day; this meat is

*most tender and flavorsome, so use
every bit.)*
*12 small white onions: should be uniform
in size*
4 medium-sized, firm ripe tomatoes
2 large green peppers
8 small fresh mushrooms
*½ teaspoon dry thyme (Use no more;
too much thyme creates a bitter taste.)*
1⅔ cups instant rice
1 cup finely cut parsley

PREPARATION TIME:

about 10 minutes

BROILING TIME:

about 8 minutes

1. Mix cup French dressing: Peel and
   split garlic clove; place in small deep
   bowl with paprika, dry mustard, salt
   and vinegar. Mix well. Slowly stir in
   olive oil. Adjust to taste; should not
   be too sharp, or too oily.
2. Put lamb cubes in large bowl. Add
   each vegetable as it is prepared:

   Peel onions; do not cut up.

   Wash tomatoes; cut in quarters.

   Wash peppers; cut in quarters, discarding seeds and stem.

   Wipe fresh mushrooms with damp
   paper towel; do not wash or peel.
   Cut stems even with caps. Refrigerate stems for another meal; add
   caps to bowl.
3. Salt all lightly. Scatter in thyme. Pour
   on French dressing. Mix well with
   spoon so that all foods are well saturated. Let stand in marinade as long

as possible, though 10 minutes is
enough.
4. String foods on 4 long skewers, alternating them in appetizing arrangement: tomato, lamb, onion, pepper,
   lamb, mushroom, etc. Suspend skewers over shallow pan; pour on all of
   French dressing in bowl.

   *Or: Arrange foods in shallow pan and
   pour all of French dressing in bowl
   over them.*
5. Begin broiling only 9 minutes before
   serving. Place pan 3 in. below high
   flame of broiler. Broil 4 minutes.
6. Turn skewers over; baste with pan
   juices.

   *Or: Mix foods broiling in pan with a
   spoon.*
7. Broil about 4 minutes more, depending on intensity of your flame. Lamb
   must be rare (pink inside) for tenderest eating.
8. While foods broil, cook instant rice
   according to directions on package.
9. When lamb is properly cooked, remove pan from broiler. Lay a bed
   of rice on serving platter; arrange
   skewers (or foods in pan) attractively
   on top. Scatter parsley over all.
10. Spoon some of pan juices over lamb.
    Pour the rest into gravy boat. (If all
    were poured over platter, rice would
    absorb all, leaving none for lamb.)

NOTE:

Steps 1 through 3 should be done well in
advance of serving. Step 4 may also be
done well in advance.

mixed grill

4 servings

COMBINATION I:

*4 slices of beef tenderloin: each only ½
in. thick*
8 pre-cooked pork sausages
  (Or: 4 fairly plump beef frankfurters)
*4 slices calves' liver: not too large, and
only ½ in. thick. Have butcher remove
thin membrane from edge of each
slice, and any bits of hard fiber inside.
(Or: ¾ lb. fresh chicken livers)*
*8 or 12 slices lean bacon. (Thick-cut slices
are wonderful.)*
Flour
Salt
*2 tablespoons French dressing (See page
116.)*
*½ teaspoon dry thyme (Use no more;
too much thyme creates a bitter taste)*
Prepared mustard (if serving frankfurters)

PREPARATION TIME:

about 3 minutes

BROILING TIME FOR "RARE":

about 6 minutes

1. Lay beef tenderloin and sausages (or
   frankfurters) in shallow pan. Lightly
   salt and flour liver; lay in pan. Pour
   French dressing over all; sprinkle with
   thyme.
2. Eight minutes before serving, put bacon in large skillet; fry over low heat
   until crisp but not brittle. Drain off
   grease as it collects; do not let grease
   smoke.

3. Place pan 3 in. below high flame of broiler. Broil only 3 minutes on first side. Pre-cooked pork sausages need only browning.
4. Turn bacon over; watch closely from now on.
5. Turn meats over; broil 3 minutes more. If cooking too fast, turn broiler flame down a bit; beef and liver should be served rare.
6. Drain cooked bacon on paper towels.
7. Arrange mixed grill on a warm platter the moment beef and liver are ready or they will continue to cook even if broiler is turned off. Pass mustard if serving frankfurters.

NOTE:

Step 1 may be done well in advance of serving.

COMBINATION II:

4 loin lamb chops: each ¾ in. thick
4 slices calves' liver; not too large, and only ½ in. thick. Have butcher remove thin membrane from edge of each slice, and any bits of hard fiber inside.
   (Or: ¾ lb. fresh chicken livers)
4 lamb kidneys
   Have butcher remove outside fat casing and thin membrane, if necessary, and split in half lengthwise.
8 or 12 slices lean bacon. (Thick-cut slices are wonderful.)
Salt
4 tablespoons French dressing (See page 116)

½ teaspoon dry thyme (Use no more; too much thyme creates a bitter taste)
Flour

PREPARATION TIME:

about 1 minute

BROILING TIME:

about 9 minutes

1. Lay lamb chops in shallow pan. Salt lightly; pour 1½ Tbsp. French dressing over all. Sprinkle each with a tiny pinch of thyme.
2. Ten minutes before serving, place pan 3 in. below high flame of broiler. Broil 3 minutes.
3. While chops broil, lightly salt and flour liver; lightly salt split kidneys.
4. Eight minutes before serving, put bacon in large skillet; fry over low heat until crisp but not brittle. Drain off grease as it collects; do not let grease smoke.
5. Place liver and kidneys in pan with lamb chops. Pour 1½ Tbsp. French dressing over them; sprinkle with remaining thyme. Broil 3 minutes.
6. Turn bacon over; watch closely from now on.
7. Look at lamb chops. If nicely browned, turn over; moisten with remaining French dressing.
8. When liver and kidneys have broiled 3 minutes, turn over; broil all meats 3 minutes more. If cooking too fast, turn broiler flame down a bit; lamb kidneys and liver should be served while still pink inside.
9. Drain cooked bacon on paper towels.

10. Arrange mixed grill on a warm platter the moment lamb and liver are ready or they will continue to cook even if broiler is turned off.

NOTE:

Steps 1 and 3 may be done well in advance of serving.

COMBINATION III:
(MONGOLIAN GRILL):

4 Belgian endive
4 slices, ⅛ in. thick, of each of the following vegetables:
   eggplant
   sweet potato (peeled)
   Bermuda onion
   green pepper
Salt
6 tablespoons French dressing (See page 116)
4 slices beef tenderloin: each only ⅛ in. thick
4 slices milk-fed veal: each only ⅛ in. thick, about 4 in. square
4 slices uncooked chicken or turkey breast: each only ⅛ in. thick. Buy enough breasts to provide these slices; have butcher cut them.
¼ lb. butter

PREPARATION TIME:

2 minutes, once foods are sliced

BROILING TIME:

about 5 minutes

1. Cut washed stalks of endive in half lengthwise. Place in shallow pan with

vegetable slices. Salt lightly; pour about 3 Tbsp. French dressing over all.

2. Six minutes before serving, place pan 3 in. below high flame of broiler. Broil 3 minutes.
3. Turn vegetables over; dot with butter. Add slices of meat and poultry; salt lightly and moisten with remaining French dressing. Broil about 1 minute, until lightly browned.
4. Turn meats over; dot with butter. Broil another minute or less, until meats are lightly browned. (Meats so thin require very little cooking.)
5. Serve as soon as ready, or everything will continue to cook even if broiler is turned off.

NOTE:

Step 1 may be done well in advance of serving.

ratatouille provençale with pork sausages

4 servings

½ cup olive oil
2 large yellow onions
3 cloves of garlic
1 large eggplant, or 2 small ones
2 large green peppers
3 medium-sized zucchini: these are green squash shaped like cucumbers
    Or: 2 packages frozen zucchini
1 (8 oz.) can peeled Italian plum tomatoes: should be seasoned with basil
Salt and pepper

½ teaspoon dry thyme
½ teaspoon dry oregano
16 or 20 pre-cooked pork sausages

PREPARATION TIME:

1 minute or so to wash and wipe vegetables

COOKING TIME:

about 30 minutes

1. In attractive casserole, heat olive oil over medium flame on top of stove. (If casserole is earthenware, use an asbestos pad over flame.)
2. Slice vegetables directly into casserole in this order, so each gets required amount of cooking. Mix with spoon as you go along.
   Peel onions and garlic; slice very fine.
   Peel eggplant if you wish; it's not essential. Cut into 1½-in. cubes.
   Wash and dry peppers; remove stems and seeds. Cut into 1-in. round strips.
   Wash and dry zucchini; remove stems. Do not peel. Cut into slices a good ¼-in. thick.
   Or: Add frozen zucchini; do not cut up.
3. Drain tomatoes; save juice in case you need to add liquid to casserole later.
4. Add tomatoes to casserole. Salt and pepper all well. Stir in thyme and oregano.
5. Taste for flavor; adjust if necessary. Add a little extra olive oil if not velvety enough.
6. Stir in pre-cooked sausages. (Before adding uncooked pork sausages, sim-

mer in water for 10 minutes to dispose of fat. Do not allow skins to break.)

7. Cover casserole; use heavy aluminum foil if you have no cover that fits. Cook over medium flame about 15 minutes more, stirring occasionally.
8. When eggplant is soft but not mushy, casserole is ready to serve. Just taste sauce to make sure it lacks nothing.
9. Serve directly from casserole, with plenty of warm French bread.

NOTE:

Steps 1 through 6 may be done well in advance of serving. If you wish dish to cook in less time, cut vegetables smaller.

sautéed calves' liver

4 servings

4 slices fresh calves' liver: each should be ½ to ¾ in. thick. Have butcher remove thin membrane from edge of each slice, and any bits of hard fiber inside.
Salt
Flour
½ lb. butter

PREPARATION TIME:

2 minutes

COOKING TIME FOR "RARE":

about 6 minutes

1. Lightly salt and flour both sides of liver slices.
2. In a large skillet (or two skillets, if nec-

essary), melt 4 Tbsp. butter. Do not brown.

3. Lay in liver slices; they should lie flat. Cook first side gently 3 minutes. Add more butter as needed, and keep flame very low, so liver does not fry hard.
4. Turn liver over: baste with pan juices. Cook gently only 3 minutes more.
5. Examine for rareness: Cut small gash in center of 1 slice. If too raw, cook another minute or less; look again. (Calves' liver is delicious, tender and succulent if served somewhat pink inside. Overcooking dries and toughens it. So watch closely.)
6. Place liver on warm platter the moment it is ready or the heated skillets will continue to cook it. Pour pan juices over.

NOTE:

Step 1 may be done well in advance of serving.

VARIATION:

CALVES' LIVER, VENETIAN STYLE: Instead of butter, use olive oil. Add 1 lb. of onions, thinly sliced; cook gently to light golden color. Cut liver into ½-in. strips; salt and flour lightly. Add to skillet; cook gently only 2 or 3 minutes. Serve immediately, with halves of lemon on the side. Lemon adds a delightful flavor when squeezed on just before eating. It also cuts the richness of the olive oil.

104

sautéed veal kidneys

4 servings

4 fresh veal kidneys
  Have butcher remove outside fat casing and thin membrane, if necessary
Salt
Flour
½ lb. butter
½ lb. medium-sized fresh mushrooms
  (Or: 2 small (3 or 4 oz.) cans of sliced or button mushrooms)
1 heaping teaspoon dry tarragon
⅓ cup cognac (or bourbon)
½ cup dry white wine or dry vermouth
1 juicy lemon
½ cup heavy sweet cream
Paprika

PREPARATION TIME:

about 8 minutes

COOKING TIME:

15 minutes

1. Wash kidneys quickly in running cold water; dry with paper towels. Cut across into slices ⅛-in. thick. Lightly salt and flour on both sides.
2. In large skillet slowly melt 6 Tbsp. butter. Do not brown. Lay kidney slices into skillet; cook gently 4 or 5 minutes. Do not brown.
3. Wipe fresh mushrooms with damp paper towel; do not wash or peel. Discard dry ends of stems. Slice caps evenly down through stems directly into skillet.

   Or: Open canned mushrooms. Drain well; place in skillet.

4. Add more butter if necessary; there should always be enough to bubble in skillet. Cook gently 1 or 2 minutes.
5. Crumble in tarragon. Stir in cognac (or bourbon).
6. As soon as cognac is hot, (after about 2 minutes), ignite with lighted match.
7. When flame dies, add white wine or vermouth. Taste sauce; you may want to add a dash of lemon juice or salt to bring out flavor.
8. Stir in heavy sweet cream; cook 3 or 4 minutes to thicken slightly. If sauce gets too thick, add a little more cream, or white wine or vermouth.
9. Place kidney slices on warm platter; pour sauce over. Decorate top with paprika.

NOTE:

Steps 1 through 7 may be done well in advance of serving.

filets of sole normandy

4 servings

4 filets of fresh lemon or grey sole
  (Or: 4 filets of fresh flounder. Better than frozen sole.)
¾ lb. large fresh shrimp: shelled and cleaned, but not cooked
  (Or: ¾ lb. uncooked shelled and cleaned frozen shrimp)
½ lb. butter
Salt
Flour
12 fresh oysters in their liquor
  (Or: 1 (8 oz.) can small oysters)

¼ lb. medium-sized fresh mushrooms
(Or: 1 small (3 or 4 oz.) can of sliced
mushrooms)
1 teaspoon dry tarragon
1 juicy lemon
½ cup dry white wine or dry vermouth
2 egg yolks
½ pt. heavy sweet cream
1 cup finely cut parsley

PREPARATION TIME:

3 to 4 minutes

COOKING TIME:

about 20 minutes

1. Wash filets and shrimp quickly in running cold water. Remove any visible
black cords from shrimp. Pat all dry
with paper towels.
2. Place a long attractive shallow roasting
pan over two burners on top of stove.
Put 4 Tbsp. butter at each end; melt
over gentle heat, then swish around
to cover bottom. Do not let either
flame get too hot.
3. Salt and flour filets lightly on both
sides; lay into center of pan.
4. Continue to cook gently as you add
other ingredients to pan. Add more
butter as needed; it should always
bubble around ingredients:

Lay shrimp in uniform arrangement
along one side of filets.

Open oysters; drain well. Remove any
bits of shell. Lay tastefully along other
side of filets.

Wipe fresh mushrooms with damp
paper towel; do not wash or peel. Discard dry ends of stems. Slice caps

evenly down through stems. Lay in
even arrangement between filets.

*Or: Open canned mushrooms; drain
well. Lay in even arrangement between
filets.*

5. Crumble tarragon over all. Squeeze on
juice of ½ lemon. Pour on white wine
or vermouth. Cook gently another 3 or
4 minutes, basting all with pan juices.
Do not turn or move anything.
6. Meanwhile, in a large cup stir up egg
yolks with fork. Mix in most of cream;
then pour over all. Cook very gently
so mixture thickens slightly into a nice
creamy sauce. No need to cover. Cook
10 to 15 minutes more, basting all with
sauce every 5 minutes.
7. Taste sauce for flavor; add more salt,
or a dash of lemon juice if needed.
When serving a sauced dish like this,
you should not serve extra lemon at
the table. If sauce thickens too much,
stir in a little more cream or wine.
8. Turn off heat. Decorate top with
parsley.
9. Serve directly from roasting pan.

NOTE:

Steps 1 through 6 may be done well in
advance of serving.

VARIATIONS:

I. FILETS OF SOLE VERONIQUE: Omit
shrimp, oysters, mushrooms, tarragon
and parsley. Cook sole as above, basting
frequently with butter to keep flesh succulent. Do not turn over. Five minutes
before serving, add 1½ cups peeled
seedless white grapes.

II. FILETS OF SOLE AMANDINE: Omit
shrimp, oysters, mushrooms, tarragon
and parsley. Cook sole as above, basting
frequently with butter to keep flesh succulent. Do not turn over. Five minutes
before serving, decorate top with ¾ cup
slivered almonds. Pop under broiler until
almonds are golden brown. Takes only 2
or 3 minutes.

broiled fish

4 servings

½ lb. butter
1 (3½ lb.) fresh fish. Or 2 smaller fish,
each weighing 1¾ to 2 lbs. Must be
fresh catch of the day. Good broiling
fish are sea bass, striped bass, whitefish, bluefish, boned shad, and red
snapper if absolutely fresh. Have dealer
clean, cut off most of tail, and split in
half. Do not have him skin. Head may
be left on if you like. I do, since a whole
fish looks better than a headless one.
Salt
1 tablespoon French dressing
(See page 116.)
3 juicy lemons
1 heaping teaspoon dry tarragon
1 cup finely cut parsley

PREPARATION TIME:

6 minutes

BROILING TIME:

15 minutes

1. Lay 4 small pieces of butter in a large
shallow pan.

2. Rinse fish quickly in running cold water. Pat dry with paper towels. Salt lightly on both sides. Lay on top of butter, flesh side up.
3. Pour French dressing and the juice of 1 lemon over all. Crumble on tarragon. Dot in 5 or 6 places with big lumps of butter.
4. Begin broiling only 15 minutes before serving. Place pan 2½ in. below high flame of broiler. Fish must be broiled close to high flame; otherwise it will exude moisture and be ruined. Broil 7 minutes.
5. Baste with pan juices; add more butter if needed. If browning too fast, lower pan slightly or turn flame down. But do not turn down too much. Broil 4 minutes more.
6. Baste fish again. Frequent basting is essential if you want to keep fish from drying out. Do not turn over; fish will break. Watch carefully from now on, so fish does not overcook. Broil 4 minutes more.
7. Examine fish for doneness: Prick thickest area with a fork. If flesh flakes easily but is still moist, fish is done. If too raw, broil 1 minute or less; look again. (Fish cooks very quickly, and overcooked, dried-out fish is one of the least palatable foods I know.)
8. Remove pan from broiler the second fish is ready, or it will continue to cook even if broiler is turned off. Run metal spatula under fish to be sure nothing sticks to pan. Then slide carefully to warm platter.
9. Scatter on parsley; pour pan juices over. Place 8 quarters of lemon on edge of platter, and serve.

NOTE:
Steps 1 through 3 may be done well in advance of serving.

zuppa di pesce
4 servings

4 fresh fish heads
Salt and pepper
2 bay leaves
2 large yellow onions
Dry oregano
Dry basil
4 slices young cod (scrod): each 1½ in. thick
4 slices young halibut: each 1½ in. thick
1 (2½ lb.) striped bass, black bass, or sea bass. Or any other tasty fresh fish of same size. Have dealer remove head; clean and cut into 4 chunks.
1 eel (optional)
Have dealer skin and cut into 2½-in. pieces.
½ cup olive oil
4 cloves of garlic
1 green or red pepper
3 tablespoons tomato sauce
3 juicy lemons
½ cup dry white wine or dry vermouth
16 or 20 fresh mussels
Have dealer scrape shells clean.
1 cup finely cut parsley

PREPARATION TIME:
3 minutes

COOKING TIME:
about 30 minutes

1. Rinse fish heads in running cold water. Place in saucepan; cover with cold water. (Should be at least 2½ cups.) Add 2 tsp. salt, 2 bay leaves, a little dry oregano and dry basil and 1 large onion, split in half. Bring to boil; cook actively 15 minutes to obtain a fish bouillon.
2. While bouillon cooks, remove slices and chunks of fish from refrigerator; wash quickly in running cold water.
3. Now make sauce for zuppa di pesce: In attractive casserole, heat olive oil over medium flame on top of stove. (If casserole is earthenware, use an asbestos pad over flame.)

Peel garlic cloves and remaining onion; remove stem and seeds from pepper. Sliver all into casserole. Cook slowly, stirring occasionally, until soft. Do not brown.

Add 3 Tbsp. tomato sauce, salt and freshly ground pepper; then crumble in 1 tsp. each of oregano and basil. Mix well. Taste; sauce should have pronounced herb flavor.

Slowly add about 2 cups hot fish bouillon, cooking and stirring constantly. After 1½ cups are added, taste to see whether sauce is a perfect blend—not too oily, not too thin and watery. Add more oil or bouillon, whichever is needed, until you have a very tasty sauce in which to cook fish.

4. When sauce is ready, lightly salt fish and eel. Squirt with lemon juice and lay into casserole, heaviest chunks on the bottom.
5. Add white wine or vermouth. Cover casserole; use heavy aluminum foil if you have no cover that fits. Cook quite actively about 6 minutes.
6. While fish cooks, wash mussel shells thoroughly.
7. Taste sauce. With a baster, baste sauce in bottom of casserole over top layer of fish. You need plenty of sauce for serving. If necessary, combine remaining fish bouillon with a little tomato sauce, olive oil and wine. Season with pepper, oregano and basil. Taste. When flavor pleases you, add to casserole.
8. Lay mussels on top of fish. Cover casserole well so mussels will steam open; this takes about 12 minutes.
9. As soon as all mussels have steamed open, casserole is ready to serve. Just taste sauce to make sure it lacks nothing. Sprinkle parsley over top.
10. Serve directly from casserole. Pass 2 lemons, cut in half, and plenty of warm French or Italian bread.

NOTE:

Steps 1 through 7 may be done well in advance of serving.

TO SERVE ZUPPA DI PESCE:

1. Be sure each guest has a soup spoon and fork, and a separate bowl in which to put fish bones and mussel shells.
2. Use largest soup plates you have. With two large spoons, serve each guest a portion of every kind of fish. Pile some mussels on top; then ladle over as much sauce as soup plate will hold.

broiled lobsters

4 servings

2 large fresh lobsters: each should weigh 2½ lbs.
Ask for females; besides the delicious green liver (tomalley) present in all lobsters, females have red roe, or "coral," a great delicacy. Have dealer split in half, clean and crack large claws.
4 juicy lemons
4 tablespoons French dressing (See page 116.)
½ lb. butter

PREPARATION TIME:

3 or 4 minutes

BROILING TIME:

about 20 minutes

1. Spread lobster halves flat, flesh side up, in two shallow pans. Break ends of tails open completely to prevent their curling up when broiling.
2. Over each half pour the juice of ½ lemon and 1 Tbsp. French dressing. Dot generously with butter.

3. Begin broiling only 20 minutes before serving. Place each pan 2½ to 3 in. below high flame of broiler. Lobster must be broiled as close to high flame as possible without scorching; otherwise it will exude moisture, and be ruined. Broil 5 minutes.
4. Baste lobsters with pan juices. Add more butter if needed. If tops are beginning to brown, lower pans slightly. But do not lower too much. Broil 13 to 15 minutes more, basting every 5 minutes to keep lobsters juicy. Do not turn lobsters over; they would lose juices. Frequent basting will cook them properly.
5. In 18 or 20 minutes, lobsters should be done. You can tell by looking. Remove from broiler immediately, to prevent drying out.
6. Place on a warm platter; pour pan juices over. Add ½ lemon for each guest. Be sure to have a nutcracker or lobster cracker at the table if claws are not thoroughly cracked.

NOTE:

Steps 1 and 2 may be done well in advance of serving. You must have two broilers to do 2 lobsters, because each must be close to broiler flame at all times. One oven broiler, unless it is much wider than average, will just not accommodate 2 lobsters spread out flat. Of course, if you have a supplementary electric broiler, you have no problem, provided lobster pan will fit.

baked alaska

4 generous servings

4 egg whites
   *Be sure not to have any yolk in the
   whites or they will not beat stiff. (Yolk
   may be picked out easily with a broken
   egg shell.)*
¾ cup sugar
*1 layer of spongecake: 7 in. long, 5 in.
   wide, 1 in. thick.*
*1 quart brick of ice cream: any flavor
   Keep solidly frozen until baking.*
1 small package of slivered almonds

PREPARATION TIME:

10 minutes

BAKING TIME:

about 4 minutes

1. Pre-heat oven to 450°; put serving
   platter in refrigerator.
2. Beat egg whites, slowly adding sugar,
   until very dry and glossy. (Egg whites
   should not slide when bowl is partially
   inverted.) This is your meringue.
3. Lay cake on small bread board; center
   solidly frozen ice cream on top. Cake
   should be just slightly larger than ice
   cream.
4. Quickly cover all with meringue. Swirl
   surface of meringue into attractive
   peaks with spatula. Sprinkle with
   almonds.
5. Place on middle rack of oven; bake
   only 3 or 4 minutes, until meringue is
   lightly browned. Watch closely. (If you
   prefer to brown it under high broiler
   flame, it takes less time. So watch even
   more closely.)

6. Remove from oven the moment it is
   ready. With two wide spatulas, slide
   onto chilled platter; serve immediately. Cut into fairly thick slices at the
   table.

NOTE:

Step 2 may be done well in advance of
serving.

VARIATION:

NORWEGIAN BAKED ALASKA: Before
centering ice cream on cake, the Nor-
wegians usually spread a layer of jelly or
jam over cake. Especially good if jelly is
first thinned with a little Cointreau or
cognac to make spreading easier.

chocolate mousse

4 servings

*1 (8 oz.) package unsweetened baking
   chocolate*
*1 heaping Tbsp. drip grind coffee: break-
   fast blend or after-dinner roast*
1¼ cups sugar
Salt
1½ cups (¾ pt.) heavy sweet cream
1 California orange
⅓ cup Cointreau
*1 (4 oz.) package unsweetened cocoa:
   "Droste's" is especially good.*

PREPARATION TIME:

about 20 minutes

CHILLING TIME:

about 20 minutes

1. Half-fill lower part of double boiler
   with warm water. Bring to active boil
   as you place top in position and
   break baking chocolate into it. (Need
   not be broken small; heat and coffee
   will melt it quickly.)
2. Meanwhile, make 1 cup strong black
   coffee: In small saucepan, bring 1¼
   cups fresh cold water to a near boil.
   Then stir in coffee. Let boil up to top
   of pan; turn off heat.
3. Quickly pour this coffee through a
   fine sieve over the chocolate in top
   of double boiler. Stir in 1 cup sugar
   and dash of salt.
4. When fully melted, chocolate should
   look smooth and glossy. If granular,
   stir in water, a little at a time, until
   chocolate shines.
5. Remove top of double boiler from
   bottom. Grate outer skin of 1 orange
   into chocolate. Stir in Cointreau.
6. Taste; add more salt or Cointreau if
   desired. Place in refrigerator to cool
   for about 5 minutes.
7. Meanwhile whip 1½ cups heavy
   sweet cream until firm but not dry.
   (Should stand in soft peaks when
   beater is lifted.) Add ¼ cup sugar
   while beating.
8. Fold whipped cream into cooled
   chocolate mixture, lifting with spoon
   from bottom to top. Do not stir
   around and around. When all is
   smooth-textured, transfer to serving
   bowl. Place in coldest part of refrigerator, but not in freezing compartment.
9. At least half an hour before serving,
   remove mousse from refrigerator so
   it will not be served ice cold. Tastes

best when only slightly chilled.

10. Just before serving, cover top with ¼-in. layer of unsweetened cocoa. Do not add sugar.

This is a soft mousse, not the solid ice-cold one cooked with egg yolks; I prefer it.

NOTE:

Steps 1 through 8 can be done well in advance of serving.

mocha mousse

4 servings

16 fresh white marshmallows (1 small box): "Campfire" is a good brand.
2 tablespoons drip grind coffee: breakfast blend or after-dinner roast
1½ cups (¾ pt.) heavy sweet cream

PREPARATION TIME:
about 20 minutes

CHILLING TIME:
about 20 minutes

1. Place marshmallows in deep bowl; set a fine sieve next to bowl.
2. Make 1 cup double-strength black coffee: In small sauce pan, bring 1¼ cups fresh cold water to a near boil. Then stir in coffee. Let boil up to top of pan; turn off heat.
3. Quickly pour this coffee through sieve into bowl with marshmallows. Stir well; then beat into smooth cream with rotary beater. Put bowl in coldest part of refrigerator (but not the freez-

ing compartment) for about 15 minutes to chill well.
4. Meanwhile, in a large deep bowl whip heavy sweet cream until firm but not dry. (Should stand in soft peaks when beater is lifted.) Do not add sugar.
5. Test refrigerated coffee-marshmallow mixture with finger; it *must* be well chilled. If so, pour very slowly into whipped cream, folding it in with a spoon as you pour. (Lift spoon from bottom to top. Do not stir around and around.) You may not use all of coffee-marshmallow mixture; stop pouring when whipped cream is smooth-textured and the consistency of the frozen custard you buy at highway stands in summer. Blend should not be too "thin." (I cannot be more exact than this about the amounts because marshmallows differ considerably in composition.)
6. Transfer blend to dessert bowl. Put back in coldest part of refrigerator until serving. But do not freeze. Mousse should be creamy and light, not solid.

NOTE:

Steps 1 through 6 can be done well in advance of serving.

zabaglione

4 servings

6 egg yolks
6 tablespoons sugar
Salt
1 cup dry Marsala wine

PREPARATION TIME:
about 3 minutes (for water to boil)

COOKING TIME:
about 6 minutes

1. Half-fill lower part of double boiler with warm water. Cover; bring to active boil.
2. In interim, place egg yolks in top of double boiler. Mix in sugar and dash of salt. (I like a wire whip for this.)
3. As soon as water comes to boil, turn off heat. Place top of double boiler in position for 1 minute to warm egg yolks slightly. Remove and immediately begin stirring eggs with wire whip.
4. Repeat this sequence of heating eggs, then stirring them, 2 or 3 times, or until water is no longer too hot.
5. Then leave top of double boiler in position while you beat eggs with rotary beater, slowly adding Marsala. Work in all the mixture on bottom and sides of pan. Continue until all Marsala is beaten in and eggs are cooked to the right consistency; takes about 5 minutes. (Mixture should become creamy and fluffy, somewhat like the frozen custard you buy at highway stands in summer.)

IMPORTANT:

If mixture does not seem to be cooking, the water beneath is too cool. Turn on heat for only 1 minute. Then turn heat off, or very, very low. Remember, egg yolks cannot stand sustained heat.

If mixture starts to thicken too fast,

into a sort of spongecake consistency on bottom or sides of pan, there is too much heat below. Immediately lift off pan and stir mixture with spoon from bottom up so all is well blended. (Small solid parts on sides or bottom of pan may be safely mixed into the creamy center, but do not overdo it.) When all is well blended, place top of double boiler on lower part, and continue as before.

6. As soon as zabaglione is ready, spoon into stemmed glasses (or dessert dishes), removing every bit from pan with rubber spatula. Serve immediately; wine and eggs separate on standing.

VARIATIONS:

PEACHES ZABAGLIONE: Fill cavities of canned peach halves with freshly made zabaglione.

PEARS ZABAGLIONE: Fill cavities of canned pear halves with freshly made zabaglione.

RHUBARB ZABAGLIONE: Use zabaglione as a topping for freshly baked rhubarb.

Amenities

how to buy:

First of all, choose a good wine merchant. His stock will be varied, his selections first-class, and he will be glad to give you all the help he can. He will not over-charge you. In fact, he often offers out-standing values. Moreover, he stores his bottles properly, so the wines you buy will be at their best.

Here is what you should know about red, white and rosé wines before buying.

red wines:

Serve with all red meats, roasts, game, cheese.

Always serve at room temperature. Open as early in the day as possible, or even the night previous, so wine can breathe. Lay carefully in wine basket. Serve from basket.

NOTE:

Connoisseurs disparage such choices as "Sparkling Burgundy."

white wines:

Serve with all fish and shell food.

Many people enjoy a white wine with less heavy roasts such as chicken, veal, and even pork. Goes very well with all sautéed meats. It's really a matter of indi-vidual preference.

White wines are always served ahead of red, if more than one wine is served at a dinner.

Always serve well chilled; never pour over ice. Place in refrigerator as early in day as possible, or even the night pre-vious. Open bottle just before serving. No need to lay in wine basket, since there is no sediment to agitate. Do not envelop bottle in napkin. Guests often like to see what you are serving, particularly if they enjoy it.

pink (rosé) wines:

May be served with all red meats except heavy roasts and game; may substitute for white wine almost any time. Pink wine is often served throughout a dinner, particularly in summer. Always serve slightly chilled; never pour over ice. Open bottle just before serving. No need to lay in wine basket.

how to keep:

For long storage, red, white and pink (rosé), should be kept in a closet having a temperature between 55° and 75°. They should be stored lying down, so cork is always moist.

how to open:

Before opening the wine, remove all of the metal capsule around the cork. Wipe off cork and top of bottle with a damp cloth. Withdraw cork gently; try not to move bottle any more than you have to. Wipe the lip of the bottle to remove cork particles.

how to serve:

The ideal wine glass is clear thin crystal with a roomy bowl. For grace of han-dling, the stem should be about the same height as the bowl. Fill glasses only half-full or a little more to enjoy a wine's aroma.

THE WINES OF FRANCE

A surprisingly large number of excellent wines from all areas of France are avail-able for around $2.00 a bottle. Many times they cost much less. All are delight-ful accompaniments to a meal.

Here is a list to guide you when buying. It is based on present New York prices for the excellent 1959 vintage. However, great vintage wines from well-known vineyards are necessarily more costly. Wines, like many other products, vary in price across the country, and are subject to price fluctuations.

MODERATELY PRICED WINES

red bordeaux:

Also called "Clarets." Bottles are distinc-tive — have straight sides which curve in sharply to make a clearly defined neck. Outstanding years: 1952, 1953, 1955, 1959 and 1961.

Médoc . . . .$1.50 a bottle
St. Emilion . . . .$1.75 a bottle

red burgundies:

Most red Burgundies reach their prime in 5 to 7 years and fade after 15. Bottles are larger at the bottom than Bordeaux and taper gradually to a neck. Outstanding years: 1952, 1953, 1955, 1959 and 1961.

Côte de Beaune .... $2.80 a bottle
Beaujolais* .... $2.00 a bottle
*Beaujolais is properly drunk when young.
  Several of the best Beaujolais are:
        Moulin-à-Vent
        Fleurie
        Juliénas
        Brouilly
        Lamartine

red rhones:

Bottles look like Burgundy bottles. Outstanding years: 1952, 1955, 1957, 1958, 1960 and 1961.

Châteauneuf du Pape .... $2.00 a bottle

white bordeaux:

These wines are less dry than whites from other areas. Graves is moderately dry, and may accompany dinner. Sauterne is sweeter, therefore best served with dessert. It keeps better than most whites. Bottles are identical to red Bordeaux bottles. Outstanding years: 1955, 1959 and 1961.

Bordeaux Blanc .... $1.25 a bottle
Graves .... $1.50 a bottle
Sauterne .... $2.00 a bottle

white burgundies:

Bottles look like red Burgundy bottles. Outstanding years: 1960, 1961, 1962.

Pouilly-Fuissé .... $2.00 a bottle
Chablis .... $2.00 a bottle

white loire wines:

Bottles look like red Burgundy bottles. Outstanding years: 1959, 1960 and 1961.

Muscadet .... $1.75 a bottle
Vouvray .... $2.00 a bottle
Pouilly-Fumé .... $2.50 a bottle
Sancerre .... $2.00 a bottle

alsatian wines:

Bottles look like German wine bottles; they are made of green glass, and are tall and slim. Outstanding years: 1959 and 1961.

Sylvaner .... $1.50 a bottle
Riesling .... $2.00 a bottle
Gewurztraminer .... $2.00 a bottle

pink wines of france (vin rosé):

Bottles vary in shape, depending on the wine's geographic origin. Outstanding years: 1959 and 1961.

Rosé of Bordeaux .... $1.25 a bottle
Tavel (Rhone) .... $2.00 a bottle
Rosé of Anjou (Loire) .... $1.75 a bottle
Rosé of Provence .... $1.50 a bottle

COSTLIER WINES

When buying exceptional wines from renowned vineyards, ask the advice of a first-class wine merchant. However, you can be guided by these suggestions. For the red Bordeaux, red Burgundies and white Bordeaux, I refer to 1959 vintage.

The red Rhones are 1958 vintage, and the white Burgundies, 1960.

red bordeaux:

Château Lascombes
   (Margaux) .... $3.50 a bottle
Château Beychevelle
   (St. Julien) .... $4.00 a bottle
Château Latour (Pauillac).. $8.00 a bottle
Château Margaux
   (Margaux) .... $8.00 a bottle
Château Haut-Brion
   (Graves) .... $8.00 a bottle

red burgundies:

Beaune .... $3.00 a bottle
Nuits-St. Georges .... $3.50 a bottle
Corton .... $4.00 a bottle
Pommard .... $4.00 a bottle
Clos de la Roche .... $4.50 a bottle
Vosne-Romanée .... $4.50 a bottle
Chambertin .... $5.00 a bottle

red rhones:

Côte Rôtie .... $3.50 a bottle
Hermitage .... $3.50 a bottle

white bordeaux:

Château La Tour Blanche
   (Sauterne) .... $3.00 a bottle
Château Climens (Barsac).. $3.00 a bottle
Château Haut-Brion
   (Graves) .... $5.50 a bottle

white burgundies:

Chablis . . . . $3.00 a bottle
Puligny Montrachet . . . . . . $3.00 a bottle
Meursault Charmes . . . . . . $3.50 a bottle
Bâtard Montrachet . . . . $4.75 a bottle

AMERICAN WINES

The best American wines come from northern California, and are counterparts of the French types. Sometimes the name of the corresponding French wine (Bordeaux, Burgundy, etc.) appears on the label. More often the names of grapes are used to differentiate them. It is important to look for the name of a good vineyard when buying. Here are my preferences:

Almaden   Louis B. Martini
Beaulieu (BV)   Paul Masson
Buena Vista   Wente Brothers
Inglenook   Christian Brothers
Charles Krug

red wines:

Bordeaux Types — Labeled for the grape
    "Cabernet Sauvignon"—$1.75 a bottle.
Burgundy Types — Labeled for the grape
    "Pinot Noir"—$1.90 a bottle.

white wines:

Bordeaux Types — Labeled for the grape
    "Sauvignon Blanc"—$2.00 a bottle.
Sauternes — Labeled for the grape
    "Semillon" — $1.70 a bottle.

Burgundy Types — Labeled for the grape
    "Pinot Blanc" — $1.90 a bottle.
        Labeled for the grape "Pinot Chardonnay" — $2.50 a bottle.

pink wines:

All labeled "pink" in one form or another
    —$1.50 a bottle.

Some American wines can be purchased in half-gallon jugs. They are enjoyable, but not comparable to the bottled wines listed. For serving, decant into a pitcher or nice-looking bottle. The best sell for about $2.60 a half-gallon:

Almaden (red or white)
Louis B. Martini (red or white)
St. Michel (red or white)

ITALIAN WINES

Look for the names of good shippers: Bertani, Bolla, Brolio, and Ruffino.

reds:

Chianti . . . . $1.50 a bottle
Valpolicella . . . . $1.50 a bottle
Bardolino . . . . $2.00 a bottle

whites:

Orvieto . . . . $1.50 a bottle
Soave . . . . $2.00 a bottle
Verdicchio . . . . $2.25 a bottle

GERMAN WINES

Liebfraumilch
    (a white Rhine) . . . . $2.00 a bottle
Bernkasteler
    (a white Moselle) . . . . . . $2.00 a bottle

PORTUGUESE WINES

Mateus (rosé) . . . . $1.75 a bottle
Dao San Pedro Branco
    (white) . . . . $1.50 a bottle
Dao San Pedro Tinto (red) . $1.50 a bottle

SPANISH WINES

Rioja (red) . . . . $2.00 a bottle
Rioja (white) . . . . $2.00 a bottle

SWISS WINES

Neuchâtel (white) . . . . $1.75 a bottle
Dezaley (white) . . . . $2.00 a bottle

13

Bread and butter are an important factor in any meal. As noted below, there is a right kind of bread for every sort of dish. Use good sweet butter, generously spread to the edges.

french or italian bread
(fresh or partially baked)

Both are delicious eating, and perfect for most dinners, as suggested in the menus. If a long loaf, cut into 2-in. chunks. If a round loaf, cut into ½-in. slices, then cut loaf in half. Butter slices well on one side. Lay on pan in loaf shape and heat in hot oven before serving. (5 minutes for fresh bread; about 15 minutes for partially baked.)

"gem" rolls
(sometimes called "butterflake" rolls)

An American specialty. Light and delicious, they are made of several segments of rich dough layered together. Go extremely well with creamed soups and dishes in a creamy sauce, particularly at luncheons. Butter between each segment and heat rolls in hot oven for 5 or 6 minutes before serving.

french brioches and croissants, and french baguettes

Hot brioches and croissants are great with your breakfast coffee. The long very thin French loaves (called baguettes), bought fresh at good French bakeries, are a great favorite for cocktail bites and hors d'oeuvres.

very dark rye bread or pumpernickel
(sliced or in loaves)

Thinly sliced pumpernickel, well buttered, is delicious with oysters or clams on the half shell, and with Nova Scotia salmon. Fairly thick slices of fresh, very dark rye go well with hamburgers, steak tartare (Page 94) and beef Stroganoff (Page 93). The Germans serve dark pumpernickel whenever they serve sauerkraut. The Danes cut very dark bread in thin slices, spread heavily with sweet butter, and place in refrigerator; when well chilled, they serve this "ice brod" with cold radishes, scallions, cherry tomatoes (the tiny ones), or with sardines, smoked eel, and the like.

russian black bread
(often called "health bread")

This is a unique kind of rye bread, darker and coarser than other rye. It's sold in small loaves, or by the pound, cut from an enormous round loaf. When served with whipped butter or a good country butter, it's sensational on a buffet table — particularly with cold ham, good sliced sausages, and cheeses such as Swiss or Italian provolone, and many others.

Recipes for French dressing and sauce vinaigrette on page 116.
Recipe for seafood sauce on page 116.

hors d'oeuvre salads
Serve well chilled

Avocados—Cut in half just before serving and sprinkle with lemon juice to retain color. Fill cavities with tiny shrimp or fresh crabmeat mixed with seafood sauce.

Marinated Hearts of Artichokes — Lay out on a plate, with or without sliced fresh (or canned button) mushrooms. Dress with French dressing, or sauce vinaigrette.

Mixed Cold Vegetables — Arrange chilled vegetables such as boiled leeks, marinated hearts of artichokes, and freshly cooked or canned asparagus stalks attractively on a platter. Dress with sauce vinaigrette.

Salad Niçoise—Turn out a can of tuna fish in center of a platter; surround with sliced tomatoes, green pepper rings, onion rings (or scallions cut 3½ in. long), hard-boiled eggs cut in halves, ripe or Greek olives and can of anchovies. Dress with French dressing.

salads to follow a main course
Serve well chilled

ONE-INGREDIENT SALADS:

Asparagus—Chill freshly cooked or canned asparagus stalks. Dress with French dressing and crumbled hard eggs or sauce vinaigrette. Also a splendid hors d'oeuvre course.

Avocados — Cut just before serving and sprinkle with lemon juice to retain color: Cut in half; fill cavities with French dressing or French dressing and blue cheese. Or peel, then cut into crescents and pour French dressing over.

Belgian Endive—Quarter stalks lengthwise into salad bowl. Salt lightly. Crumble blue cheese over top; pour on French dressing. Or mash blue cheese with enough French dressing to make a thick creamy sauce. Blue cheese counteracts slight but interesting bitterness of endive.

Boston Lettuce—Keep leaves whole. Salt lightly; toss with French dressing.

Cucumber — Peel; slice thin. Salt well and chill. Pour off liquid accumulated. Dress with fresh dill or parsley.

Escarole—Break (do not cut) leaves into 2½ to 3-in. lengths. Salt lightly; toss with French dressing.

Hearts of Palm (a canned Brazilian import) — Drain and dress with French dressing. Also a great hors d'oeuvre salad.

Iceberg (Head) Lettuce — Separate into leaves, or cut head into quarters or fifths. Salt lightly. Crumble blue cheese over top; pour on French dressing. Or mash blue cheese with enough French dressing to make a thick creamy sauce.

Romaine—Break (do not cut) leaves into 2½ to 3-in. lengths. Salt lightly; toss with French dressing.

Spinach — Cut stems off fresh spinach leaves. Toss with 1-in. pieces of crisp bacon and French dressing.

Tomatoes — Cut into ¼-in. slices; salt,

and sprinkle with freshly cut parsley or dill, or fresh or dry oregano or basil. Serve with or without French dressing.

Water Cress — Should be perfect large leaves. Cut off stems. Salt lightly. Toss with French dressing.

SALAD COMBINATIONS:

Belgian Endive and Water Cress (with or without crescents of avocado) — Place water cress leaves in bowl; slice several 1-in. sections from base of each endive into bowl and add separated upper leaves. Salt lightly; toss with French dressing.

Avocado, Belgian Endive and Mushrooms —Slice avocado into crescents directly into salad bowl; sprinkle with lemon juice. Slice several 1-in. sections from base of each endive into bowl; add separated upper leaves. Wipe fresh mushrooms with damp paper towel; do not wash or peel. Discard dry ends of stems; slice caps evenly down through stems directly into bowl. Salt lightly; toss with French dressing.

Sliced Avocado and Tomatoes — Arrange tastefully on a platter; salt lightly; dress with French dressing.

Tomatoes and Water Cress — Place water cress leaves on platter; arrange sliced tomatoes on top. Salt lightly. Pour French dressing over. Or place water cress and quartered tomatoes in a bowl; toss with French dressing.

Tomatoes and Whole String Beans—Slice tomatoes; surround with bunches of chilled freshly cooked (or canned) string beans. Salt lightly; pour French

dressing over. Decorate tomatoes with freshly cut parsley.

Tomatoes, Anchovies and Black Olives— Dress sliced tomatoes with strips of anchovies, pitted black olives, and French dressing.

Escarole and Chicory—Break (do not cut) leaves into 2½ to 3-in. lengths. Salt lightly; toss with French dressing.

Mixed Salad—Combine any of the following. Salt lightly; toss with French dressing.
Romaine, escarole or chicory leaves, broken into 2½ to 3-in. lengths; water cress leaves; thin slices of fresh mushrooms, radishes or cucumbers; thinly sliced onion, or white and green parts of scallions cut very small; avocado crescents; quarters of tomatoes; slices of hard-boiled eggs.

Danish Spring Salad — A refreshing salad course for a hot-weather luncheon. Slice cucumbers, radishes, white and green parts of scallions (or onion), green pepper and tomatoes very thin. Mix with sour cream. Add fresh dill if you like.

Caesar Salad—A hearty salad; grand after a light main course. Combine romaine lettuce broken into 2½-in. lengths, 1 cup croutons and 2 raw or coddled (slightly cooked) eggs. Toss lightly. Then add 4 or 5 Tbsp. French dressing. Toss well. Salt lightly; sprinkle in ½ cup grated Parmesan cheese, as you toss.

15

DRESSINGS AND SAUCES

Although French sauces number in the hundreds, most of the popular ones are based on French dressing, mayonnaise, hollandaise, or sauce béchamel (a hot white sauce). Here are the first three, with some of their variations. Sauce béchamel has not been mentioned elsewhere in the book, so is not included here.

I. french dressing:

An authentic French dressing is the simplest of mixtures.

To make ⅔ cup: Peel and split 1 clove of garlic; place in small deep bowl with ½ tsp. each of paprika, dry mustard and salt. Add dash of pepper and 3 Tbsp. vinegar or lemon juice; mix well. Slowly stir in 6 Tbsp. olive oil (two times as much oil as vinegar). Taste; correct dressing to a perfect balance of vinegar and olive oil —not too sharp, not too oily. Add more vinegar or oil, whichever is necessary. Remove garlic now, or just before using dressing, depending on how much garlic flavor you like. *Never add sugar as is sometimes suggested.*

sauces based on french dressing:

Sauce Verte. Italians use this successfully on hot or cold boiled meats, on sliced tomatoes and on salad greens.

Add to French dressing enough roughly cut parsley to thicken it into a sauce. Add cut-up onion, too, if you wish; I do not.

Sauce Vinaigrette. For cold boiled fish or meat or vegetables. Add to French dressing cut-up fresh herbs: 1 Tbsp. parsley, 1 tsp. tarragon, 1 tsp. chervil, 1 Tbsp.

chives (or 1½ Tbsp. finely cut onion). Crumble hard-boiled egg yolk over top.

II. mayonnaise (a cold sauce):

To make 2 cups: In cold bowl, with electric mixer at slowest speed, beat together 2 fresh egg yolks, ½ tsp. dry mustard, ½ tsp. salt and dash of pepper. Then beat in 1 cup olive oil — at first drop by drop, then in a slow thin trickle. (Curdling occurs when olive oil is added too rapidly.) At the end add 1 Tbsp. lemon juice. Refrigerate (this is not essential).

If curdling occurs, wash and dry your beater. Then, in a fresh bowl place 1 new egg yolk; add curdled mayonnaise a tablespoon at a time, beating constantly.

sauces based on mayonnaise (bought or homemade):

Seafood Sauce. For all cold shell foods. Mix mayonnaise with half as much sour cream; add salt, lemon juice and Worcestershire sauce to taste. (Use about 1 Tbsp. each of lemon juice and Worcestershire sauce for every 4 heaping Tbsp. of mayonnaise.) Result should be slightly pungent but not too lemony. If so, add more mayonnaise or sour cream.

Sauce Ravigote. For cold crab and fish salads.

Mix mayonnaise with a tiny squeeze of anchovy paste, finely cut shallots (or onion) and hard-boiled egg white, capers, minced parsley and chervil. Taste; should have a pleasant piquant flavor.

Sauce Rémoulade. For cold boiled or

bottled vegetables such as whole leeks, asparagus and hearts of artichokes when used as hors d'oeuvres.

Mix mayonnaise with finely cut sour pickles or gherkins, prepared mustard, capers, minced parsley, tarragon and chervil. Taste; add more of whatever you like.

Sauce Tartare. For sautéed soft-shell crab or frogs legs. Mix mayonnaise with finely cut sweet pickles or gherkins, green olives, shallots (or onion), prepared mustard, and minced parsley and tarragon to give a good-tasting piquant green sauce.

Green Mayonnaise. For cold poached salmon.

Mix mayonnaise with enough of these cut, crushed greens and herbs to give flavor and color: water cress, parsley, fresh chives, tarragon, chervil, and a bit of dill.

III. hollandaise (a hot sauce):

For hot asparagus, broccoli and boiled cauliflower. This is an easy sauce once you get the method. Just remember that it will curdle if too much heat is applied, since fresh egg yolks are sensitive to too much heat. If curdling occurs add Tbsp. or more hot vegetable liquid and mix smooth.

To make 1 generous cup: Bring water in lower part of double boiler to a boil. Turn off heat. Put 3 fresh egg yolks in upper part of double boiler, and place it over lower part. Beat eggs briskly with wire whisk or fork until light and lemon-colored. Leave top of double boiler in

116

position while you beat in about ¼ lb. softened butter 1 in. at a time. Let mixture thicken slightly after each addition. Be sure to beat mixture on bottom and sides of pan. When all butter is beaten in and mixture is the consistency of a medium thick cream sauce, add dash of cayenne pepper, a little salt and a good squeeze of lemon juice. Taste; should be slightly piquant. Add more lemon juice if needed. Whole process takes about 8 minutes or less.

If sauce is slow in blending, you may need to reheat the water below for a minute or two. (But do not let it boil.) Then turn heat off, or very, very low. Remember, egg yolks cannot stand sustained heat.

If sauce gets too thick, add 1 Tbsp. of hot water from the vegetable you are cooking.

Europeans — particularly the French, Italians and Scandinavians — are proud of their fine cheeses, and frequently serve them as dessert. Breads, not crackers, invariably accompany them. In Scandanavian countries, one gets black breads, well buttered with that incomparable Danish butter. In France and Italy one gets hard-crusted breads and, very often, apples, pears and grapes.

For best-looking presentation, serve a whole form (or half of a large form), instead of individual portions. However, buy only what is needed for a particular dinner, because most cheeses are hard to keep. This is particularly true of the types which must be flowing inside. When cheese is left, wrap loosely in aluminum foil, refrigerate, and serve again as soon as possible. Remember to remove from refrigerator well ahead of serving. All these cheeses should be served at room temperature.

soft cheeses

BRIE — French, American and Danish brie are available. Half of a whole form should serve 4 adequately.

French Brie—At best when absolutely soft to touch, and flowing inside. Product labeled "Babette" is my preference.

American Brie — At best when soft and flowing inside, like the French. A very good product, slightly less expensive than the French.

Danish Brie — Choose when good and creamy; does not become as flowing as French and American brands. But very good.

CAMEMBERT—French and American Camembert are available. A whole form should be enough for 4.

French Camembert — Must be soft to touch, and flowing inside.

American Camembert — Must be soft to touch, and flowing inside, like the French. Somewhat less expensive.

PONT L'EVEQUE — (French) Ripe when soft to touch; does not flow inside.

REBLOCHON — (French) Slightly milder than Pont l'Eveque. Buy when soft to touch; does not flow inside.

semi-soft mild cheeses

French — Beaumont, Cantal, Crème Chantilly, Gourmandise, Hable, Ile de France, La Grappe, Tomme de Savoie, Triple Crème.

American— Monterey Jack.

Canadian — Oka.

Danish — Crema Danica, Tilsit.

English — Wensleydale.

German — Muenster.

Italian — Bel Paese, Fontina, Tallegio.

semi-soft sharp cheeses

Danish — Blue.

English — Stilton.

French — Roquefort.

Italian — Gorgonzola.

firm cheeses

Canadian and English — Cheddar.

Dutch — Edam, Gouda.

Swiss — Emmental, Gruyère.

AFTER-DINNER COFFEE

Coffee should never be served with dinner. It should be served after, and it should be much stronger than breakfast coffee. Follow these pointers and your coffee will be a fitting finale to your dinner.

5 rules for perfect after-dinner coffee

1. Use a rich roast. Combine Italian after-dinner roast with your breakfast coffee, half and half. Or use all Italian or all French roast, if you prefer.
2. Use a fine grind. Regardless of the roast you use, always choose drip or filter grind. Gives far more flavor than the coarser percolator or all-purpose grind.
3. Use any coffeemaker you like. You can even use a saucepan, as is suggested in *Last-Minute Coffee* below. To use filter grind coffee in a percolator, place a paper filter at base of coffee compartment. Will keep coffee clear and help you get every bit of flavor.
4. Start with fresh cold water. (To retain flavor, keep coffee cans in refrigerator once they have been opened.)
5. Measure both water and coffee carefully; 1 well-rounded Tbsp. coffee for each cup or more, as you find you like it.

Last-Minute Coffee
For each cup you wish to serve, measure into saucepan 1 coffee cup of running cold water. Heat just to the boiling point. Throw in 1 well-rounded Tbsp. of filter or drip grind coffee for each cup of water. (Use combination of breakfast blend and Italian after-dinner roast if you like it.) Let all come to a quick boil to top of pan, stirring coffee into water as it boils. Watch carefully; pan can boil over in a minute. Turn off heat; let stand a minute so grounds settle. Pour through a small sieve into a warmed pot or directly into cups. (To warm a coffee pot, fill with hot water and let stand a few minutes.)

festive coffees

Coffee Brûlot
Have each guest lay a lump of sugar into his spoon and hold over his cup of hot black coffee. Saturate sugar with some cognac or brandy; ignite it with a match. When flaming is finished, sugar is dropped into coffee, giving it a tasty flavor. Pass some slivered orange and lemon peels so each guest can twist a piece of each into his cup.

Caffé Poncino
An Italian invention made with filter grind Italian roast coffee (Medaglia d'Oro). Looks delightful in a stemmed glass.
Into each serving of hot black coffee, pour 1 Tbsp. rum. Add a twist of lemon peel, and serve. Pass sugar for those who may want it.

Irish Coffee
Sometimes called "James Joyce" coffee. This is one of the most delightful special coffees.
To each cup or glass of sweetened hot black coffee, add 1 or 2 Tbsp. Irish whiskey (not Scotch whisky), depending on size of cup. Float a teaspoon of cold heavy sweet cream on top. Do not stir in

Index

*These items, not indexed, should
be kept on hand to save you shopping time.*

DRY HERBS: Basil, Garlic, Onions,
Oregano, Sage, Shallots, Tarragon, Thyme

LIQUORS: Calvados or Applejack,
Cognac or Bourbon, Cointreau,
Madeira (Dry), Marsala (Dry),
Sherry (Dry), Vermouth (French)

CANNED ITEMS:
    Soups: Beef Bouillon, Chicken
    Bouillon, Clam Broth, Madri-
    lene, Onion (Dehydrated),
    Turtle
    Vegetables: Artichokes (Mari-
    nated), Artichokes (Plain), Car-
    rots (Baby), Mushrooms (Button),
    Mushrooms (Sliced), Peas (Tiny),
    Tomatoes (Italian Plum)
    Fish: Anchovies, Tuna (Solid
    White)
    Dessert: Cherries, Chestnut
    Purée, Crepes Suzette, Figs
    (Preserved), Peaches (Sliced)

STAPLES: Almonds (Slivered),
Apples, French Bread or Rolls,
Sliced Pumpernickel, Bread
Crumbs (Seasoned), Butter
(Sweet), Capers, Coffee (Break-
fast Blend, Drip Grind, Italian
After-Dinner), Cream (Sour),
Eggs, Flour, Lemons, Mustard
Dry, Prepared [Dijon, German,
Bahamian]), Olive Oil, Oranges,
Parmesan Cheese (Grated), Pep-
per (Cayenne, Ground Regular,
Paprika, Whole Peppercorns),
Rice, Salt, Sugar (White, Brown),
Vinegar, Worcestershire Sauce